D1561429

Israel's Security Networks

Since the establishment of the State of Israel in 1948, particularly after the Arab–Israeli War of 1967, a highly informal but simultaneously potent security network has influenced Israel's domestic sphere. Composed of acting and former security personnel and their partners in the state's various civilian spheres, this security network has affected Israeli culture, politics, society, economy, public discourse, and foreign relations. This book discusses this major sociopolitical phenomenon and its effects in a comparative and theoretical perspective.

Gabriel Sheffer is a professor of political science at The Hebrew University of Jerusalem. He is the author of numerous books, journal articles, book chapters, and edited volumes, including *Middle Eastern Minorities and Diasporas* (2002), *Diaspora Politics: At Home Abroad* (Cambridge, 2003), *Militarism and Israeli Society* (2010), and *The Jewish Diaspora and the Jerusalem Question* (2012).

Oren Barak is an associate professor of political science and international relations at The Hebrew University of Jerusalem. He is the author of *The Lebanese Army: A National Institution in a Divided Society* (2009) and co-editor, with Gabriel Sheffer, of *Existential Threats and Civil-Security Relations* (2009) and *Militarism and Israeli Society* (2010).

Israel's Security Networks

A Theoretical and Comparative Perspective

GABRIEL SHEFFER
The Hebrew University of Jerusalem

OREN BARAK
The Hebrew University of Jerusalem

CAMBRIDGE UNIVERSITY PRESS
Cambridge, New York, Melbourne, Madrid, Cape Town,
Singapore, São Paulo, Delhi, Mexico City

Cambridge University Press
32 Avenue of the Americas, New York, NY 10013-2473, USA

www.cambridge.org
Information on this title: www.cambridge.org/9781107034686

First published 2013

Printed in the United States of America

A catalog record for this publication is available from the British Library.

Library of Congress Cataloging in Publication data
Sheffer, Gabriel, author.
  Israel's security network: a theoretical and comparative perspective / Gabriel Sheffer,
  the Hebrew University of Jerusalem, Oren Barak, the Hebrew University of Jerusalem.
    pages cm
  Includes bibliographical references and index.
  ISBN 978-1-107-03468-6 (hardback)
    1. National security – Israel. 2. Social networks – Israel. I. Barak, Oren, author.
  II. Title.
  UA853.I75S54 2013
  355'.033095694–dc23   2012044894

ISBN 978-1-107-03468-6 Hardback

Contents

Acknowledgments

This book could not have been completed without the generous help of numerous individuals and institutions.

We thank the Van Leer Jerusalem Institute for its generous help in launching the Workshop on Israeli Security and Society, where we had the opportunity to develop many of the ideas that culminated in this book.[1] We also thank the Leonard Davis Institute for International Relations at The Hebrew University of Jerusalem for helping us organize a conference at which we presented and further developed our ideas.[2] In recent years, we presented various parts of this project at meetings of the Association for Israel Studies, the International Studies Association (ISA), the Inter-University Seminar on Armed Forces and Society, and the Israel Political Science Association. We also presented these ideas in department colloquia at several universities in Israel and abroad. We thank participants in all of these conferences and seminars for their helpful comments and suggestions.

Many individuals in Israel and abroad have given us feedback on our project in various stages and we are indebted to them. We thank Sarai Aharoni, Eyal Ben-Ari, Oded Löwenheim, Amiram Oren, Shaul Shenhav, Mario Sznajder, and Eyal Tsur from The Hebrew University of Jerusalem; Stuart Cohen from Bar Ilan University; Zoltan Barany and Ami Pedahzur from the University of Texas in Austin; Richard Kohn from Duke University; Jonathan Caverley and Hendrik Spruyt from Northwestern University; and Christopher Dandeker from Kings College.

At Cambridge University Press, we thank our editor, Lewis Bateman; Shaun Vigil; and two anonymous referees who offered valuable feedback on the

[1] The proceedings of the workshop were published in Sheffer, Barak, and Oren (2008) and Sheffer and Barak (2010) as well as in a special issue of the journal *Israel Studies*.
[2] Its proceedings were published in Barak and Sheffer (2009a).

manuscript. We also thank Theresa Kornak and Colette Stoeber for copyediting the manuscript.

We also thank Chanan Cohen and Einat Vadai for valuable research assistance.

Research for this book was made possible by grants from The Harvey L. Silbert Center for Israel Studies and the Levi Eshkol Institute for Social, Economic and Political Research in Israel, both at The Hebrew University of Jerusalem.

Introduction

Since the establishment of the State of Israel in 1948, and particularly after the Israeli–Arab War of 1967, a highly informal but at the same time very potent security network, composed of acting and former security personnel and their partners in the state's various civilian spheres, has influenced Israel's domestic sphere, including culture, politics, society, economy, public discourse, and foreign relations. This book discusses this major sociopolitical phenomenon and its impacts in a comparative and theoretical perspective.

The book has six main goals. First, we define Israel's security network and situate it in a broad, theoretical and comparative perspective. Second, we explain how Israel's security network came into being and how it managed to acquire a hegemonic position in the area of national security and foreign policy, shaping various strategic and tactical views, policies, and actions of the state. A third goal is to provide details on the actors, their cultural values, and the mechanisms that make up the security network. Fourth, we discuss the multitude of roles that Israel's security network has come to play both domestically and externally, including but by no means limited to the area of national security and foreign policy. Fifth, in discussing other relevant cases, we point out the similarities and differences between these cases and Israel. Finally, we aim to provide general analytical and theoretical conclusions that would help explain kindred phenomena in these and other states and would also help to study these significant issues better.

ISRAEL'S SECURITY NETWORK – A PRIMER

The main argument advanced in this book is that the civil–security relations in Israel, as well as in some other small states, are characterized by the existence of an informal powerful security network made up of acting and former security personnel and their partners in the state's various civilian spheres. At the same time we will show that occasionally a number of competing and even clashing subnetworks appear within Israel's security network, and that this phenomenon has become more conspicuous in recent years.

Israel's security network is a type of an informal "policy network" in which one of its members' most significant concerns is security. Thus, we refer to it as a "security network" that has had a significant impact on domestic and external policymaking and concrete strategic and tactical policies in recent decades. Although Israel's security network is quite heterogonous, and despite occasional disagreements between some of its members, its common features, interests, and ultimately its exceptional ability to influence many aspects of public life in Israel, make it a subject worthy of increased attention. In addition, because the Israeli case is not unique, it can be applied to other similar cases.

Three types of actors make up Israel's security network: first, acting and former members of the state's large and powerful security sector, particularly the military, that is, the Israel Defense Forces (IDF); second, former lower-ranking security personnel, also mainly from the army; third, influential actors operating within various civilian spheres (politics, the economy, and civil society), including politicians, bureaucrats, wealthy private entrepreneurs, academics, and journalists.

Such actors can be regarded as members of Israel's security network for a number of reasons: They are interconnected by informal, nonhierarchical links and ties; they share common values and perceptions on Israel's various policy areas, and particularly security, which, despite differing views on how to promote it, they see as paramount; they have identical or similar individual and collective interests; and they are capable of joining hands in order to influence policymaking on different levels and in various spheres.

Despite the relatively large size of Israel's security network – a conservative estimate of membership would be some hundreds per decade since 1948 – and notwithstanding its considerable impacts on policymaking and concrete policies in recent decades, this network is an understudied topic in the otherwise extensive literature on the country's culture, politics, economy, and civil society. Particularly striking is its absence from most debates over Israel's pattern of civil–military relations, which, despite certain advances in recent years, still attach great importance to the state's formal institutions and their positions and relations and overlook more informal factors and their impact on planning, policymaking, concrete policies, and actions.

The scholarly gap regarding the role of policy networks in the area of national security, however, extends beyond the Israeli case. Despite the growing attention to informal aspects of the relationship between the civilian and security spheres, particularly since the end of the Cold War, many studies are still preoccupied with its formal aspects and tend to emphasize them when dealing with both Western and non-Western states.[1] In this book, we address

---

[1] A notable exception is Wedel (2009), whose book raises important questions about the role of networks in the area of foreign policy in non-Western and Western states.

this notable gap by closely examining Israel's security network, emphasizing its own specific characteristics but also juxtaposing it to a number of other relevant cases, and developing a more general conceptual framework for studying this phenomenon. In the remainder of this introduction, we provide an overview of the Israeli case, and present the plan of the book.

AN OVERVIEW OF THE ISRAELI CASE

On May 14, 1948, after the termination of the British Mandate in Palestine, the State of Israel proclaimed its independence, and two weeks later it formed its own army – the IDF. In practice, however, Israel's security agencies, like its political and bureaucratic institutions, can be traced back to the period of the Yishuv, the Jewish community in Palestine during the time of British Mandate.

The pre-state voluntary security institutions included, first and foremost, the Hagana and its regular fighting force, the Palmach, but also smaller military organizations such as *Etzel* and Lehi (Horowitz and Lissak 1977; Pa'il 1979; Gelber 1986; Ostfeld 1994; Ben-Eliezer 1998; Segev 2000). In addition, Jewish youth served in foreign armies, most notably in the British Army during the Second World War (Gelber 1986: 552).

The circumstances surrounding Israel's independence were by no means hospitable to the new state. When it was established, the long-time conflict between the Jewish and Arab communities in Palestine had already escalated into a full-fledged civil war, and after the end of the British Mandate in Palestine, the armies of several Arab states, mainly Egypt, Transjordan, Syria and Iraq, intervened. Consequently, a host of foreign volunteers came to fight alongside the two belligerents (see, e.g., Malet 2010: 101–2). In 1949, the conflict was terminated not by formal Israeli–Arab peace treaties, as some Israeli leaders expected, but by armistice agreements signed between Israel and each of Egypt, Lebanon, Transjordan, and Syria, but not with Iraq or the Palestinians, under the auspices of the United Nations (Bialer 1990: 202).

In the next decades, Israel was involved in several wars with the neighboring Arab states (in 1956, 1967, 1969–1970, 1973, and 1982), and launched military operations against Palestinian and Lebanese nonstate armed factions (in 1978, 1982, 1993, 1996, 2006, and 2008–2009). Eventually, Israel did manage to reach formal arrangements with some of its Arab neighbors, including two peace treaties signed with Egypt in 1979 and with Jordan in 1994. However, two agreements, signed between Israel and Lebanon in 1983 and between Israel and the Palestine Liberation Organization (PLO) in 1993, were not so successful. On a more informal level, Israel established a working relationship with Jordan and reached certain tacit understandings with Syria concerning Lebanon in 1976. It also reached informal understandings with a Lebanese nonstate armed faction, Hizbullah, in the 1990s, and with Palestinian nonstate armed factions such as the PLO in the early 1980s and Hamas since 2003. But these did not prevent occasional outbreaks of violence in Israel, Lebanon, and the Palestinian Territories.

Following the First Israeli–Arab War (1947–1949), Israel's leaders decided that in view of the state's volatile security situation, all Jewish citizens, both male and female, should be drafted to the IDF at the age of 18, and that men would serve there for 30 months and women for 24 months.[2] In practice, men have served for 36 months since 1967.[3] It was also decided that most members of Israel's Palestinian Arab community would be exempted from military service, though small groups within this sector, such as the Druze, the Circassians, and some Bedouins, were later drafted (Peled 1998; Krebs 2006; Kanaaneh 2009).[4] Those exempted from military service also included ultrareligious Jewish men and women and all married Jewish women.

In addition to these conscripts, the IDF was to have a reserve force comprising men and women who had completed their mandatory military service. The reservists, who were to undergo periodic military training, could be fully mobilized during national emergencies. The most important part of the IDF, however, was its standing force of career officers and noncommissioned officers (NCOs), who were not drafted separately but rather recruited from among its conscripts (Horowitz and Lissak 1989: 195–230; Van Creveld 1998: 113–5). As we shall see, many serving and retired members of this third group, particularly from among its highest echelons, can be regarded as the "core" of Israel's security network.

The missions and tasks of the IDF in 1949 were, first and foremost, military: to defend the long and meandering borders of the new state and protect Israeli citizens from any Arab attack, and to prepare for a possible, and according to some Israeli leaders, inevitable, "second round" with the Arab states that refused to recognize Israel. In order to achieve these ends, Israel's military and political leaders decided in the early 1950s to adopt an offensive–defensive military strategy that stipulated the launching of preemptive strikes against imminent threats to the state's security. This new military strategy led to the development of a powerful air force with long-range strike capabilities; an armored corps and infantry capable of penetrating the enemy's lines; and a large intelligence community, with the IDF's Intelligence Branch as its most important part, entrusted with determining whether Israel is under threat and if so by whom (Handel 1994; Oren 2002; Oren, Barak, and Shapira, 2013). Later, Israel also developed a nuclear capability, though it never acknowledged this officially, and eventually also antimissile systems (Cohen 1998).

However, from the outset the IDF was also entrusted with civilian tasks such as education, settlement, and the absorption of the hundreds of thousands of Jewish immigrants arriving in Israel in its early years. In conceptual terms, the

---

[2] Religious Jewish women can serve within the framework of the National Service, which, in recent years, has expanded to include some Palestinian Arab citizens.

[3] Some conscripts serve in the Border Guard, which is part of the Israeli police.

[4] Military service became mandatory for the Druze and Circassians in 1956.

IDF played a pivotal role in Israel's process of state formation and development. By this last term, we mean three interrelated and often-overlapping sub-processes that, together, helped produce the modern state in the West and later in other regions: first, state-building, which consists of measures that produce "territorial consolidation, centralization, differentiation of the instruments of government, and monopolization of the means of coercion" (Tilly 1975: 42); second, "statecraft," or state-construction, defined as the "processes or mechanisms whereby a state enhances its power and authority," using its formal agencies but significantly also an array of informal, including cultural, means (Davis 1991: 12; see also Foucault 1979; Mitchell 1991; Steinmetz 1999); and third, national integration, which involves centrally based efforts to inculcate the state's entire populace with a common identity (Gellner 1983; Smith 1986; Hobsbawm 1990; Anderson 1991). This role has accorded the IDF a senior position in the politics, economy, society, and public culture of the new state.

In the decades after the establishment of the state, the boundaries between its civilian and security spheres have remained, by and large, extremely porous and almost nonexistent, and this important factor has enabled the IDF, as well as Israel's informal security network, to wield considerable influence on all areas of public and private life. This factor, in turn, contributed to the continued lack of differentiating boundaries between these spheres. These processes are discussed in the text that follows.

In conceptual terms, which we elaborate upon in Chapter 1, Israel can thus be defined as a "small state" that has faced real or imagined, but in any case perceived "continuous existential threats" since its independence.

Concerning the question of whether Israel is a unique case in this regard or does it have parallels in other countries, we wish to emphasize that we do not view the Israeli case as being essentially *sui generis* and hence as incomparable to other relevant cases. While the view that Israel is "unique" is held by some Israeli politicians, who have sometimes used it to justify special arrangements, positions and actions for Israel (e.g., in the nuclear realm; see Cohen 1998: 160), as well as by some students of the Israeli case, we suggest that scholars, particularly from the social sciences, who make comparisons as part of their research, should treat such claims with caution (see the discussion in Barnett 1996). The question is, therefore, to *which* other cases should one compare Israel, and what insights can be gleaned from such an approach. In the following chapters, we elaborate on our position on this important issue first by presenting a critical appraisal of previous studies on Israel's civil–security relationship, including the comparative dimension, and then by placing this case in the most appropriate reference group as per our research.

RATIONALE AND STRUCTURE OF THE BOOK

This book sheds light on Israel's security network by examining its emergence and scope in connection with the development of the Israeli political system, demonstrating its impact on the domestic sphere and on Israel's foreign

relations, and situating this phenomenon in a broad theoretical and comparative perspective.

Chapter 1 presents the theoretical and comparative tools that we use to analyze Israel's security network. These include theories that explain, and at times
also prescribe, the relationship between the state's civilian and security spheres,
as well as studies that focus on small states that have faced real or imagined,
but in any case perceived, continuous existential threats. It demonstrates that
general studies on civil–security relations, as well as those that deal with small
states, tend to overlook the more informal aspects of this relationship, and
especially the role of security networks in shaping policymaking, concrete policies, and actions. The chapter addresses this notable gap by discussing studies
on policy networks and other relevant theories and asking how they can be
applied to the realm of national security.

The goals of Chapter 2 are twofold: First, we aim to demonstrate how our
concept of the security network relates to, and informs, the ongoing debate
concerning the relationship between Israel's civilian and security sectors.
Second, we explain the emergence, persistence, and strength of Israel's security
network and its connection to Israel's political culture and political system. We
show how it has developed through the years and identify the major milestones
in this process. Although we especially focus on Arab–Israeli confrontations (in
particular the 1967 War) and peacemaking efforts, we also consider important
domestic developments, such as the formation of successive National Unity
Governments in Israel, and other changes in its political, social, economic, and
cultural spheres.

In Chapter 3, we focus on Israel's security network itself and ask who its
members are and where they are situated in Israel's broadly defined political system, economy, and civil society. We then inquire about the formal and
informal mechanisms and institutions that have facilitated the operation of
Israel's security network and helped its members promote their individual and
collective interests and goals, and discuss some of their shared values and con-
ceptions, particularly with regard to Israel's national security, and how they
relate to general cultural values of the Jewish community in Israel. One of the
issues that we mention in this chapter and demonstrate later is the appearance
in recent years of competing and even clashing subnetworks within Israel's
security network.

Chapter 4 discusses the impact of Israel's security network and, in certain
cases, of subnetworks operating within it, on the domestic arena. This is done by
highlighting some of the manifold influences members of the security network,
or the subnetworks, can have on major decisions and actions in various civilian
spheres in Israel, particularly the political system and the economy. Ultimately,
the chapter asks whether the persistence and strength of the security network
can help explain why and to what extent Israel is a "formal democracy" and
not an "effective democracy."

Chapter 5 discusses the long-term effects of Israel's security network on the state's foreign relations and defense. After providing additional evidence for the hegemonic position acquired by Israel's security network in war and peacemaking, particularly in comparison with other relevant actors, we present two concrete cases that highlight the role of the security network in shaping Israel's policymaking and concrete policies in the external realm.

The goal of Chapter 6 is to situate our discussion of Israel's security network and its impact in a broad perspective by comparing the Israeli case to some other small states that have faced continuous existential threats. In particular, we inquire about the type of relationship that emerged between these states' civilian and security sectors and its impact on the domestic sphere, including their regimes, and on their foreign relations.

Finally, in the Conclusion, we present our main analytical and theoretical findings concerning Israel and the additional cases that we have examined. We also call attention to the implications for future research on security networks generally and in other states and suggest how they can be better comprehended and studied.

I

Security Networks

A Theoretical and Comparative Perspective

In the introduction to this book we posited that Israel is a small state that has confronted continuous existential threats, real or imagined, since its establishment as an independent state in 1948. We also suggested that the best way to comprehend the relationship between Israel's civilian and security sectors is in terms of a highly informal but very influential security network that comprises acting and former security personnel and their partners in the state's various civilian spheres. This chapter provides the necessary "tool-kit" that will allow us to analyze Israel's security network and kindred phenomena in other relevant states. First, we discuss several major approaches to the relationship between the civilian and security sectors. We then focus on the category of states that best approximates Israel, that is, small states that have faced real or imagined continuous existential threats, and discuss the relationship that developed between their civilian and security sectors. Finally, we present several additional tools that can help analyze security networks in Israel and elsewhere.

Before proceeding with the actual discussion, we will briefly explain the main concept used in this chapter. Since the term "civil–military relations" refers to the military but not to states' other security services, we prefer to speak of the relationship between states' civilian and security sectors. "Civilian sector" as used here not only refers to cultural aspects but also encompasses the political system, the economy, and civil society, broadly defined, including civil society groups, the media, and the educational system. The "security sector," in its turn, includes the military but also other law-enforcement agencies, such as the police, the paramilitary forces, the border guards, and, if relevant, the coast guard, the intelligence and internal security services, as well as the military industries and the nuclear authority. The professional, that is, the nonpolitical, components of the Ministry of Defense can also be considered part of the security sector. Although this book is concerned mainly with the military, which in

Israel and in many other states, including continuously threatened small states, is the most powerful security service in terms of its size, missions, and role in the process of state formation and development, we do mention other security services when they are relevant to the discussion.

THE RELATIONSHIP BETWEEN THE STATE'S CIVILIAN AND SECURITY SECTORS

In the last decades of the twentieth century, the study of the relationship between states' civilian and security sectors was neglected by political scientists and students of International Relations (IR), though not always by sociologists and anthropologists (see, e.g., Bland 2001: 527; Bruneau 2006: 2). However, since the turn of the twenty-first century, and particularly since the terrorist attacks of 9/11 and the launching of the wars in Afghanistan and in Iraq by the United States and its allies, there has been a renewed interest in this field. Whereas political scientists, especially from the subfield of comparative politics, either revisit the "traditional approach" (Nielsen and Snider 2009; Croissant, Kuehn, Chambers, and Wolf 2010) or raise new questions (such as how to build "democratic armies" as part of the efforts to export democracy to non-Western regions and/or restore a legitimate political order in the aftermath of civil wars: see, e.g., Barany 2009: 178–9), IR specialists express interest in civilian control of the military, which, they posit, "is not merely a means to promote democracy, but it is also a force in favor of peace" (Sechser 2004: 771; see also Choi and James 2008: 37).

Among the many approaches to the study of the relationship between the state's civilian and security sectors, we choose to focus on four major ones. The first is the "traditional approach" with its two major strands, the "political approach" and the "sociological approach," which dominated the field until the end of the Cold War and is still very influential today. Second, we refer to several "critical" perspectives, which, though less popular than the traditional approaches, have nonetheless stimulated the academic and public debate on these issues, and, we must add, have also inspired this book. Third, we consider studies that have focused on the relationship between the civilian and security sectors in non-Western states. Finally, we discuss more recent works that address the changing relationship between the civilian and security sectors since the end of the Cold War. Rather than presenting an exhaustive account of these approaches, which would exceed the scope of this book, we focus on the major questions that each addresses.

Traditional Approaches

The main question that the "traditional approach" posed with regard to the relationship between states' civilian and security sectors, namely, how states guarantee civilian control of the military, was not new. What authors who adopted this approach did offer, however, was the first systematic attempt to analyze this relationship based on empirical evidence and the formulation of a set of theoretical and normative assumptions that had a clear prescriptive dimension.

The major strands within the traditional approach – the "political" and "sociological" approaches – were developed in established states in the West, particularly in the United States, in the period of the Cold War. This fact has considerable bearing not only on these theories themselves but also on their applicability to other periods and to other regions of the world. Indeed, these theories were soon complemented by works that sought to explain the relationship between civilian and security sectors in the socialist and communist countries in Eastern Europe and elsewhere (for an overview, see Segal 1994), in Latin America (see, especially, Stepan 1988) and in the "new states" in the Third World, which are sometimes referred to as the "postcolonial" or the "developing" states.

The first of these traditional approaches – the political approach – is associated with the works of Samuel Huntington (see, especially, Huntington 1957), who posited that the best way to guarantee that the military remains answerable to the state's civilian leaders is to establish "objective civilian control" over it. This, Huntington later explained, stipulated "1) a high level of military professionalism and recognition by military officers of the limits of their professional competence; 2) the effective subordination of the military to the civilian political leaders who make the basic decisions on foreign and military policy; 3) the recognition and acceptance by that leadership of an area of professional competence and autonomy for the military; and 4) as a result, the minimalization of military intervention in politics and of political intervention in the military" (Huntington 1996: 3–4). The state's civilian and military spheres, in other words, were to be fully separated from one another: A civilian leader was to be the commander in chief in all respects, a separate civilian body was to be entrusted with approving the military's budget, and the military itself was to be a professional institution that enjoyed autonomy in military affairs in return for its total obedience to the civilian leaders. Many observers have noted that the political approach has been dominant in the United States and in other Western states for many decades (Segal 1994; Burk 2002; Nielsen and Snider 2009).

The second traditional approach – the sociological approach – is identified with the works of Morris Janowitz (see, especially, Janowitz 1960). In contrast to Huntington's political approach, Janowitz posited that effective civilian control over the military would not be achieved by removing it from society and professionalizing it, but rather by integrating it into society. To this end, the boundaries between the military and society were to be permeable, and the military itself composed not of specialists in military affairs but rather of "civilian-soldiers" whose values and perceptions were to be greatly influenced by those of their fellow citizens (Segal 1994; Burk 2002). Although less popular and influential than the political approach, the sociological approach did appeal to many scholars not only in the United States but also in other regions of the world, including in newer states such as Israel.

In the decades that elapsed since they were formulated, both the political and the sociological approaches have had a considerable impact on the field of civil–security relations (Feaver and Seeler 2009: 85–9). But both also elicited criticism. The former, which stipulated rigid boundaries between the civilian leaders and the military, "had eventually given way to a military willing to involve itself, if only tentatively at first, in politics" (Cohen 2002: 205). The latter, in its turn, was of limited use to political scientists since it did "not [focus] on answering political questions about control and decision making" (Feaver 2005: 9).

Critical Perspectives

At about the same time that the traditional approaches to the relationship between the state's civilian and security sectors were introduced, critical perspectives emerged, also in the United States. These sought to grasp the potent fusion of security and civilian interests in periods of major security threats to a state and particularly during large-scale conflicts, which were liable to overshadow all other considerations.

First among these was the "garrison state," a concept put forth by Harold Lasswell as early as 1941, during the Second World War. According to Lasswell, the "total wars" of the 20th century were characterized by little separation between the state's civilian and military realms and by the accumulation of unprecedented power by the military, which far exceeded that of the political leaders. In situations such as these, he posited, the imperatives of the conflict were liable to push the military command to demand, obtain, and maintain overall superiority even without seizing formal political positions and power (Lasswell 1941).

A second critical perspective, which dates to the early years of the Cold War, revolved around the notion of the "power elite." According to C. Wright Mills, who introduced this concept, the continuous wars waged by the United States in the late nineteenth and early twentieth centuries led to the rise of a particular kind of social elite in the country, whose members were state functionaries, heads of large corporations, social leaders, and army generals. The members of this power elite, Mills posited, were now in positions to make decisions that could have major consequences for their fellow countrymen (Mills 1956: 4).

Another critical perspective was the "military–industrial complex," a term that, unlike aforementioned concepts, was coined not by an academic but by a former army general who became a political leader: U.S. President Dwight Eisenhower. In his farewell address in 1961, Eisenhower warned his fellow citizens of a situation in which the combined interests of the military establishment and big industrialists in the United States, which he referred to as the "military–industrial complex," could lead to the "disastrous rise of misplaced power" that would come at the expense of the public good (Eisenhower 1961; Ledbetter 2011).

Taken together, these critical perspectives challenged the traditional approaches to the relationship between the civilian and security sectors. They called attention to structural, cultural, and rational (or interest-based) factors that were either overlooked or rejected by the traditional writers, but that were liable to affect, or, according to some, were already significantly influencing this relationship. These factors were the results of the profound changes that took place in the nature of war, which included the emergence of the "total wars" in the 1930s and 1940s and the Cold War in the late 1940s and early 1950s; the shared experiences, values, and perceptions of members of a country's social elite, which set them apart from their fellow citizens; and the potent mix of economic and military considerations that became a factor to be reckoned with.

Although these critical perspectives also elicited criticism (see, e.g., Desch 1999: 1–2) and despite the fact that some of them did not establish how the particular factors, or actors, that they identified, influenced policymaking and concrete policies,[1] it would be a mistake to dismiss them offhand. First, and as we shall see in the next chapters, some of these concepts have been applied to cases besides the United States, particularly to small states, such as Israel, facing perceived continuous threats, in order to define their emerging pattern of civil–security relationship. Second, these theories can help elucidate the predicament of great powers such as the United States, which since 9/11 has been engaged in a new kind of open-ended war – the War on Terror (Johnson 2004; Kohn 2009: 198; Ledbetter 2011: 14).

The Situation in Non-Western States

Although they were presented as general theories that could be applied at different periods and in various states' settings, the traditional approaches to the relationship between the security sector and the civilian sector have been relevant mostly to established states in the West, and particularly the United States (cf. Huntington 1996). Indeed, the political approach was based on the premise that the political system is effective and that the political leaders are more powerful than their military counterparts. These assumptions, at least at the time, applied mainly to Western states. The sociological approach suggested that society is vibrant and that the civilian values espoused by its members are more robust than those prevailing in the military, and that this, too, was the case mainly in the West. Whether or not these assumptions were applicable to

---

[1] Some of these writers did not deal with this question. Mills (1956: 21) writes, "The idea of the power elite implies nothing about the process of decision-making as such: it is an attempt to delimit the social areas within which that process, whatever its character, goes on."

non-Western states, especially to the new states in the Third World, however, remained a question.

Some traditional authors, including Samuel Huntington (1968) and Morris Janowitz (1977), did acknowledge the difficulties inherent in applying their theories to the new and partially democratic states. However, some of the prescriptions they and their colleagues proposed, such as that the military would become the driving force for establishing a Western-type political order in these states (Huntington 1968), were problematic. First, this prescription could be interpreted as an encouragement for the military to seize power in these states, and for Western powers, chiefly the United States, to support its essentially authoritarian rule (see, e.g., Migdal 1997: 220–1). Second, it was not at all clear whether the military in these new states would be at all capable, or willing, to play such a role. "Armies," Roger Owen has observed, "have their own institutional imperatives which mean that their technological, educational or administrative resources are not simply available to the rest of society for whatever civilian purpose they may happen to be needed" (Owen 2000: 178).

Other students of the non-Western states presented their own theoretical frameworks for studying the relationship between their civilian and security sectors, which were more congruent with the situation there at the time (see, e.g., Finer 1962; Luckham 1971; Perlmutter 1974). However, these studies, useful as they were, were also heavily influenced by Western theories, especially of the traditional type. Moreover, they could not account for important political and social changes that took place in these states in later periods, especially the decline of military coups and the partial "civilianization" of the military regimes and governments in some non-Western states (see, e.g., Alagappa 2001).

More recent works, however, have been more successful in this regard. Drawing on the works of Morris Janowitz and Robin Luckham, Roger Owen has posited that non-Western militaries, like their Western counterparts, have unique characteristics such as hierarchy, defined borders, and professionalism; that they seek to achieve complete control of how they recruit, train, and promote their officers; and that they try to protect themselves against threats to their integrity and particularly their politicization. The result, he argued, is that the military's place in society is not fixed but changes over time: The military tries to obtain more resources and define and establish its role in the state's national security, and the civilian leaders attempt to impose their control over the military. Both sides manipulate public opinion, forge alliances, and either divide their prominent opponents or shift them to their own side. In this process of bargaining, the military's relative power is judged by the extent to which it succeeds in getting its share in the state budget, the size of the military industry, and whether or not it has to share power with the state's internal security agencies. The relative strength of the army and the politicians is determined by the prestige of the army, its ability to intimidate or override the decisions of the civilian government, the cohesion of the army's senior officers, and the extent to which the state is seen as facing a military threat (Owen 2000: 178–80. See also Croissant, Kuehn, Chambers, and Wolf 2010).

But this analysis, too, has its drawbacks, mainly because of the informal connections, ties, and understandings that exist between, on the one hand, the military and other security services and, on the other hand, various civilian actors such as politicians, businessmen, journalists, former security officials, and so forth. In Turkey, for example, the military has in recent years reached a tacit understanding with the politicians, including Prime Minister RecepTayyip Erdoğan, head of the pro-Islamist Justice and Development Party, that the military would no longer intervene in politics and the politicians would not undermine the core values of the Turkish Republic. In addition, the military has connections to a "collective of associations [that] have periodically fanned the fears of security risks, from destructive challenges of ethnic and ideological movements to those of 'foreign enemies', and in doing so have helped to 'securitize' public opinion" (Aydinli 2009: 590). Indeed, some authors have used the term "deep state" to describe the influence of the Turkish military and its civilian partners, referring to the network of individuals within the military and the intelligence agencies, the executive branch, academia, the media, and even civil society that planned a military coup against Erdoğan's party in what has come to be known as the "Ergenekon case" (Kaya 2009; Ünver 2009; Aydinli 2011). In Lebanon as well, especially during the presidencies of former General Fouad Chehab and his successor, Charles Helou (1958–1970), but also in later periods, in particular since the end of the civil war of 1975–1990, close ties emerged between acting military officers and civilian politicians and journalists who had considerable influence on the state's day-to-day affairs (Barak 2009). Finally, Egypt under President Hosni Mubarak saw tacit understandings between, on the one hand, the state's large and powerful security sector and, on the other hand, some actors within civil society. According to these, the security sector protects the state against the threat of takeover by radical Islamic groups, and civil society actors accord legitimacy to the security sector's meta-political position in the state (Barak 2011).

As we will see in Chapter 6, other small states, especially continuously threatened ones such as Singapore, Taiwan, South Korea, and South Africa until the demise of Apartheid, have also exhibited informal ties and connections between their powerful security sector and various civilian actors.

It should be emphasized, however, that the growing attention being given to the informal aspects of the relationship between the state's civilian and security sectors is by no means limited to non-Western states, where focus on military coups and military governments has shifted to an interest in "the diverse and often subterranean forms of military political influence under civilian or democratic regimes" (Luckham 2003: 10) and to various strategies of "coup-proofing" (Quinlivan 1999). Indeed, in recent years, and particularly since the end of the Cold War, one can identify an "informal turn" in the study of the relationship between the civilian sector and the security sectors in established states in the West.

Before we elaborate on this significant development let us mention two additional issues that are highly relevant to this relationship in many non-Western states, including Israel, but that are not always accorded due attention. These are, first, the role of the military and the other security services in the process of state formation and development as defined earlier; and second, the particular relationship that exists between the security sector, on the one hand, and the pattern of intersectoral relations in the state, on the other, in divided or heterogeneous societies where ethnic, national, tribal, clan, regional, or other identities are salient and politically relevant.

With regard to the first issue, many studies underscore the pivotal role of the military and other coercive institutions in the process of state formation and development. One group of authors (Tilly 1975, 1990; Evans, Rueschemeyer, and Skocpol 1985; Mann 1986; Anderson 1987) focuses on the institutional aspects of this process and emphasizes the role of coercion in building the state's military, bureaucracy, and physical infrastructure, mostly in a positive correlation with war-making (see, especially, Tilly 1975: 42). A second group of writers highlights the role of military institutions in the social construction of the state as an actor that is considered to be "autonomous" from society (Foucault 1979; Mitchell 1991). Finally, a third group of authors (Finer 1975; Mosse 1990; Barak 2009) highlights the role played by the military in national integration, though others (Krebs 2006) are more skeptical in this regard.

At the same time, there is evidence that militaries can, sometimes, become an obstacle to the process of state formation and development. First, attempts to influence politics either by launching military coups or by penetrating the political system in an informal and hence less costly manner can undermine the differentiation between the state's various functions, which is a crucial part of the process of state formation and development, and prevent effective civilian control of the military. Second, when militaries and other security services openly identify with some sectors of a heterogeneous or divided society and antagonize and even repress others, the process of national integration is inevitably impaired (see, e.g., Salih 1996 with regard to Iraq).

This last issue raises the interesting question of what kind of relationship exists between the security sector and the various social sectors of a divided or heterogeneous society. Generally speaking, two models exist for describing such relationships. The first is characterized by "control," and describes such societies in which (1) one sector is dominant; (2) national security is, essentially, the security of the dominant sector; and (3) the military and the security sector in general are under the dominant sector's exclusive control (Enloe 1980; Horowitz 1985; Peled 1998). The second model is one of "power-sharing" that describes divided or heterogeneous societies in which none of the societal sectors is dominant and decisions on all matters of national security are reached by consensus (Barak 2009).

The Informal Turn in the Post–Cold War Period

The end of the Cold War resulted in the reorganization of most Western militaries and other security services. These were accorded new roles, missions, and tasks, in particular peacekeeping, "nation-building," and counterterrorism. But it also led to renewed efforts to understand the relationship between the security and civilian sectors and to identify continuity and change in this context. This section, which charts the major developments in the field in the last two decades, identifies (1) studies that attempt to grasp mainly the structural changes in the post–Cold War period by considering them from a broad socio-economic and historical perspective and (2) studies that focus on the civil–military interface and analyze it using rational or interest-based tools, cultural tools, or a combination of both.

The first type of works includes, first and foremost, the "postmodern military," a concept introduced by Charles Moskos (2000). It holds that the U.S. military in the 1990s, that is, in the "postmodern era," was different from its predecessors in the modern period (1900–1945) and in the late modern period (1945–1990) in several important respects. These include the major threat facing the state, the military's structure, the central mission of the military, the identity of the dominant military professionals, public attitudes toward the military, the relationship between the military and the media, the role of civilian employees in the military, the role of women in the military, the role of parents and spouses of military personnel, and the status of homosexuals and conscientious objectors in the military. By examining all these factors in the modern, later modern, and postmodern periods, Moskos suggested that the structure, composition, and goals of the U.S. military, and perhaps of other militaries, were changing much like the transformation of society at large. Other studies examined issues such as the changes in the state's threat environment and how they affected civilian control of the military (Desch 1996, 1999; for criticism, see Tzeng 2009; Woo 2011); the linkage between the process of democratization in some non-Western states, especially in Latin America, Eastern Europe, and East Asia, and these states' civil–security relationship (Huntington 1996; Alagappa 2001; Cawthra and Luckham 2003; Croissant and Kuehn 2009)[2]; the privatization of some of the military's traditional functions; and the challenges this privatization posed for civilian control of the military generally

---

[2] Another example is Croissant et al. (2010), who inquire about the influence of the civilian and military leaders in different policy arenas, such as elite recruitment, public policy, internal security, national defense, and military organization, and whether this is indicative of civilian control of the military. While this attempt to disaggregate the civil–security relationship certainly has its merits, this approach is not without problems, especially when dealing with more informal (including cultural) aspects of this relationship.

and particularly in the new conflicts in this period (Avant 2000, 2005; Mandel 2002).

The second group of works in the post–Cold War era reflects a growing dissatisfaction with the aforementioned traditional approaches to civil–security relations, specifically with what they regard as the overly formal-institutional nature of the political approach and the nonpolitical character of the sociological approach. Focusing on the relationship between the state's political and military leaders, these authors have raised the question of whether the former exercise effective as opposed to merely formal control over the military, and, if so, how they attain this both in a general sense and on a day-to-day basis (Cohen 2002; Feaver 2005).

Accordingly, some recent studies give more attention to the questions of whether and how the army protects democratic values and practices, with some proposing a type of federal model of civil–military relations (Burk 2002) and others proposing a regime composed of principles, norms, and rules to govern the civil–military relationship (Bland 2001). Others seek to better understand the decision-making process concerning national security, describing it as problem solving, in which military personnel contribute their expertise on security, and military and civilian relations are more collegial than hierarchical in nature (Roman and Tarr 1998). Still other writers, who observe the meeting between civilian policymakers and high-level military officers, raise the question of which of the two groups has more experience in security matters (Gibson and Snider 1999). Some authors look at the nature of the dialogue between the political leaders and the security officials and ask whether it is unequal (Cohen 2002: 208–24) or equal (Betts 2009: 40), and whether the military, or certain actors from within it, are capable of influencing this dialogue by defining the concepts employed in its course (Michael 2007), even when formal civilian control of the military is in place. Finally, some posit that the relationship between the political and military leaders in some states, including both Western (e.g., the United States) and non-Western (e.g., India and Israel), is in fact characterized by a concordance. This refers to informal understandings between the country's civilian and military elites that, according to these authors, are more meaningful and effective than the formal subordination of the military to the civilian institutions (Schiff 1995, 2009).

In view of these developments in the field of civil–security relations, and based on his own research on Latin America, it is thus not surprising that David Pion-Berlin has asked in a recent piece whether "informalities within specific countries [are] the exception or the rule," and whether "informal routines so consistently substitute for the formal ones [that] they should constitute the dominant focal points for the analysis of civil-military interactions?" (Pion-Berlin 2010: 15). As this book clearly demonstrates, in the case of Israel, as well as in several other states that have faced similar situations, the answer to both questions is yes!

ISRAEL AND OTHER CONTINUOUSLY THREATENED SMALL STATES

As mentioned earlier, the War on Terror launched by the United States and other Western democracies in the aftermath of the terrorist attacks of 9/11, the antiterrorist policies adopted by these states, and the launching and persistence of the wars in Afghanistan and Iraq have all raised new questions about the predominance of the civilian sector over the security sector in "effective democracies," namely, states where "democratic practices have spread throughout society, governing not only relations between states and citizens but also public relations between citizens" (Heller 2000: 487–8).[3]

The question of civilian control over the security sector, however, is even more relevant to "formal democracies," which are states where "[f]unctionally and geographically, the degree of public legality ... remains severely constrained" and "the component of democratic legality and, hence, of publicness and citizenship, fades away at the frontiers of various regions and class, gender and ethnic relations" (Heller 2000: 487–8). Indeed, in these formal democracies, the extent to which the control of the security sector by the civilian sector, represented by a state's politicians, is effective and not merely formal is doubtful (Luckham 2003: 10).

Among this second group of states, a particularly interesting subcategory consists of several small states that have relatively scarce human and natural resources and limited power or influence in the international system (see, especially, Keohane 1969; Baehr 1975; Amstrup 1976; Handel 1981; Wiberg 1987; Elman 1995; Inbar and Sheffer 1997; Ingebritsen et al. 2006). These are states that, in spite of facing continuous existential threats since independence, have nonetheless retained their formal democratic regime or witnessed a transition from an authoritarian regime to a formal democracy, though not to an effective democracy. In this section we introduce this subcategory of "continuously threatened small states," focusing on the interplay between the continuous existential threat facing the state, on the one hand, and the relationship between the state's civilian and security sectors, on the other. In addition to Israel, which is the focus of this study, this subcategory of states includes Taiwan, South Korea, and South Africa in the period of Apartheid – three states that have successfully transformed from authoritarian regimes into formal democracies in recent decades – as well as Singapore, which is considered to be "partially free."[4] Later in this book we will discuss in more details the nature and quality of Israel's democracy and its development through the years, and we will elaborate on the additional cases and draw comparisons between them and the

[3] In the United States, these events only highlighted long-term processes in this regard. See Gibson and Snider (1999); Kohn (2002, 2009).
[4] According to the recent Freedom House report on democracy in the world, these states received the following combined rating: Israel–1.5 (Free); South Korea–1.5 (Free); Taiwan–1.5 (Free); South Africa–2 (Free); Singapore–4.5 (Partially Free) (see Freedom House 2010).

Israeli case. This will help us to draw some general analytical and theoretical conclusions.

The term "continuous existential threat" refers to a long-term threat to a state's independence, sovereignty, and basic security. Many states in the world face domestic or external security threats and some states face both types; however, existential threats, which can be actual or imagined, stem from one or all of the following factors: first, the particular circumstances in which the state was established; second, the history of the state (and sometimes also the pre-state community) before and/or after independence; third, the state's contested legitimacy in the eyes of domestic actors, foreign actors, or both; and fourth, extraordinarily high levels of hostility toward the state demonstrated by some or all these actors. By underlining the continuous nature of these existential threats, we call attention to the possibility that they will have an impact not only on the state's institutions, namely, the political system, the bureaucracy, the security sector, and the educational system, but also on informal links between various actors operating within the state's civilian and security sectors. At the same time, we wish to emphasize that continuous existential threats not only *influence* these formal and informal actors but can also be *nurtured and sustained* by them. In particular, continuous existential threats affect and are affected by the particular relationship that exists between the state's civilian and security sectors.

A survey of the existing scholarly approaches to existential threats (for details, see Barak and Sheffer 2009b) reveals the absence of a detailed discussion of actors that are both able and willing to present domestic and/or external challenges to the state as existential threats. Scholars of the realist tradition in IR (e.g., Desch 2009; Maoz 2009), for example, speak of threat manipulation and inflation without explaining how these claims are presented and accepted. Furthermore, members of the Copenhagen School in IR elucidate the process of "securitization," whereby threats in general and existential threats in particular are represented and recognized and, moreover, influence the organization and behavior of political and social actors (Buzan, Wæver, and De Wilde 1998; Williams 2003; Stritzel 2007; Wilkinson 2007). However, they often do it without explaining who securitizes and why, and do not consider cultural values that may facilitate securitization.

In view of this theoretical and analytical gap, we specifically focus in this book on the role of informal security networks in presenting challenges to states and their citizens as security challenges and in framing these in existential terms. Indeed, as will be shown in the next chapters, in Israel, and to some extent also in other continuously threatened small states, the growing impact of the security sector, particularly the military, has been paralleled by the rise of informal security networks, whose members are capable of, and who have an interest in securitizing challenges to the state, framing security threats in existential terms in a way that resonates within society at large and suggesting "adequate" responses to these threats that, ultimately, promote these members' individual and collective interests.

WHAT ARE SECURITY NETWORKS?

In a well-known story, three blind men approach an elephant and touch it in order to identify it. Each of the three blind men, however, having touched only one part of the large mammal, concludes that the entire elephant looks like only that particular part, and disagreement among them ensues. The dispute is resolved only when a fourth man, who is not blind, steps in and tells the three blind men that, in fact, elephants have all of the features that they had identified.

In this vein, as far as security networks are concerned, we contend that they have rational (or interest-based), structural, and cultural dimensions (on this useful differentiation, see Lichbach 1997) and that to grasp them fully it is not enough to "feel" only one of their "parts." One must consider all of these dimensions, as well as their interplay. In the paragraphs that follow, we first elucidate each of these dimensions and then present an integrative definition.

From a rational, or interest-based, perspective, security networks are a particular type of policy network (see, especially, Knoke 1990) operating in the realm of national security. The concept of a "policy network," defined as "a cluster of actors, each of which has an interest, or 'stake' in a given ... policy sector and the capacity to help determine policy success or failure" (Peterson 2003: 1) was developed as a way to describe, explain, and predict the outcomes of policymaking via such hybrid arrangements (Marsh and Smith 2000: 6; see also Marin and Mayntz 1991; Marsh and Rhodes 1992; Marsh and Stoker 1995: 292–4). This emphasis on political outcomes sets the concept of "policy network" apart from the more general concept of "social network," which, in recent years, has received increased attention from scholars (see, especially, Aldrich and Zimmer 1986; Burt 1982, 2001; Lin 2001; Wasserman and Faust 1994; Wellman 1999). Although security networks are not formally hierarchical in nature, it can be argued that some of their members are more influential than others: Acting and former security officials have more impact than junior security personnel; and both senior and junior security personnel have more say than civilians in security matters as well as in additional spheres that are securitized. As the Israeli case suggests, a number of competing and even clashing subnetworks can appear within a particular security network.

From a structural perspective, security networks are the informal structures of power that emerge when the boundaries between the state's security sector and various civilian spheres, such as the political system, the economy, and civil society, are porous in nature (cf. Mitchell 1991). The stability of these informal structures, as well as their impact on policymaking and concrete policies, depends, first and foremost, on the continued lack of differentiation between the state's security and civilian spheres, which enables their members to move, and sometimes move back and forth, between the security sector and these various civilian spheres, and on the ability of these structures to exclude various "others" from policymaking and the execution of concrete policies.

Last but certainly not least, from a cultural point of view, a security network has several meanings. First, a security network can be seen as a particular type of an "epistemic community," a network of experts who share a common understanding of the scientific and political nature of particular problems (in this case, security-related issues). Their influence on policymakers, especially under conditions of uncertainty, stems from the fact that they have "epistemic authority," that is, that they are widely held to be authorities in their areas of expertise (Haas 1990: 55; Haas 1997; Adler 1997, 2005). Second, as noted previously, members of security networks have the capacity to securitize civilian issues and to present security challenges to the state and its citizens as existential threats in a way that is acceptable to the state's leaders and large segments of the general public. In Israel, securitization is very often successful, particularly in the Jewish community, because of a potent mix between widely held societal views and beliefs, such as ethno-national fears, collective traumas, and feelings of imminent danger from Israel's enemies (Bar-Tal, Halperin, and Magal 2009). Third, members of security networks have shared norms, values, and perceptions that they express in action and in word.

Security networks, in sum, are complex and fluid relationships between acting and former security officials and civilian actors in the state, which enable these actors to shape policymaking, in general, and particularly determine concrete policies and their implementation. These networks are composed of officials in the area of national security who are considered as experts in this field, have shared values, norms, and perceptions, and are capable to tap on to widely held societal views and beliefs. These individuals occupy key social, political, and economic positions that enable them to promote their particular (and to some extent collective) interests by cutting across ostensibly separate spheres and effectively bypassing official institutions and procedures. At the same time, security networks are not necessarily homogeneous and sometimes feature a number of competing and even clashing subnetworks.

CONCLUSION

This chapter's discussion of the main scholarly approaches to the relationship between the state's civilian and security sectors opened with the traditional approaches and the critical perspectives developed in the formative period of this academic field and continued with a discussion on to studies on non-Western states and more recent developments. Three conclusions can be drawn from this discussion. The first is that there has been increasing attention given to informal, including behavioral and cultural aspects of the civil–security interface. This trend can be seen not only with regard to new states in the non-Western regions, where the boundaries between civilian and security sectors have been and to an extent remain porous, but also in established Western states, including the United States and some European states. Second, existing theories about the relationship between the civilian and security sectors appear to find it very difficult to describe, let alone prescribe, this relationship in periods of major or open-ended conflict, that is, when the national security of the state is at stake. A third conclusion is that in order to consider the complex relationship between the state's civilian and security sectors in a comprehensive way, that is, taking into account its rational (or interest-based), structural, and cultural aspects, we need to develop new terms. In our view, the concept of the security network represents a first step in this direction.

2

The Making of Israel's Security Network

This chapter discusses the emergence of Israel's "security network" which, we posit, was closely interconnected to the process of state formation and development in Israel and to the consolidation of its democratic regime. We begin our discussion with the period of the Yishuv – the Jewish community in Palestine during the time of the British Mandate – which was the formative period not only of the state and the democratic regime in Israel but also of its informal security network. We then discuss the period from Israel's independence in 1948 until the present. Our main focus is on the major milestones in the emergence of Israel's security network, in particular the numerous Arab–Israeli confrontations (most notably the Arab–Israeli War of 1967), that created real and imagined existential threats to Israel and resulted in successful and failed peacemaking efforts between the state and its neighbors. But we also consider important developments that occurred within Israeli society and its political system and economy, which are also very relevant to the discussion.

STATE FORMATION, SECURITY, AND DEMOCRACY IN THE YISHUV AND IN ISRAEL

The establishment of a Jewish state in Palestine was first conceived by the leaders of the Zionist Movement in the late nineteenth century. However, the actual processes that led to the realization of this goal commenced during the late 1930s and gained further impetus during and immediately after the Second World War and the Holocaust in Europe. In any case, already in the 1930s the Jewish community in Palestine had firmly established its communal political and social organizations and its initial military capabilities and agencies under the British Mandate.

There is no question that the establishment of autonomous Jewish military capabilities during that period was strongly prompted by the challenge posed to the Yishuv by the Palestinian Arab community (and, later, also by the Arab states). But this process, which some see as the militarization of the Yishuv, also stemmed from a deep-seated perception of threat that emanated from collective memories of suffering and persecution that prevailed among the Jewish people, including those living in Mandatory Palestine during that period. The growing hardships that the Jews confronted as a result of the immense anti-Semitism in Europe and, later during the Holocaust, reinforced these collective memories, and the result was an aspiration not only for an independent Jewish state but also for significant military capabilities that would guarantee its continued existence. We will return to this important historical-cultural factor when we discuss the factors that have facilitated the predominant role of the security network in Israel since 1948.

In addition to its significance for Israel's process of state formation and development, including the formation and development of its security agencies, the period of the Yishuv is also critical when trying to account for the formal, rather than effective, character of Israel's democracy since 1948. Indeed, with certain minor modifications, which resulted mainly from the inclusion of a sizeable Arab Palestinian community in the state after the First Israeli–Arab War, Israel's political system can best be seen as a continuation of the political institutions that were established in the period of the Yishuv. This observation relates to the following main attributes of Israel's democracy: First, whereas the people (and, since 1948, the citizens) enjoy certain liberties, such as freedom of speech, of movement (including migration) and the freedom of organization and participation in elections, political power rests mostly in the hands of the politicians. These politicians initially included also the political parties and other social and economic actors, but the influence of some of these actors, such as the Kibbutz Movement and the political parties, declined later (Sternhell 1995). Second, security matters, which were are seen critical and indeed existential in Israel (and also in the Yishuv), are to be dealt with by the security experts, which in the early years of statehood included several civilian leaders (e.g., David Ben-Gurion, Israel Galili) but also the emerging and very powerful security sector. Third, one of the main goals of Israeli democracy is to enable its dominant Jewish community, which is anything but homogeneous, to govern itself successfully and to promote its collective interests. Indeed, although members of Israel's Palestinian Arab community have enjoyed certain religious, social, political, and economic rights since 1948, there is little doubt that the Jewish majority is the predominant factor in all internal spheres, policies, and actions, and that it often excluded and marginalized Israel's Palestinian Arab citizens (cf. Gavison 1999; Smooha 2002; Yiftachel 2006; Berent 2010). Finally, a significant portion of political life and public life in Israel in general is mediated through informal practices and procedures, which created the basis for and consequently the emergence of numerous informal aspects, arrangements, and procedures in the area of policymaking, decision taking, and activities in all spheres, and especially in the area of national security (Sharkansky 1999).

Together, these basic characteristics of Israeli democracy can help explain the emergence of policy networks in general and security networks in particular in the Israeli case. They also help account for the high level of autonomy of the security sector and security networks, and for their power and abilities to deal with major social, political, and even some economic matters in Israel.

CIVIL–SECURITY RELATIONS IN ISRAEL: MAIN APPROACHES AND GAPS

In recent decades, numerous works by authors from various academic disciplines have tackled the relationship between Israel's civilian and security spheres. We identify three major scholarly approaches to this relationship: the "traditional," the "critical," and the "new critical" (see Barak and Sheffer 2006, 2007). We briefly present these approaches and then discuss the main differences between them and our own approach (for previous discussions of these studies, see Peri 1996; Sheffer 1996b; Ben-Ari, Rosenhek, and Maman 2001: 1–39; Rosenhek, Maman, and Ben-Ari 2003; Cohen 2008).

The "traditional approach" was inspired by the traditional theories of civil–military relations that emerged in the United States, especially by Morris Janowitz's sociological approach. The writers belonging to this approach, who were also influenced by structural–functional theories dominating Israeli social sciences until the 1980s, focused on the formal structural and functional features of what they perceived as two distinctive subsystems of the Israeli state – the civilian and military – which were separated according to this approach only by "fragmented" boundaries. These writers' overall argument was that the civilian sector in Israel was, traditionally, the dominant among these two sectors (see, especially, Eisenstadt 1967, 1985; Perlmutter 1969; Luttwak and Horowitz 1975; Horowitz and Lissak 1989; Ben-Meir 1995; Lissak 2001).

It is easy to understand the disregard by members of this approach of many important features of the Israeli case, especially since 1967. In particular, they did not realize that some of the informal aspects of the relationship between what they considered to be two separate spheres, especially the social networks between civilians and army officers (Maman and Lissak 1996), would ultimately hinder, rather than strengthen, effective civilian control of Israel's security sector.[1]

---

[1] A recent study argues in the same vein that "Israel's national security establishment, at least at senior levels, is comparatively small, and most officials come to know each other personally. The 'old boys' network' facilitates development of a 'common language' and understanding of the issues and, further, creates a level of personal and professional intimacy. Perhaps most important of all, it enables ease and speed of communications through informal, personal ties that cut through various areas and levels of responsibility. Furthermore, the comparatively small size of the establishment makes it easier to identify those who are responsible and capable of dealing with an issue" (see Freilich 2006: 660).

The second approach – the "critical approach" – was also influenced by Western theories of civil–military relations, but unlike the traditional approach, it was informed by other theoretical advancements in the field. Moreover, unlike members of the traditional approach, who were closely linked to Israel's process of state development in its early decades, these authors were part of a more general trend characterizing Israeli social scientists in the 1980s and 1990s to reexamine the history of the Yishuv and the first decades of Israel's independence, including the societal and political arrangements that influenced the relationship between the state's civilian and security sectors.

Accordingly, proponents of this second approach dealt more critically with the underlying ideological positions of both the civilian sector and the security sector in Israel. They focused, for example, on the continuous involvement of political parties, especially Mapai, the dominant party in the state's early decades, in the development, organization, and policies of the Israel Defense Forces (IDF) since 1948. In addition, these authors emphasized the IDF's growing involvement in Israel's political system since the 1967 War, and the ways in which the latter has turned into a lodestone for former security officials. Still, members of the critical approach spoke of two clearly distinguishable security and civilian/political spheres, and their conceptualization of the relationship between them, including instances of cooperation and conflict, was sometimes vague and not very different than the traditional approach (see, especially, Peri 1983, 1996, 2006; Michael 2007; Sela 2007).

Finally, the third, or "new critical," approach has been influenced by the postmodernist tradition in the social sciences, which percolated into the Israeli social sciences during the 1990s. Unlike the previous approaches, this one emphasized the cultural factors underlying Israeli politics and society, especially what it referred to as the "militaristic" tendencies that, in its view, characterized the Zionist project since the period of the Yishuv. With regard to Israel itself, these authors criticized the near-absence of a vigorous civil society in Israel, that is, of organizations and movements that are not only autonomous from the state but also espouse civil values, which permitted Israel's powerful security sector, especially the IDF, to play a major role in the state (Kimmerling 1993: 197–8; Ben-Eliezer 1995, 1997, 1998; Lumsky-Feder and Ben-Ari 1999; Levy 2007, 2010a).

The emphasis on cultural factors, which are assumed to be the most important in the Israeli case, however, led some of these authors to overlook other important factors that could account for the IDF's domineering role in Israel and the weakness of its political institutions and civil society. These include the long-time predominance of the state's agencies, including the security sector, the bureaucracy, but also a host of quasi-formal agencies such as the Jewish Agency and the Jewish National Fund, over society; the vast financial, technical, and communication resources available to these agencies' members; the considerable lag in the active involvement of civil society groups in politics; the continuous economic hardships experienced by many Israelis that forced them to rely on the state and its agencies and, later, on privately owned charity organizations; and finally, the strong inclination toward individualization processes in Israel in recent decades, which replaced traditional values such as social solidarity.

The theoretical and analytical approach advanced in this book, which employs the concept of the security network, is different from these three approaches in several important respects. First, our approach adopts different theoretical tools and compares Israel to other cases. Despite certain disagreements, both the traditional and critical approaches were influenced by Western theories concerning the relationship between the state's civilian and security sectors. However, Israel has never in fact exhibited a Western-type relationship between its civilian and security sectors, particularly after the 1967 War, making it necessary to look elsewhere for relevant theories and for additional cases that are comparable to the Israeli case.

The third approach, the "new critical approach," rejected the paradigm of civil–military relations (Ben-Eliezer 1998: 339–40) and instead emphasized Israel's incomplete process of state formation and development, which precluded a discussion of its separate civilian and military realms and, ultimately, of their relations. However, in practice, writers who adopted this approach also compared Israel to Western democracies, especially when these faced severe crises (e.g., France during the Algerian War), but *not* to non-Western democratic and democratizing states. Yoram Peri (1996) attributes this shortcoming to these authors' uncritical use of the concept of "militarism," but it seems to us that other, deeper factors have also played a part in this context.

In this book, we adopt an entirely different approach. In our view, the use of Western models of civil–military relations, which are applicable to established states that are effective but not formal democracies, to analyze the Israeli case, which is only partially Western and which, moreover, exhibits a formal democracy, was problematic from the outset and became even more inadequate after 1967. This is mainly because of Israel's unending conflicts and confrontations with Arab states and with the Palestinians and, consequently, its blurred boundaries, which have impinged on the relationship between its civilian and military sectors and obstructed the processes of the state's formation and development. Another factor is the considerable expansion of the security network in Israel and its significant impact over various domestic spheres, including culture, politics, society, and the economy, as well as the state's foreign relations. This phenomenon, which does not have parallels in Western states, does, however, make Israel comparable to several continuously threatened small states. Accordingly, the next chapters attempt to map the scope of Israel's security network, explore its domestic and external impacts, and compare the Israeli case to other relevant cases.

The second area in which our approach differs from existing approaches is our basic characterization of the Israeli case. Consistent with its Western inclination, the traditional approach presents Israel as a "nation-in-arms," or, in the words of one author, as a "civilianized military in a partially militarized society" (Horowitz 1982: 77). While also employing the concept of a nation-in-arms, critical writers speak of a "political–military partnership" between some members of Israel's security and civilian sectors, adding that in the earlier decades of independence, Israel's pattern of civil–military relations was, in fact, characterized by "apparatus control" by Mapai over the security sector (Peri 1983). The new critical approach, for its part, depicts Israel as a "garrison state" or as a "praetorian state" that is, imbued with a "militaristic" culture (Kimmerling 1993; Ben-Eliezer 1995).

Our approach is different. Instead of employing vague theoretical concepts, such as militarism, we conceive of the Israeli case as one that has been characterized by the existence of a security network that has structural, rational, and cultural facets. This network operates in the realm of national security and in other civilian spheres, and has had a considerable impact both domestically and on the state's defense and foreign relations.[2] Hence, we examine the various ways that this security network affects Israel's domestic arena, including its culture, politics, economy, and the broadly defined civil society, and the state's external behavior, in relation to issues such as the perceived continuous real or imagined existential threat that Israel faces; its enduring conflict with its neighbors; its actions in the Arab territories it occupied in the 1967 War; the orientation of its economy; and its public discourse and political culture. Here, too, it is worthwhile to compare Israel to other small states that, like Israel, have not completed their process of state formation and development; perceive themselves as facing continuous domestic and external existential threats, or both; and are engaged in protracted conflicts with their neighbors.

The third major area in which our own approach differs from existing approaches to the Israeli case is in our understanding of the nature of the boundaries that exist between the state's civilian and security sectors. As has been mentioned previously, traditional authors speak of fragmented boundaries between Israel's purportedly autonomous civilian and security spheres and the IDF's "role expansion" into the civilian sphere, often at the initiative of the dominant civilian sector. Though critical authors do accept the notion of fragmented boundaries, they speak of a political–military partnership of members of both spheres. Finally, some members of the new critical approach contend that no meaningful boundaries exist between Israel's dominant military sphere and the subaltern civilian sphere.

Unlike the followers of these approaches, we argue that for most of Israel's history the security network has been a major factor working against a meaningful differentiation between the state's civilian and security sectors, as well as

---

[2] A recent study that examines continuity and change in Israel's security policy by employing the concept of networks is Erez (2009).

against the strengthening of civilian values such as efficiency, transparency, and accountability in Israeli society. Instead, the security network creates a high level of mutual penetration and interdependency, wherein security officials expect their civilian partners, who occupy key positions in the Israeli government, the Knesset, and other institutions, to cooperate with them, and in return they support their civilian partners' decisions and actions. The persistence of this state of affairs renders the notion of the IDF's role expansion or contraction (Lissak 2001) or the notion of a "crisis," or crises, in civil–military relations in Israel (Peri 2006), redundant. This is because all of these terms imply the existence of two clearly delineated and stable subsystems that are more or less equal in strength and that interact voluntarily.

We argue, by contrast, that the boundaries between Israel's security and civilian spheres, which were deliberately kept porous by the state's founding fathers, who sought to employ the IDF and the other security agencies to promote the process of state formation and development, ultimately allowed acting and former security officials to penetrate the civilian sector and to forge ties with influential actors there. The connections between these individuals, together with their shared values and perceptions, have given rise to Israel's security network, which became one of the most influential political, economic, and social factors in the state, eclipsing its civilian leaders. The continued existence of Israel's security network, especially since 1967, has hindered the emergence of more differentiated civilian and military spheres in Israel; contributed to the chaotic development of the state and its political system, economy, and civil society; encouraged militant views and *modi operandi* among the state's leaders and in society; and reinforced the perception of a continuous existential threat to the state.

Last, but not least, our approach differs from the other approaches to the Israeli case in that it offers a more dynamic appraisal of the relationship between the state's civilian and security sectors. Traditional writers posit that in Israel, civilian control of the security sector has been preserved despite domestic and external developments. However, even Eliot Cohen, who praises David Ben-Gurion's style of command in the early years of Israel's independence, concedes that "before long retired generals, rather than true civilians, came to exercise the real control over the conduct of Israel's military affairs" (Cohen 2002: 171). Critical authors argue that Israel's civil–security relationship has changed considerably, especially since 1967; but apart from several works published in the 1980s, which identified a military–industrial complex in Israel (Mintz 1985; Peri and Neubach 1985), these writers have clung to the notion of a political–military partnership in the state's highest policymaking circles, but not elsewhere. Finally, many new critical approaches, and especially those that adopt a cultural standpoint, offer a rather deterministic view of the Israeli case, including the relationship between the state's civilian and security sector, and though some works deal with the changing relationship between the IDF and Israeli society (Levy 2007, 2010a; for a different approach, see Cohen 2008), their view of both spheres is, in the end, quite rigid. This relates to the basic approach of these authors to the different ethnic, religious, and peripheral sectors of Israeli society, as well as to the military itself, in which they do not always differentiate between its conscripts, its reserves, and its standing force.

As we suggest later, there was nothing inevitable in the emergence of Israel's security network and the power that it managed to accumulate in the state since 1948, and the security network itself has a dynamic and ever-changing character. Before discussing these issues in more detail, we briefly mention how this concept relates to the main general approaches to the field.

First of all, the nominal separation that has existed between Israel's security sector and its civilian sector, in combination with the considerable weakness of Israel's political system, render the political approach's notion of objective control of the military (i.e., a professional army separated from society by clearly delineated boundaries and controlled by the political leadership) inapplicable in the Israeli case. Indeed, only a few works have analyzed the Israeli case in these terms, and even these are prescriptive in nature (Shelah 2003). The same is true with respect to the sociological approach and its model of a society of citizen-soldiers in which the armed forces are effectively woven into civilian society. In Israel, civilian influence over the military, as stipulated by the sociological approach, is very limited, while military values penetrate and influence most civilian spheres.

At the same time, our concept of the security network does bear a certain resemblance to, and in a sense can be seen as a conflation of, three critical concepts conceived of during the Cold War to explain the potent fusion of security and civilian interests that comes at the expense of other national interests and public goods in periods of major conflict. These are Harold Lasswell's notion of a garrison state, C. Wright Mills' notion of a power elite, and President Dwight D. Eisenhower's notion of a military–industrial complex. Yet, considerable differences exist between our concept of the security network and these perspectives, in that our concept, which is informed by the expanding literature on policy networks, also highlights the informal structure, capabilities, and actual impact of the security network on policymaking and concrete policies in Israel.

Turning to the post–Cold War literature on the relationship between the civilian and the security sectors, our approach is no doubt part of the informal turn because it focuses on the role of informal ties and connections in the realm of national security and elsewhere. However, our emphasis is not only on the dialogue between civilian and security officials in the realm of national security. In Israel, this dialogue is more often than not conducted between acting security officials and former security officials-turned-politicians. We also ask how this relationship itself is affected by, and how it helps shape, the larger political, societal, economic, and cultural context in which it takes place.

THE EMERGENCE OF ISRAEL'S SECURITY NETWORK

The emergence of Israel's security network and the pivotal role that it has come to play in the civilian and security spheres in the state can be explained in several ways.

From a new critical perspective, this development is seen as part of the emergence of a military culture and militaristic politics in the period of the Yishuv and, later, in the independent Israeli state (Kimmerling 1993). Indeed, even traditional writers speak of the *Diktat of Defense* in Israel, particularly among its dominant Jewish community (Dowty 1998: 87). Without reiterating the debate over whether Israel is a "nation-in-arms," or exhibits a type of "civil militarism" (Kimmerling 1993; Ben-Eliezer 2000; Levy 2010a), consecutive public opinion polls taken in Israel have shown that a majority of its citizens, especially members of its Jewish community, consider security matters and concerns to be the most paramount issue that worries them. In addition, the heads of Israel's security sector, especially the IDF, are widely considered to be more credible than Israel's civilian politicians (see, e.g., Arian 1999–2003). Indeed, for many years, but, as we have already noted, especially since 1967, army officers and other security officials in Israel have enjoyed an unparalleled reputation as public servants who are interested primarily in promoting the national interest and not their own personal goals.

We will elaborate on this sociopolitical cultural factor, which has undoubtedly facilitated the emergence of Israel's security network and helped its members a great deal in advancing their individual and collective goals, especially when they met resistance by civilian politicians and civil society groups. Still, when trying to explain the emergence of the security network and, moreover, identify the turning points in this process, other important factors must also be taken into consideration.

The first factor that comes to mind in this context is the considerable growth in Israel's security sector, particularly the IDF, the volume of the weapons systems that it has acquired, and the rising budgetary allocations for security purposes in Israel, especially in the wake of the 1967 War and the 1973 War (Shiffer 2007). No less important has been the expansion of Israel's military industries, which began to produce weapons systems such as the *Merkavah* tank, the *Arrow* antimissile defense system, and the *Amos* and *Ofeq* satellites (Dvir and Tishler 2000). This process, too, has accelerated after the 1973 War, when Israeli security officials realized that if they produced cutting-edge weapons systems by themselves rather than acquiring weapons from the United States, Israel's main arms supplier, U.S. leaders would be less capable of withholding these weapons from them (Eilam 2009: 226–7). The need to maintain such a huge enterprise turned the IDF into one of the largest Israeli customers and producers in the domestic and foreign markets, and this had profound implications, as the IDF determined standards of products and influenced demand and supply of numerous commercial goods.

Another domestic implication was that the IDF and, to a lesser extent, other
security agencies in Israel, became major participants in all aspects of R&D
in Israel: They not only initiated and financed numerous scientific studies,
including in the fields of strategy, psychology, education, and the experimen-
tal sciences, but they also operated special higher educational programs for
their officials with the cooperation of Israel's universities. The technological
advancements attained by Israel's security sector, in turn, "spilled over" into the
Israeli economy and, among other factors, contributed to its flourishing high-
tech industry. Indeed, the "boom" witnessed by Israel's high-tech industry since
the early 1990s was due, at least in part, to some fifty enterprises launched by
former security personnel, and in 2003, the market value of fifteen of the firms
established by former members of the army's principal intelligence-gathering
unit, 8200, was estimated at $10 billion (*Haaretz* August 15, 2003; see also
Greenberg 1997).But the growth of Israel's security sector also had external
implications. As a result of its ownership of military industries, Israel became
not only a significant importer but also a major exporter of weapons systems,
electronic devices, and know-how. Thus, defense products and weapons systems, which accounted for 32% of Israeli industrial exports (Dvir and Tishler
2000: 35), have risen from an average of less than $1.5 billion per annum in
the early 1990s to an average of $2.8 billion per annum in later years, reaching
a total of $20 billion in the period 1993–2003. In 2002, for example, it reached
$4.18 billion (*Haaretz* June 9, 2003, September 5, 2003, January 22, 2004).
In late 2009, it was reported that Israel's defense exports for 2008 were $6.3
billion and that Israel was the world's third largest defense exporter after the
United States and Russia (*Globes* October 6, 2009). According to one defense
official, in 2008 Israel's revenues from its defense exports had reached $6.75
billion (Defense Update Business Report 2010), and a report by Israel's State
Comptroller from 2012 states that in the period 2008–2010, the export contracts signed reached $7.12 billion per annum while the actual export was
$5.41 billion per annum (State Comptroller 2012: 1545). To be sure, a num-
ber of attempts were made to reduce the total budgetary allocation to Israel's
security sector, and this in response to harsh economic conditions in the early
1950s and mid-1980s; hopes for regional peace in the late 1970s and in the
1990s; and the relative economic recession in Israel and the changes in its geo-
strategic environment in the early twenty-first century. By 2000, for example,
the percentage of public resources allocated to security had dropped to 8.6%
of the Gross Domestic Product (GDP; Dvir and Tishler 2000: 34), and in 2010
military expenditures were estimated at 6.5% of the GDP (SIPRI 2012). But
these attempts, which were not always very successful, have not reduced the
security sector's predominant position in Israel nor led to the dismantling of
the security network. In fact, the opposite is the case. The outbreak of the
second Palestinian Intifada, for example, saw defense expenditures in Israel
rising by 16% in the period 2000–2002, and although they were reduced in
2003–2004, they rose again in 2005, on account of the construction of Israel's

Separation Barrier in the West Bank and its withdrawal from the Gaza Strip, and were still 8% higher than in 2000 (Shiffer 2007: 196). The war between Israel and Hizbullah in 2006 also resulted in a rise of defense expenditures in Israel, and in any case, the fact that Israel's GDP has risen in almost every year in the last decade and a half means that defense expenditures in Israel have not declined in absolute terms and are high relative to those of both Western *and* non-Western states (*The Marker* July 1, 2011).

The second relevant factor is the relatively early retirement age of senior members of Israel's security sector, particularly the IDF. The cycles of these retirements began as early as the mid-1950s. This factor, resulting from pressures by the IDF on the government in the wake of the 1956 Suez War, created a growing group of relatively young former security officials (i.e., army officers and senior members of the other security services) seeking opportunities for second careers and enjoying at the same time financial backing in the form of generous state pensions (*Haaretz* March 14, 2003). Moreover, the fact that these former security officials receive their pensions from the state and continue to serve in the IDF's reserves has contributed to their unmitigated loyalty and allegiance to the security sector and to the state, and thus reinforced their ties to other members of the security network.

The third factor that can be mentioned with regard to the emergence of Israel's security network are the many political, administrative, and business opportunities offered to former security officials who showed a strong commitment to the security sector, especially to the IDF. A telling example is the area of arms trade, weapons export, and the provision of security services to other countries in the world, which has attracted many former IDF officers as well as civilians who were employed by the security sector since the early 1960s. In the early 1980s, in response to the growing demand for Israel's expertise in securing facilities and persons, a vibrant branch catering to the local and foreign markets emerged. The terrorist attacks on the United States on 9/11 reinforced this trend. Thus, the demand for Israeli security experts has grown, consequently opening up new possibilities for the security network and its members.[3] As one report, discussing the expansion of Israeli firms into the realm of security and safety, explains it:

The State of Israel would naturally prefer to offer the world Jaffa oranges, polished diamonds, Hi-Tech and colorful flowers, which it has been successfully exporting for many years. However, this country's unique geo-political situation has forced it to also focus on security, and develop ... state-of-the-art know-how, products and systems related to maintaining alert and security and fighting terror. (Israel Diplomatic Network, n.d.)

---

[3] One example is the decision of EL AL President David Hermesh to create a commercial unit for training security agents at foreign airlines in the wake of the 9/11 attacks. It is noteworthy that Hermesh's appointment elicited criticism due to his ties with his former army superior, Minister of Transportation and former Chief of Staff of the IDF Lieutenant General (res.) Amnon Lipkin-Shahak.

A fourth factor is the growing demands for the services of former security officials in civilian markets, which increased greatly after Israel's military victory in the 1967 War and the creation of the myth of the IDF's "infallibility." Subsequently, the numbers of security officials who became senior managers of, and advisers to, both public and private economic enterprises grew further. Three main advantages that former security personnel have over civilians helped Israel's security sector become the prominent institution for training officials for both public administration and in significant parts of the economy. As mentioned earlier, these officials have financial backing in the form of generous pensions and other benefits that facilitate their integration in civilian enterprises. In addition, institutions such as the Retirement Division of the IDF organize workshops whose aim is to help former officers and noncommissioned officers (NCOs) find their way in civilian life. In addition, the purported and actual qualifications of these security personnel are considered to be applicable, and hence attractive, to both public and private firms. To this one must add the personal connections that these individuals have with other members of the security network, which are institutionalized through organizations such as Tzevet, the IDF Veterans Association. This organization, which has some 30,000 members, not only helps in the assignment of former security officials in various civilian spheres but also serves as a lobby, or pressure group, that promotes their collective and personal interests.[4]

But these various factors, important as they may be, are only part of the answer to why and how Israel's security network emerged, spread, and acquired such a considerable influence on policymaking and concrete policies in Israel. No less important is the increasing role of Israel's security sector in policymaking (not only in the realm of national security but also in other civilian spheres) and the growing involvement of former security officials (especially retired high-ranking officers in the IDF) in Israel's political system, which began in the mid-1950s and was enhanced by major events, especially the confrontations between Israel and its Arab neighbors. It is the convergence of these two processes, which we discuss in the remainder of this chapter and in Chapter 3, that has greatly contributed to the spreading, persistence and, ultimately, the influence of Israel's security network.

THE INCREASING ROLE OF ISRAEL'S SECURITY SECTOR IN
POLICYMAKING

In some instances, the process whereby the security sector in Israel, particularly the IDF, came to play a pivotal role in determining the state's national security policy resulted in more bellicose behavior by Israel toward its neighbors, and in others, it contributed to more peaceful relations with them. But what is more important in our view is how the area of national security in Israel became

---

[4] This could be gleaned from a cursory look at its publication, *Ruach Tzevet* [Team Spirit].

monopolized by the "experts" – that is, members of Israel's security network who effectively marginalized other actors, especially the country's civilian leaders, from "their" turf. During the first two decades after Israel's independence, conflicts and disagreements occurred mainly between the state's civilian and security, especially military, leaders; however, since 1967 the conflicts that have taken place have been, in many cases, between groups of acting and former security officials and their civilian allies, and can thus be regarded as struggles within Israel's security network itself.

As we have noted previously, because of an inherent continuity in its historical development, any discussion of the process of state formation and development in Israel and the making of its political system, economy, and civil society, including the relationship between its civilian and security sectors, must begin with the Yishuv, in the last two decades before 1948 (Eisenstadt 1967; Horowitz and Lissak 1977; Ben-Eliezer 1995, 1998; Sternhell 1995). This observation also applies to the structure and roles of the Yishuv's voluntary military forces. The emphasis of the following paragraphs is on the latter forces and their penetration into and shaping of the cultural, political, social, economic, and discursive subsystems of the Yishuv.

Until the Second World War, the Yishuv mainstream, known as the Organized Yishuv, established and commanded two paramilitary organizations, the Hagana and its regular fighting force, the Palmach, whereas the Revisionist Movement had an autonomous organization, the *Etzel*. A fourth paramilitary organization, the Lehi, later split from the latter. Initially, these paramilitary forces were small, utterly dependent on the relevant parties and political institutions, and reliant on few "professionals," mostly volunteers. Except for certain, tactical military decisions, quite primitive weapons production, and storage facilities, these militias did not extensively penetrate other subsystems of the Yishuv and particularly not the higher echelons of the political system.

This pattern changed first during the late 1930s and then, even more so, in the years immediately before 1948, which saw an expansion and penetration of military commanders into the political arena of the Yishuv. In addition, personal changes occurred within the security sector itself. First, Jewish soldiers, who during the Second World War had served in the British army, joined the military forces of the Yishuv, and especially the Hagana. The politicians in the Yishuv, who respected the professional capabilities of these individuals, encouraged this trend. This marked the beginning of the professionalization of the command of the security sector of the Yishuv, which was purportedly nonpolitical but that reflected the politicians' goal of weakening the politically connected militias and establishing an army for the Jewish State (Cohen 2002). Second, there was a significant increase in manpower, material resources, and purchase of weapon systems and equipment for the Jewish militias, and hence also a significant increase in budgetary allocations. Interconnected, the third development was a gradual penetration of these armed organizations into other subsystems of the Yishuv, especially the production and procurement of arms and the establishment of various facilities, such as camouflaged weapons storage caches, camps, offices, and R&D (Eisenstadt 1967, 1985; Luttwak and Horowitz 1975; Bar-Zohar 1975, 1:510–38; Gelber 1986: 1–72; Horowitz and Lissak 1989; Ben-Eliezer 1998; Cohen 2002).

Thus, to all intents and purposes, it was during the period from the early 1940s to 1948 (especially in the period 1945–1948), that what we refer to as Israel's security network was created, began to expand, and became active and influential in the various civilian subsystems of the Yishuv. Indeed, although the senior politicians were purportedly running the show in this period (Cohen 2002), in fact an increasing number of functionaries, especially "professional" military personnel and civilian officials, became intimately involved in policy and decision making, and their activities helped expand and increase the impact of the security network (cf. Ben-Eliezer 1998).

The First Israeli–Arab War only expedited these processes. On the one hand, Israel saw the simultaneous dismantling of all three underground militias by the state, their partly voluntary and partly coercive amalgamation, and the establishment of a unified military – the IDF; a rapid substantial increase in the latter's size; and an increase in size and importance of the secret services – the Mossad[5] and the Shabak.[6] On the other hand, the political and bureaucratic institutions of the Yishuv were transformed into state agencies and a number of young army officers retired. All of these events and processes created security organizations that developed autonomously.

One pattern did not change, however, and that is the intimate informal connections between individuals involved in security affairs and politics. Moreover, since the three major pre-state militias were established by political parties that held firm ideological views, the members of these militias generally shared these ideologies. Put differently, since the early days of Israel's independence, close links have been inherent between ideology, politics, and the military and other security service. This pattern was maintained in the newly established IDF and in the secret services, in which certain positions and units were "reserved" for members of particular political movements, especially Israel's ruling party, Mapai. Among other things, this state of affairs created a tradition wherein Israel's security sector was deeply involved in the ideological and strategic debates that determined the state's politics, to the point that this was perceived as natural and legitimate (Luttwak and Horowitz 1975; Peri 1983; Gelber 1992).

As mentioned in the introduction, the First Israeli–Arab War ended in 1949 in armistice agreements (rather than peace agreements) between Israel and several Arab states, including Egypt, Transjordan, Lebanon, and Syria, but not with others such as Iraq and, most importantly, the Palestinians. This unfortunate ending from Israel's perspective created an ingrained perception

[5] In English: the Institute for Intelligence and Special Operations.
[6] In English: the Israel Security Agency. In Israel's early decades it was referred to as *Shin Bet*.

among its political and security elites that the new state would continue to rely on its sword for many years to come. The frequent clashes with neighboring Arab states and the Palestinians that occurred in later decades, along with the open hostility that these and sometimes also other actors expressed toward Israel, also fostered a persistent self-image in Israel of a state facing a continuous existential threat. Indeed, many authors speak of a "security complex" (Brecher 1972: 564)[7] or a "siege mentality" in Israel since its independence (Maoz 2006: 489).

This volatile situation was, however, advantageous to Israel's security sector, because it entailed a permanent need for its expertise, planning, and actions. Thus, in the decades that followed, Israel invested enormous resources in its security agencies, especially in the IDF. The combination of Israel's political–military–economic isolation, which fostered a strong sense of the need for self-reliance; the persistent image of a continuous existential threat or threats to the state; and the substantial resources placed at the disposal of Israel's security sector all created the foundations for the expanding autonomy of the security sector and for its members' dominating involvement in matters far beyond the strict defense issues.

An early proof of the deep involvement of the IDF in most civil spheres in the country and of its disregard of due procedures is provided by the protocol of an Israeli government meeting held in November 1948, just six months after independence. During that meeting, minister after minister complained about the IDF's penetration into their areas of responsibility and its acting according to its commanders' whims. Thus, the minister of transportation pointed to the IDF's construction of roads and airstrips wherever it chose; the minister of agriculture complained that the IDF built camps and held military exercises on agricultural lands without the ministry's approval; and the minister of finance charged that the IDF had far exceeded the budgetary allocations approved by the government and the Knesset.[8] It should be noted in this context that in later years the IDF remained in control of vast territories in Israel and had influence over sizeable others, including ones that had been owned by Palestinians before 1948 (see, especially, Oren and Regev 2008; Oren 2009).

These complaints and later ones, however, did not prevent the IDF from establishing its predominance in the spheres of strategic and tactical planning in the intertwined areas of defense and foreign relations in Israel, in fact effectively marginalizing the Ministry of Foreign Affairs (Sheffer 1996a; Barak and Cohen 2006). An important milestone in this process occurred in 1953, when, following the recommendation of the IDF, the Israeli government, under Prime

---

[7] Writing in 1972, Michael Brecher spoke of "the hegemony of the 'Security Complex'" among Israel's elite, "which pervades all foreign policy decisions of substance, even when 'security' is marginal or irrelevant to the issue" (Brecher 1972: 564; see also Freilich 2006: 637).

[8] "Protocol of Meeting of the Temporary Government," November 21, 1948, *Israel State Archives.*

Minister David Ben-Gurion, decided on a shift from a defensive–offensive to an offensive–defensive military strategy. This landmark decision originated in the IDF and served, moreover, to further empower this institution, which was invested with the critical task of identifying the threats to Israel's security that necessitated the launching of preemptive military strikes (Oren 2002; Oren, Barak and Shapira, 2013).

It should be noted, however, that the IDF was not the only security agency that acquired such a predominant position in this period. Israel's secret services, chiefly the Shabak, became the main source for information, assessment, and policies regarding Israel's Arab Palestinian citizens, a role that it maintained even after 1966, when the Military Administration imposed on this community was lifted (Bäumel 2007; Cohen 2010). Since the 1967 War, moreover, the Shabak has performed the same functions vis-à-vis the Palestinians in the occupied West Bank, the Gaza Strip, and East Jerusalem. Simultaneously, also the Mossad increased its capabilities, activities, and influence on security decisions and actions.

The strength of Israel's security sector in the early decades of independence is demonstrated by its ability to act autonomously of the civilian politicians. During the First Israeli–Arab War in 1948, for example, various offensive operations and strategic and tactical moves were planned by the IDF, as were moves leading to (that is, the actual beginnings and endings of) various periods of ceasefire. Only some of the operations conducted during that war were discussed beforehand and approved by the government. Moreover, most military operations were of the "rolling" type, leaving the IDF with plenty of room for maneuver vis-à-vis both the civilian politicians and its Arab opponents. In addition, the decisions to end military operations that had been approved by the government[9] were, in many cases, made by the IDF. Thus, for example, it was only after immense pressure that the IDF agreed that it would not occupy the West Bank, allowing King Abdullah of Transjordan to impose its rule over it, and that it acquiesced to the civilian leaders' orders to withdraw from the areas that Israel had occupied in the northern part of the Sinai and the Gaza Strip (Bar-Zohar 1975, 2:860–1; Sheffer 1996a: 425–8; Heichal 1998).

During the 1950s, the IDF initiated and executed dozens of limited and extensive retaliatory operations against the neighboring Arab states. Frequently, the attempts of Israel's moderate politicians to control and limit these retaliatory actions failed. The IDF's goal was to push the Arab states and Israel toward a war, and these retaliations indeed paved the way to the 1956 War. In fact, the IDF's initial combative moves in the Sinai, which opened the war, were never approved by the political leaders; they were planned and executed by the IDF's chief of staff, Lieutenant General Moshe Dayan, and some of his commanders,

---

[9] Because in Israel the term "cabinet" specifically denotes the Israeli government's forum for political-security decision making, we use the term "government" throughout.

in particular Ariel Sharon (cf. Golani 1997: 397–409; Golani 2001: 49–70; Sheffer 1996a).

In May 1967, the rising political–military tensions between Israel and its Arab neighbors and the tensions between the Israeli government and the IDF command resulted in the appointment of the IDF's former chief of staff, Moshe Dayan, as defense minister, a post previously held by civilian politicians such as David Ben-Gurion, Levi Eshkol, and Pinhas Lavon. The significance of this move is evident in the fact that the overwhelming majority of Israel's defense ministers have since that date been members of the security network. This actuality attests to the widely held opinion in Israel's political system and in Israeli society in general that former security officials are the best qualified individuals to deal with Israel's complex geo-strategic challenges. These patterns still exist in Israel, and as suggested in the text that follows may have been reinforced in recent years.

It is noteworthy that during the last phase of the 1967 War, the IDF did not heed the government's instructions to avoid reaching the bank of the Suez Canal (Goldstein 2003: 569; Gorenberg 2006: 38), and that toward the end of that phase of the conflict, its units set out to occupy the Syrian Golan without the knowledge of most Israeli ministers (Mayzel 2001: 241–80; Gorenberg 2006: 39). The establishment of the ceasefire line on the bank of the Suez Canal, which obstructed the free passage of commercial ships, was among the causes for the next Arab–Israeli War, the War of Attrition in 1969–1970 (Bar-Siman-Tov 1980). The casualties inflicted on Israel during that conflict, in turn, led to Israel's decision to construct the Bar-Lev Line, an expensive system of fortifications along the waterline that offered lucrative contracts to the country's leading construction firms, which had disastrous results in the next Arab–Israeli confrontation, the 1973 War. Importantly, some members of the security network such as Major Generals Israel Tal and Ariel Sharon were opposed to the Bar-Lev Line. During the 1973 War, as well, Israeli military commanders, once again especially Ariel Sharon, who was called for reserve duty, disregarded orders coming from Israel's civilian leaders, particularly concerning the launching of an offensive over the Suez Canal with the purpose of carrying the war to its western bank (Bergman and Meltzer 2003: 221–85).

Although the IDF suffered a major blow in the 1973 War, when Egypt and Syria launched a surprise attack against it, and despite the fact that the Agranat Commission, appointed by the Israeli government to investigate the military fiasco after an unprecedented public uproar, limited its recommendations to Israel's military commanders, the security network did not lose its dominant position in the area of Israel's national security. On the contrary, its power only increased further. The main reason for this was that the 1973 War did not dramatically change the relationship between Israel's civilian and security sectors, which, as mentioned earlier, had tilted in the direction of the latter since 1967.

On the institutional level, the Agranat Commission's report pointed out the lack of an advisory body to the government independent from the influence of the IDF, the Shabak, and the Mossad, and it recommended that such a body should be established in order to expose civilian policymakers to varied outlooks on Israel's strategic status vis-à-vis its neighbors. However, members of the security network effectively thwarted this decision; hence a National Security Council was established only in 1999, and even then it did not become a major actor in the area of Israel's national security.

But more importantly, in 1974, and for the first time in Israel's history, a former chief of staff of the IDF, Lieutenant General (res.) Yitzhak Rabin, who was a member of the security network, was appointed prime minister in place of Golda Meir. Rabin, who was the IDF's chief of staff during the 1967 War, was identified with Israel's military victory, and since in October 1973, during the Israeli-Arab War, he was Israel's ambassador to the United States, he was not held responsible for the political–military fiasco. Rabin soon promoted several of his former comrades to senior positions in his government and in the security sector. Thus, Major General (res.) Yigal Allon, Rabin's commander in the Palmach, became minister of foreign affairs (the first member of the security network to occupy this position); Major General (res.) Ariel Sharon was appointed as Rabin's national security advisor[10]; and Major General (res.) Rehavam Zeevi became Rabin's special advisor for counterterrorism. Another member of the security network, Shimon Peres, former director general of the Ministry of Defense and Rabin's major rival in the Labor Party, was appointed defense minister. In retrospect, Rabin's first government was tremendously important in shaping Israel's policy in a number of critical areas, including Lebanon and the occupied Palestinian Territories, as well as with regard to Israel's Arab Palestinian citizens. But its pivotal role in strengthening the position and role of the security network, even after the military debacle of 1973, must also be considered.

The victory of the Likud Party in Israel's general elections in 1977 was a watershed event in the country's history, especially because it marked the end of the political, social, and cultural hegemony of the center-left Labor Party and the ascendance of the center-right Likud Party. Indeed, with their ethno-national-religious political agenda, which was soon reflected in Israel's domestic and regional policies, Menachem Begin and his followers in the Likud Party represented a clear break from the more secular brand of Israeli nationalism represented by its predecessors.[11]

What is often overlooked, however, is the outstanding ability of members of Israel's security network to preserve their dominant role in the national policymaking process despite this political change. Indeed, like the Rabin

---

[10] Despite their political differences – Sharon had been a Likud MK and criticized Rabin's government – both men belonged to "a clique of old military friends whose personal ties preceded politics" (see Gorenberg 2006: 318). As we note in Chapter 5, Rabin returned the favor when he consulted Sharon during the Lebanon War.

[11] This point is emphasized in Rosenblum (1996).

government before it, the Likud-led government of Menachem Begin also featured former security officials in key positions. These included Major General
(res.) Ezer Weizman as Minister of Defense; former chief of staff Lieutenant
General (res.) Moshe Dayan as Minister of Foreign Affairs; former chief of
staff Lieutenant General (res.) Yigael Yadin as deputy prime minister; Major
General (res.) Ariel Sharon as Minister of Agriculture; and former head of military intelligence and the Mossad, Major General (res.) Meir Amit, as Minister
of Transportation.[12] It should be emphasized that all of these former security officials were not "purely" civilian politicians. Rather, they maintained
their very intimate ties and relationships with other members of the security
network.[13]

In subsequent years, it was the members of the security network, rather than
the civilian politicians, who were mainly responsible for Israeli military initia-
tives, such as the bombing the Iraqi nuclear reactor in 1981. Indeed, according
to Major General (res.) David Ivry, the then Israeli air force commander, the
IDF had been planning and preparing for that operation a long time before
it was launched.[14] Israel's invasion of Lebanon in June 1982 was yet another
example of an initiative primarily taken by the IDF, in close cooperation with
Defense Minister Major General (res.) Ariel Sharon and the Mossad. Although
there were differences among these actors, for example, regarding Israel's alliance with the Lebanese Phalanges, all of them shared the view that war was in
Israel's best interest. Thus, Sharon, a veteran member of the security network,
and the IDF's chief of staff, Lieutenant General Raphael Eitan, misled Prime
Minister Menachem Begin, his government, the Knesset, and the Israeli public
about the war's true purposes: to reach Beirut, establish a pro-Israeli government in Lebanon, expel the PLO and Syria from that country, and preserve
Israel's effective control over South Lebanon (see, especially, Schiff and Yaari
1984). The long-term impact of the security network on Israel's Lebanese policy is elaborated later in this book.

After Begin's resignation and Israel's general elections in 1984, members
of the security network continued to hold key governmental positions, this
time in the National Unity governments that ruled Israel until 1990. In this
period, too, the individual and collective roles of these individuals were crucial
in making important decisions that shaped Israel's policy toward the Gaza
Strip, the West Bank, and South Lebanon, but also domestically. In addition,
members of the security network in the government, together with another
member, President Chaim Herzog, himself a former major general in the IDF,

---

[12] Another retired security official, Brigadier General (res.) Mordechai Tzipori, served as deputy
minister of defense.

[13] Another indication for this continuity was that the new government did not replace acting security officials, such as the director of the Mossad, the director of the Atomic Energy Commission,
and the military secretary of the prime minister (see Eilam 2009: 323).

[14] Interview with David Ivry, *Ynet* October 13, 2003, at: http://www.ynet.co.il/
articles/1,7340,L-2788236,00.html#n (Accessed December 14, 2010) [Hebrew].

were involved in the attempts to cover up the "Bus 300 Affair," which threatened the government's stability.[15]

The same pattern continued to affect the behavior of the security network during the two Palestinian Intifadas. Following the outbreak of the first Intifada, in December 1987, the chiefs of the IDF, together with their partners in the government, especially Minister of Defense Rabin, determined the tactics that were intended to quell the Palestinian uprising. Similarly, in October 2000, the IDF, making no secret of its combative preparations since the Oslo Agreement of 1993, played a critical role in the escalation of the conflict with the Palestinians, which stemmed, at least in part, from the army's policy of massive retaliation against Palestinian demonstrators. Later, especially after Israel suffered heavy human and material losses due to the Palestinian violence in and from the occupied Palestinian Territories, it was the security sector, with the vocal encouragement of members of the security network such as Major General (res.) Uzi Dayan, former head of the National Security Council, that determined the route of the Separation Barrier that Israel built in the West Bank. They did it without consulting key civilian officials, such as the Office of the State Attorney at the Ministry of Justice. It is noteworthy, however, that the security sector did not initiate the project. In any case, the result was a barrier that not only caused great suffering to the Palestinian civilians in its proximity, but that also had to be altered occasionally at great expense and that was difficult to defend before Israel's Supreme Court and in the International Court of Justice at The Hague (Folman 2004: 209–17).

Five episodes in Israel's military history demonstrate the problematic relations between, on the one hand, the leading officers of the IDF and other members of the security network and, on the other, Israel's civilian politicians. First was the "generals' revolt" against the civilians' control over the IDF during the 1948 War (Bar-Zohar 1975, 2:799–810; Peri 1983). Then, a second "revolt" on the eve of the 1967 War, while Prime Minister Levi Eshkol preferred to pursue a diplomatic solution, the IDF's general staff demanded the launching of a preemptive war against the Arab states. Outraged by Eshkol's "hesitancy," the IDF's generals, with the active support of other members of the security network, in effect forced Eshkol to appoint Dayan as Minister of Defense, in what was later called a "quasi-military coup" (*Haaretz* June 5, 2003; see also Goldstein 2003: 550–63; Gluska 2004; Golani 2002: 197–201). The third episode was the "Democratic Putsch" of 1999 (Peri 2003). During the general elections held that year, numerous members of the security network, including about a hundred army reserves officers, joined hands to replace Prime Minister Benjamin Netanyahu with "one of their own," the former chief of staff of the IDF, Lieutenant General (res.) Ehud Barak. In fact, this was a successful attempt

[15] For a useful summary of the affair, see: Moshe Levi, "The Bus 300 Affair, the *Shabak*, the Censorship and the *Hadashot* newspaper," at: http://www.halemo.com/info/kav300 (Accessed December 11, 2010) [Hebrew].

by the security network to preserve its hegemonic status in Israel's political system, against the backdrop of a supporting public that considered military officials to be far more credible than their civilian counterparts.[16] The fourth and fifth cases, which occurred during Israel's withdrawal from Lebanon in 2000 and in the first phase of the second Palestinian Intifada in the same year, are discussed later in this book.

One major implication of the growing involvement of Israel's security network in war-making has been that conflicts between the state's civilian and military leaders over how to conduct wars and other military confrontations with Israel's neighbors, especially before the Arab–Israeli wars of 1956 and 1967,[17] were replaced by conflicts *within* the predominant security network. But this is only part of the picture: The other part has been the decisive involvement of serving and former officers in the IDF and other security officials in negotiations between Israel and its neighbors.

Again, this pattern can be traced back to Prime Minister David Ben-Gurion, his government, and the role of the IDF leadership in the First Israeli–Arab War. After this war, many senior officers in the IDF, such as Moshe Dayan, Yigal Allon, Yitzhak Rabin, Yehosfafat Harkabi, and Mordechai Maklef, actively participated in the armistice talks held between Israel and the Arab states, having an influence on most of the agreements concerning Israel's interim borders. In addition, IDF officers participated, and in fact dominated, the armistice commissions formed in 1949 (Dayan 1976: 79–92; Chen-Shany 2002). This pattern persisted during the 1960s and early 1970s. Thus, for example, Major General (res.) Aharon Yariv was instrumental in the talks with Egypt at the end of the 1973 War, and although the IDF's Chief of Staff, Lieutenant General Mordechai Gur, was skeptical about Egyptian President Anwar Sadat's intentions in the late 1970s, former generals Dayan and Weizman, in their capacity as government ministers, played a significant role in reaching the Camp David Accords between Israel and Egypt in 1978 (Dayan 1981; Weizman 1982; Gur 1998: 293–392).

Later, in the 1990s, acting generals in the IDF, such as Lieutenant General Amnon Lipkin-Shahak, Major General Uzi Dayan, and Major General Uri Saguy, participated in most of the peace negotiations with Jordan and Syria, as well as in various contacts held with Palestinian officials after the signing of the Oslo Agreement in 1993. Again, the role of these security officials was not limited to discussing security issues relevant to the talks and they also took part in discussing political aspects and in legitimizing the talks themselves.

---

[16] According to Arian (1999), the credibility gap between Israel's military and political parties in 1999 was 23 percentage points in favor of the former.

[17] Another telling case occurred in 1954–1955, when Moshe Sharett, Israel's prime minister and minister of foreign affairs, managed to thwart the suggestions made by David Ben Gurion and Chief of Staff Moshe Dayan to adopt a revisionist policy towards Lebanon, which, at that time, was Israel's most peaceful neighbor. (See Sharett 1978, 2: 377, 4: 996; Sheffer 1996a: 574–5. See also Chapter 5).

This was particularly evident in the Israeli-Palestinian track, where security officials gradually took over the negotiations, replacing the civilians who had initiated the Oslo process. In this case, the result was a peace agreement with an overly strong emphasis on security matters. It is noteworthy that in the course of the Oslo process former security officials, such as former Shabak official Yossi Ginosar, even assumed the role of special emissaries to the Palestinian leadership.

As mentioned earlier, despite the recommendation of the Agranat Commission after the 1973 War, a National Security Council was not established in Israel until 1999. But even then this body did not become a major actor in the decision-making process in matters related to Israel's national security. The IDF, and to a lesser degree the Shabak and the Mossad, have retained their primacy as consultants to the government in general and the prime minister in particular in these matters (Freilich 2006: 641). It is no coincidence, for example, that the council's headquarters were initially located in Ramat Hasharon, a suburb of Tel Aviv, and not in Tel Aviv, the location of the Ministry of Defense, or in Jerusalem, the location of the Prime Minister's Office. Only later, the Council was relocated to Jerusalem, and in 2008 a law stipulated that it would operate there. It is also interesting that out of the eight chairmen of the National Security Council since 1999, five were former IDF officers – four were major generals and one was a brigadier general – and the other three were former Mossad officials, including one former head of the Mossad and two heads of branches.[18] The resignation in 2011 of a civilian chairman of the Council (Uzi Arad) and his replacement by a retired army officer at the rank of major general (Yaacov Amidror) is indicative of this situation.

Another officer who has had a significant impact on the civilian decision-making process in Israel is the military secretary of the prime minister. As an officer in the IDF at the rank of Brigadier General or Major General, this individual to a large extent controls the prime minister's schedule with regard to security affairs and has even filled some of the tasks of the National Security Council. Moreover, the fact that the military secretary answers to both the prime minister and the IDF's chief of staff enables the latter to exert considerable influence on the prime minister when the government faces a security challenge.

Since the outbreak of the second Palestinian Intifada, Israeli security officials have participated in various attempts to resuscitate the peace process. Some participated in the talks on the U.S.-sponsored Road Map for Peace in 2002, while others took part in drafting the unofficial Geneva Accord. The public criticism of the policy of the Sharon government vis-à-vis the Palestinian Territories by four former directors of the Shabak in November 2003 (*Yediot Achronot* November 4, 2003), which, yet again, is best explained as an intranetwork

---

[18] See: "Chairman of the National Security Council," at: http://www.nsc.gov.il/NSCWeb/Templates/NSCHeads.aspx (Accessed December 11, 2010) [Hebrew].

struggle over the best way to promote Israel's security, is also illustrative of the security network's major role in determining Israel national security policies. A similar event occurred in 2012, when another former director of the Shabak, Yuval Diskin, criticized the government's policy toward Iran and other issues, arguing that the decision making of its two most senior members – the prime minister, Benjamin Netanyahu, and the defense minister, Ehud Barak (a former chief of staff of the IDF) – was based on "messianic feelings" and that he did not trust them to lead Israel's policy toward Iran (*Ynet* April 28, 2012). Shortly after this criticism, which some observers regarded as unprecedented in its ferocity, former chief of staff of the IDF, Lieutenant General (res.) Shaul Mofaz, was invited to join the government, which already included two former chiefs of staff of the IDF (Ehud Barak and Moshe Yaalon), thus hopefully bolstering its security credentials and also dealing a fatal blow to the opposition's plans for early elections in September 2012.

The intensive involvement, dating to the state's early history but increasing considerably after the 1967 War, of members of the security network in all matters related to war and peace in Israel attests to their considerable influence on decision making in the realm of national security. But it should be emphasized that this involvement has also been accepted and even expected by large segments of the Israeli public. Indeed, opinion polls taken in Israel in 1995 and 1998, for example, showed strong public support for the involvement of security officials in peace negotiations with the Arabs (Arian, 1998). It can thus be argued that security officials have been indispensable in all matters related to war and peace in Israel not only because of their professional expertise but also because they were the only ones who could accord them legitimacy. This gave the security officials an unparalleled status in Israel and increased civilian leaders' dependence on them.

CONCLUSION

This chapter examined the major scholarly approaches to the study of the relationship between the civilian sector and the security sector in Israel. We asked how our approach, which focuses on the concept of the security network, relates to these other approaches as well as to the general theories in this field. As we have shown, our approach addresses serious gaps in the study of the relationship between Israel's civilian and security sectors, particularly concerning its informal aspects, and is commensurate with more general research trends. Employing the qualitative method, we then discussed the emergence and the development of the security network in Israel and how it effectively monopolized the realm of national security and all issues related to war and peace. In Chapter 3, we concentrate on the security network itself and inquire about its members, structure, and core values.

3

Membership, Structure, and Culture

What is the approximate size of Israel's security network and who are its members? In the introductory chapter we posited a conservative estimate to be several hundreds of members since 1948. However, the highly informal nature of Israel's security network, combined with the frequent changes in its composition due to factors such as old age, death, and loss of stature, make it difficult to determine its exact size or the actual number of its members at any given time, or even to provide a detailed description of its structure.

While acknowledging these objective limitations, this chapter provides a general categorization of the members of the security network that allows us to examine the positions they occupy in various civilian spheres in Israel: the political system, the economy, and the broadly defined civil society. This categorization will also allow us to determine the domestic and external impact of the security network. In addition, we elucidate the particular mechanisms that enable these individuals and groups to advance their individual and collective interests and goals; the values and perceptions they espouse as manifested in their public statements and actions; and some of the factors, particularly cultural ones, that facilitate their predominant role in the area of national security and, occasionally, in other spheres in the state.

WHO ARE THE MEMBERS OF ISRAEL'S SECURITY NETWORK?

Broadly speaking, members of Israel's security network can be divided into three major subgroups: first, acting and former officials in Israel's security sector, especially high-ranking officers in the Israel Defense Forces (IDF); second, former lower-ranking security personnel, also mainly from the IDF; and third, civilian actors who have close ties and connections to members of the previous two categories.

Acting and Former Officials in Israel's Security Sector

Three types of individuals make up the first subgroup of members of Israel's security network: first, senior acting and former officers in the IDF, who, in our view, constitute the "core" of the security network; second, middle-ranking active and former army officers; third, high-ranking officials in Israel's other security services, especially the Mossad and the Shabak, but also officials in the Ministry of Defense,[1] the police, the military industries,[2] and smaller security services.[3]

In the period 1948–2011, a total of 213 Israeli officers were promoted to the two highest ranks in the IDF: major general (*Aluf*), the rank of members of the general staff, and lieutenant general (*Rav Aluf*), the rank reserved to the chief of staff. Quite interestingly, an overwhelming majority (more than 90%) of these high-ranking officers have pursued a second career after their retirement, often more than one career. According to Barak and Tsur (2012: 489), former high-ranking IDF officers have occupied 120 positions in Israel's business sector, 106 positions in the political system, 40 positions in the public sector, and 10 positions in other security services. Among the latter, the most significant is the Mossad, in which five of ten former directors were retired IDF officers. In addition, there has been a significant increase in the number of high-ranking officers who served in the IDF's general staff since the late 1970s and later became owners, presidents, CEOs, and director-generals of firms in Israel's business sector and especially of security-related firms (Barak and Tsur).

In addition to these acting and former high-ranking army officers, the first subgroup of members of the security network includes active and retired army officers at the ranks of brigadier-general (*Tat Aluf*) and colonel (*Aluf Mishneh*), providing that these individuals have maintained close ties and connections with other members of the security network during their military service or after their retirement.

Until not very long ago, active and former high-ranking officials in the Mossad, the Shabak, and other security agencies in Israel did not elicit much public attention, not least because their names were not officially disclosed. But in recent decades, and especially since the outbreak of the first Palestinian Intifada in 1987, the identities of these security officials have become better known to the Israeli public, and their role in the state's civilian sector after their retirement has become more pronounced.[4]

---

[1] A noted example is Shimon Peres, who was director-general of the Ministry of Defense. Peres later served as defense minister, prime minister, minister of foreign affairs, and president.

[2] An example is Moshe Arens, who was deputy-director of the Israel Aerospace Industries. Arens later served as defense minister.

[3] An example is Rafi Eitan, former head of the Bureau of Scientific Relations, an Israeli intelligence agency that, among other things, was responsible for the Jonathan Pollard affair in the late 1980s. Eitan later served as minister in the Israeli government.

[4] Thus, former director of the Shabak, Avi Dichter, became minister of internal security; former deputy-director of the Shabak, Gideon Ezra, became minister of internal security and minister

Former Lower-Ranking IDF Security Personnel

The second subgroup of members of Israel's security network includes lower-ranking members of various security agencies, especially the IDF, who, after their retirement, maintain close ties and connections with acting or former members of the particular units or agencies where they had served. As can be expected, this second subgroup is more diverse and changing than the first one, making it even more difficult to identify its members and their exact number. However, and as we demonstrate below, there is ample evidence that these individuals are active and influential in civilian spheres in Israel, particularly in the economy.

Civilian Actors with Security Ties

The third subgroup of members of Israel's security network includes the civilian partners of members of the previous two categories. Unlike members who belong to the first two subgroups, however, members of this third subgroup forge the ties and connections with other members of the security network in the course of their civilian careers, whether in politics, the economy, or civil society. However, this does not mean that these members do not identify with the core values and perceptions of other members of Israel's security network, especially the predominance of national security in Israel. In fact, the opposite is often the case.

THE PENETRATION OF THE SECURITY NETWORK INTO ISRAEL'S CIVILIAN SPHERES

This section discusses the penetration of members of Israel's security network into the political system, economy, and civil society.

The Political System

One of the major civilian spheres in Israel in which the presence of members of its security network has become pronounced, especially since the 1967 War, is the political system. This is particularly the case in its two major institutions, the government[5] and the Knesset.[6]

---

of the environment; and former deputy-director of the Shabak, Israel Hason, became an MK. Another former director of the Shabak, Major General (res.) Ami Ayalon, also became an MK and was appointed as minister without portfolio in the government. Of the directors of the Mossad, only Meir Amit became a government minister (see Chapter 2).

[5] Data on Israel's governments was compiled from the Knesset's official website, at: http://www.knesset.gov.il/govt/heb/GovtByNumber.asp (Accessed June 28, 2011).

[6] Data on the Knesset was compiled from its official website, at: http://www.knesset.gov.il/mk/heb/mkdetails.asp (Accessed June 28, 2011).

The Government

Before 1955, the year that Israel's seventh government was formed, not a single former security official served as a government minister. During the period 1955–1961, one former security official served as a government minister, and in the period 1961–1967, two. It is noteworthy that in the latter two periods, former security officials served as ministers of transportation, agriculture, and labor, positions that although important at the time were not the most senior in the government.

In May 1967, however, a watershed event took place. During the "Waiting Period" that preceded the Arab–Israeli War, Israel's first National Unity Government was formed, and it not only had three former security officials as ministers but also featured them in two senior positions: Major General (res.) Yigal Allon as deputy prime minister and Lieutenant General (res.) Moshe Dayan, the IDF's former chief of staff, as defense minister. The next Israeli government (1969–1974) also had three former officers, while the next three governments, which followed the 1973 War and governed the state up until 1981, each had five. By then, former security officials were in charge of more civilian areas, including trade, industry and development, and information.

In the period 1974–1977, a former chief of staff of the IDF, Lieutenant General (res.) Yitzhak Rabin, served as Israel's prime minister for the first time, and another member of the security network, Shimon Peres, a civilian, served as minister of defense. But these were not the only former security officials who served in the government in this period: the total number was five.

The first Likud government (1977–1981) also had five former security officials as ministers, and the second and third Likud governments (1981–1983; 1983–1984) had three and four former security officials, respectively.

However, the three National Unity Governments that followed (1984–1986, 1986–1988, and 1988–1990) included six, six, and seven former security officials, respectively. It is noteworthy that these former security officials served as ministers of science and development/technology, communication, health, foreign affairs, police, and, of course, defense. In other words, members of the security network started to serve in more meaningful ministries than before.

The fourth Likud government (1990–1992) had five former security officials, as did the subsequent Labor government (1992–1995), which featured, for the first time in Israel's history, a former security official who held the offices of prime minister and defense minister simultaneously. The next two Israeli governments – the first Labor (1995–1996) and then Likud (1996–1999) – each had four former security officials.

The number of former security officials in Israel's next government (1999–2001) jumped again, to seven, and now included the prime minister, the IDF's former chief of staff, Lieutenant General (res.) Ehud Barak, who also served as defense minister; two of his three deputies; and the ministers of communication, housing, science, culture and sport, tourism, transportation, industry and trade, and regional development.

Israel's next government, the National Unity Government headed by Major General (res.) Ariel Sharon (2001–2003), had six former security officials, and the next government (2003–2006) started off with four and later had six. The next government (2006–2009) had seven. At the time of writing, six former security officials serve as government ministers: five were high-ranking officers in the IDF, including three who had served as chief of staff, and one served as deputy general commissioner of the police.

Examining the post of Israel's prime minister also yields interesting results. Before 1992, only two persons who occupied this position – Yitzhak Rabin (1974–1977) and Shimon Peres (1984–1986) – had a significant background in Israel's security sector, whereas all other prime ministers were party functionaries. But since 1992, only two Israeli prime ministers – Benjamin Netanyahu (1996–1999, 2009–) and Ehud Olmert (2006–2009) – had a modest security background for which they tried to compensate in various ways. In addition, and with the exceptions of Menachem Begin (1980–1981) and Amir Peretz (2006–2007),[7] the position of defense minister has not been conferred on any person without significant security (especially military) background since Dayan's appointment to this position in 1967.

It should be noted that the appointment of former security officials as ministers in the Israeli government sometimes led to the appointment of former security officials to senior positions in their ministries. This applies not only to the ministry of defense, which has employed many security officials as director generals and heads of branches, but also to civilian ministries. A telling case is the Ministry of Transport and Road Safety under Lieutenant General (res.) Shaul Mofaz. During his term (2006–2009), this former IDF chief of staff appointed several former high-ranking army officers to senior positions in the ministry, including Major General (res.) Yitzhak Harel as CEO of the Israel National Roads Company (he would later be appointed as CEO of the Israel Railways Corporation); Major General (res.) Yiftach Ron-Tal as CEO of the Israel Ports Development and Assets Company (he was replaced in 2011 by former director of the Mossad, Major General (res.) Meir Dagan and appointed as CEO of the Israel Electric Corporation); and Brigadier General (res.) Yair Dori as director general of the National Road Safety Authority. It is noteworthy that at the time of these appointments, the ministry already had two former officers in senior positions in the Civil Aviation Authority: Major General (res.) Gabriel Ofir as CEO and Brigadier General (res.) Shmuel Zakai as head of security. In internal discussions, Mofaz reportedly claimed that since the main obstacle facing the rapid development of Israel's transport infrastructure was "bureaucracy," former security officials, who deal less with

---

[7] It should be emphasized that both of these civilian defense ministers lacked real authority over the security sector. Brigadier General (res.) Mordechai Tzipori, Begin's deputy minister, later commented that "Begin was the minister of defense like I was a ballerina" (see *Maariv* June 8, 2011; on Peretz see Chapter 4).

bureaucratic issues and are more practical, could move things more quickly (*Maariv* August 26, 2007). Other Israeli security officials-turned-politicians, including former chiefs of staff Rabin and Barak, also "liked the work style" of the IDF's general staff, which displayed "flexibility, dedication, and a can-do-spirit," especially when compared to the "slow by-the-book manner of the government bureaucracy" (Peri 2006: 60).

The Knesset

The aforementioned findings about the penetration of members of the security network into the government are reinforced when examining Israel's legislature, the Knesset. The number of Members of the Knesset (MKs) with significant security backgrounds rose from nil in the period 1948–1951, to 3.4% in 1955–1965, to 4.1% in 1965–1974, to 8.3% in 1974–1977 (and again in 1981–1984), to 12.5% in 1977–1981, and to a steady portion of 10%–11.6% since 1984.

Ideologically and because of their military service, which creates certain behavioral patterns, former officers were, perhaps not surprisingly, inclined toward the more hawkish poll of Israel's political spectrum, although there have been several exceptions. Thus, although a few former security officials did join smaller parties, with more representing left-wing parties in the periods 1974–1981 and 1984–1988, and more representing right-wing parties in the period 1981–1984, and since 1988, the majority have joined parties located at the center of Israel's political spectrum. This is particularly seen in the Labor Party, with five or six such MKs since 1965; Likud with two or three MKs since 1974, except for the period 1977–1981, when it had four such MKs; and various center parties, most notably Dash with five MKs in 1977 and Kadima with five MKs since 2006. In fact, security officials sometimes approached, or were courted by both Labor and Likud ultimately accepting the highest bid.[8] In addition, several former security officials were instrumental in Israel's short-lived center parties, which played a pivotal role in the elections of 1977 and 1999,[9] and still others have been active in Israel's most recent center party, Kadima, which won the 2006 elections,[10] as well as in the Atzmaut faction that left the Labor Party in early 2011.

---

[8] This was the case, for example, with Major General (res.) Ariel Sharon, Major General (res.) Yitzhak Mordechai, Lieutenant General (res.) Shaul Mofaz, and ex-Shabak official Ehud Yatom, who wavered and finally joined the Likud Party; and Brigadier General (res.) Ephraim Sneh, Brigadier General (res.) Binyamin Ben-Eliezer, Major General (res.) Matan Vilnai, Major General (res.) Amram Mitzna, and Major General (res.) and former director of the Mossad Dani Yatom, who wavered and joined the Labor Party.

[9] Examples include Lieutenant General (res.) Yigael Yadin, Major General (res.) and former director of the Mossad Meir Amit, and Lieutenant General (res.) Amnon Lipkin-Shahak.

[10] These were Major General (res.) Ariel Sharon and Lieutenant General (res.) Shaul Mofaz. In late 2010, Lieutenant General (res.) Dan Halutz also joined Kadima, and in early 2011, Yaacov Peri, former director of the Shabak, also joined the party.

Municipal Politics

The role of members of Israel's security network can also be discerned on the municipal level. According to Barak and Tsur (2012: 489), of the 213 high-ranking officers who served in the IDF's general staff in the period 1948–2011, only four served as heads of municipalities after their retirement and few others served in municipal councils.[11] However, when considering former army officers of lower ranks, this number increases exponentially.[12] In 1993, fourteen former IDF officers were elected as heads of municipalities; in 1998, the number rose to seventeen; and in 2003, to nineteen. An article in *Ruach Tzevet*, the bulletin of Tzevet, the IDF Veterans Association, which presented this data, thus contended that "No doubt, there is a clear recognition of the managerial and executive capacities of IDF retirees in the municipalities, on all levels and positions. These retirees continue to contribute to Israel's public affairs, as they were educated and experienced in the school of the IDF."[13]

The Economy

The second major civilian sphere in which members of Israel's security network operate in increasing numbers is the economy.

We have already discussed the establishment of Israel's military industries and how the state became a leading exporter of security-related equipment and know-how, especially since the wars in 1967 and 1973. What follows from this is that acting and former officials in Israel's military industries, some of whom are themselves retired IDF officers, can also be considered as members of the security network. To these one can add former security officials, especially IDF officers, who served in combat units, who export Israeli-manufactured arms and other military equipment and security know-how to other countries and serve as advisors and trainers in foreign security services, especially in non-Western states.[14]

The presence and influence of Israel's security network extends, however, beyond the security-oriented portions of the Israeli economy to include its

---

[11] The heads of the councils include Major General (res.) Shlomo Lahat in Tel Aviv, Major General (res.) Yehoshua Sagi in Bat Yam, and Major General (res.) Amram Mitzna in Yeruham. The members of the municipal councils include Lieutenant General (res.) Yaacov Dori in Haifa, Major General (res.) Eliyahu Ben-Hur in Kiryat Shmoneh, and Major General (res.) Shmuel Eyal in Rishon Le-Zion.

[12] Examples are Brigadier-General (res.) Ron Huldai, mayor of Tel Aviv since 1998; Brigadier General (res.) Meir Nitsan, mayor of Rishon Le-Zion in the period 1983–2008; Brigadier General (res.) Tsvi Poleg, former mayor of Netania; and Colonel (res.) Benny Kiryati, mayor of Tiberias.

[13] *Ruach Tsevet*, 67 (December 2003–January 2004), 28.

[14] Examples include Lieutenant Colonel (res.) Yair Klein and Major General (res.) Yisrael Ziv. The activities of many of these former officers have been mentioned in numerous press reports in Israel, particularly by Yossi Melman from the daily *Haaretz*, as well as abroad (see, e.g., Melman's articles in *Haaretz* May 17, 2006 and in *Haaretz* July 1, 2010).

civilian spheres. Two major civilian areas of the Israeli economy in which the role of former security personnel has expanded in the last few decades are, first, large public and private firms, many of which have little to do with security, and, second, the high-tech industry.

Large Public and Private Firms

The appointment of former security officials as directors and CEOs of major economic firms has been a common practice in Israel since its independence. However, marked changes in this regard need to be mentioned. In the early decades these firms were, by and large, owned by the state or by Israel's powerful labor union, the *Histadrut*. Furthermore, the former security officials who were appointed as directors and CEOs of these firms were, in many cases, affiliated with Mapai, Israel's ruling party, and their appointment was seen as a continuation of their security service by other means.[15] In later decades, however, considerable portions of the Israeli economy were privatized, and former security officials began to be recruited to both state-owned and private firms.

Barak and Tsur (2012) examined the second careers of all high-ranking Israeli army officers who were promoted to the ranks of major general (*Aluf*) and lieutenant general (*Rav Aluf*) and served in the IDF's general staff in the period 1948–2011. According to them, the ratio of these high-ranking officers who became involved in Israel's business sector after their retirement has risen from 40% of those who served in the army's general staff in the period 1948–1957 to more than 70% who served there since the late 1970s. As mentioned previously, among the latter group there has been a significant increase of the number of owners, presidents, CEOs, and director-generals of economic firms, especially security-related firms. The exact ratios are as follows: 40% of the officers who served in the IDF's general staff in the period 1948–1957; 45.7% in the period 1958–1967; 47.7% in the period 1968–1977; 72.9% in the period 1978–1987, 77.6% in the period 1988–1997; and 63.8% in the period 1998–2007.

These findings are reinforced when we examine the second careers of the heads of Israel's two other major security services – the Mossad and the Shabak. Of the ten former directors of the Mossad, including four of the five former IDF officers who occupied this position, nine have had a second career in Israel's economy,[16] as have eight out the ten former directors of the Shabak.[17]

---

[15] Examples include Major General (res.) and former director of the Mossad Meir Amit in Coor Industries and Major General (res.) Shmuel Eyal in Hamashbir Lazarchan.

[16] These were Isser Harel, Meir Amit, Zvi Zamir, Yitzhak Hofi, Nahum Admoni, Shabtai Shavit, Dani Yatom, Efraim Halevy, and Meir Dagan. The only former Mossad director who did not have a second career in the economy is Reuven Shiloah.

[17] These were Isser Harel, Amos Manor, Yosef Harmelin, Avraham Ahituv, Avraham Shalom-Ben-Dor, Yaacov Peri, Carmi Gillon, and Ami Ayalon. The two Shabak directors who did not have a second career in the economy are Izi Dorot and Avi Dichter.

In addition, a number of lower-ranking officials in these organizations had second careers in the economy.[18]

Why were former security officials, who joined both Israeli-based firms[19] and local branches of large international firms,[20] appointed to these positions in the first place? In the early periods in Israel's history, Mapai dominated the state's civilian spheres and had considerable influence over its security sector, and local industries were based on social-democratic ideological premises. Moving from one sector to another, then, especially if one had been affiliated with or sympathetic to the ruling party, was only almost natural. However, this state of affairs changed after the rise to power of the Likud Party in 1977 and following the privatization of large portions of the Israeli economy, which, among other things, became profit-oriented. This raises the question of why security officials, who in many cases have not studied economy, business, or public management in Israel or abroad, and who can only boast of practical experience in the security sector, were appointed.

First of all, the owners of these firms may have expected these former security officials to accord their firms the high level of trust that Israel's security agencies enjoy in the eyes of the country's politicians and the Israeli public, especially in comparison to the state's other institutions. But it seems that the attraction of these former security officials also stems from their unfettered access to other members of the security network, including serving security officials (see, e.g., Erez 2009: 112). Moreover, at least some of the experiences acquired by these former security officials in the course of their military or other security service, especially their ability to be "practical" and "flexible," are seen as an important asset by leading figures in Israel's business sector, who also thought of themselves in these terms.[21] A telling example is the 2006 appointment of Major General (res.) Shlomo Yanai as president and CEO of Teva Pharmaceutical Industries, a major Israeli firm that produces generic drugs. Yanai, the former head of the IDF's Division of Strategic Planning and a former CEO of Makhteshim Agan Industries, was extolled by Teva's heads not only as "one of Israel's outstanding business leaders" but also for "bringing his extraordinary complement of operational, management development and strategic planning talents" to his new position (*Business Wire* October 18, 2006). Numerous other examples can be found in a special section of Israel's

---

[18] A noted example is Yossi Ginosar.

[19] Examples include Yaacov Peri, former director of the Shabak, who served as CEO of Cellcom Israel in the period 1995–2003; Major General (res.) Yair Naveh, who was CEO of CityPass (in 2011 he was replaced by another former IDF officer at the rank of colonel); and Lieutenant General (res.) Moshe Levy who was CEO of Derech Eretz Highways Management Corporation.

[20] Examples include Major General (res.) David Ivry of Boeing and Lieutenant General (res.) Dan Halutz of BMW.

[21] See, for example, the article by Yossi Melman in *Haaretz* September 6, 2007. See also an interview with former Mossad official Danny Biran, President of Coor, in *Mabat Malam* 44 (March 2006): 8–9.

economic magazine, *The Marker* (July 4, 2008), which discusses Israel's top fourteen business tycoons and the fact that many of them recruited former public servants, including a number of former security officials as well as other Israeli "celebs," to their firms.[22]

The High-Tech Industry

The second major civilian segment of the Israeli economy in which members of the security network operate is the country's top-notch high-tech industry. During the last two decades, Israel's high-tech industry has grown considerably, and according to a recent study the country has the "highest density of start-ups in the world (a total of 3,850 startups, one for every 1,844 Israelis)" (Senor and Singer 2009: 11). In addition, Israeli technology exports more than doubled – from $5.5 billion in 1996 to $13 billion in 2000 – and surged to almost $18.1 billion in 2008 after a lull of $11 in 2002–2003 (Senor and Singer 2009: 216).

In contrast to other segments of Israel's economy, such as those mentioned in the preceding text, members of the security network involved in the high-tech industry are, in many cases, lower-ranking security personnel who served in several units in the IDF known for their emphasis on cutting-edge technology. These include Unit 8200, the major intelligence unit of IDF that is responsible for collecting signal intelligence and code decryption; *Talpiot*, the IDF's special program for recruiting promising individuals with the purpose of enhancing its technological capacities; and MAMRAM, the IDF's major computing unit. Indeed, several recent works that attempt to account for Israel's high-tech "boom" in recent decades (Perman 2005; Senor and Singer 2009) place an emphasis on the close and indeed intimate ties between some or all of these particular military units and Israel's high-tech industry, and refer to the IDF as "an important incubator in the development of technology in Israel" (Perman 2005: 81; see also Breznitz 2005; Breznitz 2007: 47–8).

Importantly, the links and ties between Israel's security sector, especially the IDF, and the high-tech industry are not manifested only in ideas originating in

---

[22] These included Lieutenant General (res.) Dan Halutz and Major General (res.) Amos Malka, who worked for Nochi Dankner; Major General (res.) Yossi Peled, Brigadier General (res.) Baruch Spiegel, former police commissioner Moshe Karadi, and former deputy police commissioner Gabi Last, who worked for Yitzhak Tshuva; former Shabak director Yaacov Peri, who worked for Moshe (Muzi) Wertheim, himself a former Mossad employee; former director of the Mossad Shabtai Shavit and former police commissioner Rafi Peled, who worked for Yossi Meiman, who was trained by the Mossad and worked for Israeli intelligence; former police commissioner Yehuda Wilk, who worked for Shari Arisson; Major General (res.) Ehud Adam, who worked for Lev Leviev; and Major General (res.) Yom-Tov Samia who worked for Sammy Ofer. Some of the aforementioned tycoons reportedly had ties with other officers-turned-politicians, such as former Prime Ministers Ehud Barak and Ariel Sharon and Minister Binyamin Ben-Eliezer. Another business tycoon mentioned in the report, Arcadi Gaydamak, also employed two former security officials: Major General (res.) Danny Yatom, who is also a former director of the Mossad, and Brigadier General (res.) Zeev Zacharin (see *Haaretz* May 27, 2010).

the IDF's technological units and later exported to and applied in the civilian economy. They also take the form of individuals who serve in these units and who, upon leaving the security sector, join private firms owned by their former colleagues or start their own firms and recruit their former comrades as their employees. In this sense, these members of Israel's security network are similar to their senior counterparts discussed earlier.[23]

It should be added, in this context, that efforts in recent years have been made to institutionalize the connections among these units' former members. A telling example is, again, the IDF's Unit 8200, which has its own alumni association and has held a national reunion where, "instead of using the time to reflect on past battles and military nostalgia [the alumni] are focused on business networking" (Senor and Singer 2009: 69; see also Kerbs 2007; *The Marker* December 26, 2008, March 17, 2010; *Ynet* May 19, 2011). According to Senor and Singer (2009: 100), who are greatly impressed by this phenomenon, Israeli entrepreneurs "benefit from the stable institutions and rule of law that exist in an advanced democracy. Yet they also benefit from Israel's nonhierarchical culture, where everyone in business belongs to overlapping networks produced by small communities, common army service, geographic proximity, and informality." Indeed, Israel's successful high-tech industry sets it apart not only from other continuously threatened small states, particularly Singapore and South Korea (Senor and Singer 2009: 84–8), but also from other developed small states that no longer face significant security threats such as Finland, Sweden, Denmark, and Ireland (Senor and Singer 2009: 229–32).

Civil Society

The third civilian sphere in Israel in which the role of members of the security network has been apparent is civil society. By this we refer to (1) organized groups of Israeli citizens that operate in the public sphere and whose members attempt to change, or express their support for, the government's policy in specific policy areas, but without challenging Israel's democratic regime; (2) the Israeli press, which is privately owned, and the electronic media, which is partially public and partially private; and (3) Israel's educational system, including the school system and academic institutions, public as well as private.

Pressure Groups

In the last few decades, groups of former security officials have begun to organize and operate as pressure groups in Israel's public sphere. The main focus of these groups is issues related to Israel's national security, particularly the

---

[23] Quite interestingly, the founder and first chairman of a firm called Spark Enterprise, which invests in these new innovations, was Major General (res.) and former director of the Mossad Meir Amit. Another founder, Colonel (res.) Ehud Ram, had served in the IDF's Intelligence Branch (see Perman 2005: 72); "Management Team," at: http://www.spark.co.il/4.html (Accessed December 6, 2010).

Arab–Israeli conflict. However, the activities of these groups have recently extended to additional spheres.

One of the most active groups that can be mentioned in this context is the Council for Peace and Security (CPS). The CPS was established in 1988 by a group of former IDF officers led by Major General (res.) Aharon Yariv, a former head of the IDF's Intelligence Branch who briefly served as a MK and a government minister, and at that time was the head of the Jaffe Center for Strategic Studies (JCSS), later the Institute for National Security Studies (INSS) at Tel Aviv University. The CPS claims to have about a thousand members who include "former high-ranking officers" in the IDF, "former holders of equivalent positions in the Mossad and Shin Beth [Shabak] Security Services, the Israel Police, former diplomats, directors of Government Ministries and academics from various fields."[24] Although it describes itself as "a voluntary body with no party political affiliation,"[25] the CPS is nonetheless situated on the center-left of Israel's political spectrum, and has, on the one hand, voiced support of the peace process between Israel and the Arab states and the Palestinians, and on the other hand, criticized some Israeli security policies (e.g., the continued blockage of the Gaza Strip and the route of the Separation Barrier in the West Bank). As we shall see in the next section, however, the criticism voiced by the members of the CPS has certain limits. It also is noteworthy that several attempts have been made to form right-wing counterweights to the CPS.

In addition to the realm of Israel's national security, civil society movements led by former security officials have been active in the sphere of education. One example is an organization called Citizens for Education in Israel, chaired by a former air force chief and a former director of the Mossad.[26] Citizens for Education in Israel is part of the Forum for National Responsibility, a group headed by a former deputy chief of staff of the IDF, who also served as head of the National Security Council.[27] The movement, which began to operate in 2003–2004, advocated reforms in Israel's educational system, and its members have made an explicit linkage between the situation of the latter and the "qualitative edge" of the IDF.[28]

A second group in this context is the Association of Youth Leading Change, which was established "to nurture and develop young leadership and social involvement" among Israeli girls and boys coming from peripheral and low-income backgrounds to encourage them to become "good citizens in the State of Israel." The main focus of this group is the organization of a course called

[24] "About the Council for Peace and Security," at: http://www.peace-security-council.org/about.us.asp (Accessed November 17, 2010).
[25] "Council for Peace and Security," at: http://www.peace-security-council.org (Accessed November 17, 2010).
[26] Major General (res.) Herzle Bodinger and Shabtai Shavit, respectively.
[27] Major General (res.) Uzi Dayan.
[28] For positive coverage see Tzevet 67 (December 2003–January 2004): 18. For criticism, see an article by Avirama Golan in *Haaretz* December 9, 2003.

Achary (literally "After Me," named after the battle cry of the IDF). This course is described by the association as one that prepares these young people for a "substantial military service," and its crux "is based on the assumption that military service is a window of opportunity for life skills for young Israelis and that a substantial service in the IDF would be a stepping stone to the center of Israeli life." It is noteworthy that its instructors are college students who are fighters and commanders in the IDF's reserves, and that the organization's steering committee includes a former IDF colonel who was the commander of *Sayeret Matkal*, the IDF's primary elite unit; a former IDF major general; a film director who is also a former IDF lieutenant colonel and who created a TV series called *Basic Training*; and a leading Israeli industrialist. It is also interesting that the group's website features a quote from a speech delivered by former chief of staff of the IDF, Lieutenant General (res.) Yitzhak Rabin, in the first meeting of the 13th Knesset after his appointment as prime minister and defense minister in 1992: "Security is not just a tank, plane and missile ships. Security is also, perhaps even before, the individual, the Israeli citizen. Security is also an individual's education, his house, his school, his streets, the society in which he grows" (Achary n.d.).

While all of these groups claim that their actions reflect their utmost concern for Israel's security, only the CPS is active in the realm of national security in the strict sense of the term. The other two groups, as well as others that deal with additional civilian issues (e.g., anti-corruption), have in fact expanded the area of Israel's national security to include issues that inspired by statements of Israeli leaders such as Rabin they have sought to "securitize."

The Media

The second sphere of Israel's civil society in which members of the security network have been active is the public discourse on national security, which takes place mostly in the country's public and privately owned media. Since Israel's independence, with the adoption of the emergency laws introduced by the British forces in Palestine in 1945, military censorship has been imposed on all news items dealing with Israel's national security, broadly defined. However, even more significant in this context are the informal ties and connections forged between actors within the Israeli media and the security sector. These encourage many journalists to exercise self-restraint with regard to Israel's national security in return for a continuous flow of information from the security sector, as well as the continuous presence of former junior and senior security personnel in various media channels.

Historically, correspondents for security affairs in both state-owned and private radio and TV channels in Israel and in the country's major newspapers have depended almost entirely on the security sector for information about matters related to Israel's national security. Indeed, "[u]nlike other social fields, information in the realm of national security is held as a virtual monopoly. In education, economy, sports, and culture, journalists enjoy access to a variety of sources, but when it comes to national security, the sources of information are few and access to them is controlled" (Peri 2007: 84). To receive information related to Israel's national security, these correspondents must therefore abide by the rules of the game set by the IDF: they have to receive "official acquiescence" (Peri 2007: 75) from the military for covering its activities and to belong to the "pool of military correspondents," which encourages "pack journalism" (Peri 2007: 86–7). The result is that many Israeli journalists who deal with security issues more often than not reflect the positions of the security sector and serve as its "unofficial spokesmen" (Miro 2004. See also Wolfsfeld 2004).

The importance of these informal factors can be seen in several cases in which Israeli journalists covering national security who attempted to publish material the security sector considered harmful were subjected to various pressures. Reuven Pedatzur, for example, a former pilot in the IDF and a commentator on security affairs in the Israeli daily *Haaretz*, criticized the performance of the *Patriot* missile and the development of Israel's *Arrow* missile and was subsequently harassed by the security sector.[29] This modus operandi has not been limited to journalists: Avner Cohen, an Israeli academic who has written extensively on Israel's nuclear project, was subject to pressures, eventually prompting him to leave the country and reside in the United States. Israel's security sector also dislikes critical works by its own personnel. A telling example is Colonel Emanuel Wald, who in the 1980s was asked by the IDF's chief of staff, Lieutenant General Moshe Levy, to write a comprehensive report on the IDF's future development based on its past experience. When it became known that Wald's report would be critical of the IDF, Levy tried to prevent its completion and Wald could publish his criticisms only after his retirement (see Wald 1992). These examples suggest that writers who operate outside the purview of Israel's security network are strongly encouraged to play by the rules or not play at all.

As mentioned previously, the second manifestation of the security network in the Israeli media is the continuous presence of former security personnel in various public as well as private media channels, and here, too, one can differentiate between junior and senior former security personnel. With regard to the former, the IDF's influence on the Israeli media "stems from the fact that it serves as the major training college for journalists," particularly those serving in the IDF Radio (*Galei Zahal*), as well as from the fact that the "old boys' network" created during these journalists' military service continues to influence them after their retirement (Peri 2007: 88). Indeed, not only does the IDF continue to operate its own radio station, liberal as it may seem to few observers,[30]

---

[29] Two other examples, discussed below, are Uri Blau from *Haaretz* and Kalman Liebskind from *Maariv*.

[30] According to a recent report, "statements made by station's employees indicate that they are given complete independence in their work and that they abide by the professional standards required for coverage of various events, including security events. However, a review of past events that featured a deviation from the official line in times of security crisis reveals that in these periods supervision

9

but the reporters who work there, many of whom are conscripts, later join other media channels where they make use of, and continue to be influenced by, their army experience and personal connections. Noted examples are TV Channels 2 and 10, two privately owned stations that since their establishments in 1993 and 2002 respectively have drawn heavily on former personnel of the IDF Radio.

In recent decades, many former security officials, too, have become involved in the Israeli media, particularly as commentators in public and private radio and TV channels but also in the press, where they address various matters, including some that have only little to do with security. Initially, these were former lower-ranking IDF officers, mostly lieutenant colonels, who were appointed as military correspondents and commentators.[31] But in recent years, especially during the initial stage of the war in Iraq in 2003 and the war between Israel and Hizbullah in 2006, former IDF officers of more senior ranks, including several major generals, were also appointed as commentators for various radio and TV channels.[32]

Finally, several veteran Israeli media correspondents and commentators on security affairs and Middle Eastern affairs have for many decades enjoyed intimate ties to the security sector and considerable access to its agencies. Although some of these individuals have, at times, criticized certain security policies adopted by Israel (e.g., its invasion of Lebanon in 1982) and operations executed by the military, these correspondents and commentators have more often than not reflected the positions and attitudes of other members of the security network.[33]

In sum, all of these persons, who routinely reflect and present the positions, attitudes, and views of Israel's security sector, and who tend to support rather than criticize its agencies, can be considered part of Israel's security network.

The Educational System

The last sphere of Israel's civil society that warrants consideration in the context of the involvement of former security officials in various societal spheres is

of the content of the broadcasts of the station tighten and disciplinary measures are taken against the station's broadcasters on this account" (see Knesset Research and Information Center 2011). Examples cited in the report include the dismissal of reporters who presented critical views during the Lebanon War of 1982–1985 and the war between Israel and Hizbullah in 2006.

[31] Examples include Lieutenant Colonel (res.) Ron Ben-Yishai at TV Channel 1 and *Yedioth Ahronoth*; Lieutenant Colonel (res.) Yoram Hamizrachi at the Israeli Radio, *Haaretz*, *Jerusalem Post*, and *Maariv*; and Lieutenant Colonel (res.) Roni Daniel at TV Channel 2.

[32] Examples include Major General (res.) Amos Malka, former head of the IDF's Intelligence Branch, who was commentator for security affairs for TV Channels 1 and 10, and Major General (res.) Eitan Ben-Eliyahu, former chief of the air force, who was commentator for security affairs and the host of a morning program for TV Channel 2. Another host, for TV Channel 33, was Major General (res.) Oren Shahor, who also hosted a radio program. Shahor also ran for the municipal election in Tel Aviv in 2008 but was unsuccessful.

[33] Noted examples are Zeev Schiff, who was the military correspondent for the daily *Haaretz*, and Ehud Yaari, the commentator for Arab affairs for TV Channel 1 and later for TV Channel 2.

the educational system. Again, recent years have seen a gradual but nonetheless persistent penetration of former Israeli security officials into the sphere of education. Indeed, although this phenomenon also characterized early periods in the state's history, it has become more pronounced lately.

In 2004 it was announced that, according to a new project initiated by Israel's Ministry of Education and the IDF's Education Branch, active army officers at the rank of lieutenant colonel would be positioned in 74 high schools throughout the country to "accompany" students in the eleventh and twelfth grades who are nearing their military conscription until they join the IDF's ranks (*Haaretz* December 19, 2004). In fact, the program, called the "The Next Generation," which elicited resistance from some Israeli intellectuals, only served to formalize a situation that has been in place for some years: inviting IDF officers to speak before high school pupils on the military service and other defense matters was already a common practice in Israel; and various aspects of the school curriculum in Israel (e.g., physical education and *Shelah*, literally "dagger" but also an acronym for "field, nation, society," as well as the celebration of Israel's national holidays) have been geared to preparing students for military service (*Haaretz* December 29, 2004). The other side of this coin has been the appointment of a Shabak official as deputy to the head of the Arab education in Israel's Ministry of Education, a position that enables this official to be involved in, and even to veto, the appointment of Arab Palestinian principals and teachers. Finally, the integration of dozens of former security officials into Israel's educational system, as part of their growing involvement in municipal politics as mayors and members of municipal councils, had already gained momentum even without a formal program.

Moreover, in recent years, former security officials have become teachers and principals of prestigious schools throughout the country. Noted examples include *Gimnasia Hertzelia* in Tel Aviv,[34] *Gimnasia Ivrit* in Jerusalem,[35] and *Hebrew Reali School* in Haifa.[36] In addition, the appointment of a former IDF brigadier general as principal of *Blich School* in Ramat-Gan was thwarted in

---

[34] Two recent principals of this school have been Brigadier-General (res.) Ron Huldai, who later became the mayor of Tel Aviv, and Colonel (res.) Dror Aloni.

[35] Its principal in the period 1994–2004 was Colonel (res.) Ehud Praver, former deputy head of the IDF's Educational Branch, who was later appointed as head of the Department for Policy Planning at the Prime Minister's Office. See "Members of the Department," at: http://www.pmo.gov.il/PMO/PM+Office/Departments/policyplanning/peo.htm (Accessed January 12, 2010) [Hebrew]. In 2010, Praver was appointed as a temporary replacement for Israel's Civil Service Commissioner. See "Prime Minister Appoints Mr. Ehud Praver as Temporary Replacement of the Civil Service Commissioner," October 27, 2010, at: http://www.pmo.gov.il/PMO/Communication/Spokesman/2010/10/spokeminuy271010.htm Accessed January 12, 2011) [Hebrew].

[36] Its principal since 1996, except the period 2000–2002 when he served as the IDF's spokesmen, has been Brigadier General (res.) Ron Kitri. In 2008, Kitri ran for Netania's municipal council. See: http://www.reali.org.il/newsite/template2.asp?typeid=2 (Accessed January 12, 2011) [Hebrew].

2003. Another former IDF brigadier general was director of the *Amal* professional schools (Dahan-Kalev and Lebel 2004), a process that was encouraged by a special program called Tzevet ("Team")[37] funded by Israel's Ministry of Education, which prepares former IDF officers and other security personnel to serve as principals and teachers at educational institutions. According to data from 2001, more than 300 former IDF officers trained by the program were integrated in schools throughout the country since 1987 (*Haaretz* May 30, 2001). In addition, a former IDF colonel was appointed deputy director of Israel's Ministry of Education, the highest professional position in the educational system (Dahan-Kalev and Lebel 2004: 35). Put together, these factors mean that many members of Israel's security network are in a position to disseminate their positions and worldviews throughout the state's educational system. They also demonstrate the manifold formal and informal ways in which their influence is exercised.

A second process, which also has its origins in the early decades of the state, but that intensified in recent decades, is the increase in the number of former security officials employed by various research institutions in Israel's universities and private colleges.[38] One area in which these former security officials serve is the management bodies of these universities[39] and colleges,[40] which in

---

[37] This is not to be confused with the IDF's Veterans Association mentioned earlier.

[38] On the close relationship between the state and Israel's "scientific strategists," including in the area of national security, see Lissak and Cohen (2010: 18–20). Former security officials who were appointed to senior positions in Israel's higher education institutions in the past include three former presidents of the *Technion* (Israel Institute of Technology): Lieutenant General (res.) Yaacov Dori (1951–1965), Major General (res.) Amos Horev (1973–1982), and Major General (res.) Amos Lapidot (1998–2001). See "Former Presidents," at: http://www.admin.technion.ac.il/President/Eng/List_of_former_presidents_e.html (Accessed January 12, 2011). Other former security officials who were appointed to senior positions in Israel's academic institutions include Colonel (res.) Yuval Neeman, who served as president of Tel Aviv University; Major General (res.) Yohanan Ratner, who served as vice president of the Technion; and Major General (res.) Shlomo Gazit, who was president of Ben Gurion University of the Negev (1982–1985). Another former security official, Brigadier General (res.) Zvi Shtauber, was vice president of the latter university and later the director of the Institute of National Security Studies (INSS), which is affiliated with Tel Aviv University.

[39] At present, former Shabak director Carmi Gillon is the vice president of The Hebrew University of Jerusalem (see "Hebrew U. Board of Governors approves Carmi Gillon as vice-president of external relations," June 5, 2007, at http://www.huji.ac.il/dovrut/Gillon.doc [Accessed January 12, 2011]). Gillon's appointment was opposed by several faculty members (see *Haaretz* June 6, 2007). In January 2011, former Shabak director Ami Ayalon was appointed Chairman of the Executive Committee of the University of Haifa (see "Ami Ayalon Appointed Chairman of the Executive Committee," January 19, 2011, at: http://newmedia-eng.haifa.ac.il/?p=4370 [Accessed January 20, 2011]).

[40] At present, former Shabak director Yaacov Peri serves as chairman of the board of governors of the Tel Aviv-Yaffo Academic College (see https://www.mta.ac.il/about_us/Pages/board_of_governors.aspx [Accessed January 12, 2011]). Colonel (res.) Zeev Drori, former head of the IDF Radio, is director-general of the Kinneret College (see "About Us," at: http://www.kinneret.ac.il/

recent years have become increasingly independent from their faculty and susceptible to market-oriented considerations.

Equally important is the role of these former security personnel as researchers in various academic fields. In the early years of Israel's statehood, former security officials, especially from the IDF, became faculty members in Israeli universities and sometimes also in universities abroad, in fields ranging from physics[41] to archeology[42] to International Relations[43] to Arabic literature.[44] However, in recent years former security officials have, with few exceptions,[45] joined various research institutions that are affiliated with Israeli universities and private colleges, with a strong emphasis on the area of national security. Examples include the Institute for National Security Studies (INSS)[46] and the Tami Steinmetz Center for Peace Research,[47] both connected to Tel Aviv University; the Shasha Center for Strategic Studies[48] at The Hebrew University of Jerusalem; the Begin-Sadat Center for Strategic Studies (BESA)[49] at Bar Ilan University; the Forum

SiteFiles/1/3/2557.asp [Accessed January 12, 2011] [Hebrew]). The institution's board of directors includes Major General (res.) Ilan Biran, who is the director of Rafael Advanced Defense Systems, and Brigadier General (res.) Uzi Keren (see "Members of the Board of Directors, 2010–11," at: http://www.kinneret.ac.il/SiteFiles/1/335/12045.asp [Accessed January 12, 2011] [Hebrew]).

[41] Such as Colonel (res.) Yuval Neeman, who also worked at the University of Texas at Austin (see "Prof. Yuval Neeman – Physicist and Israel's first Minister of Science," at: http://www.science.co.il/people/yuval-neeman [Accessed January 12, 2011]).

[42] Lieutenant General (res.) Yigael Yadin.

[43] Major General (res.) Yehoshafat Harkabi.

[44] Major General (res.) Matityahu Peled and Colonel (res.) Menahem Milson (see below).

[45] For example, Major General (res.) Isaac Ben-Israel.

[46] Its current staff members include Major General (res.) Amos Yadlin, Major General (res.) Giora Eiland, Major General (res.) Avihai Mandelblit, Brigadier General (res.) Shlomo Brom, Brigadier General (res.) Uzi Eilam, Brigadier General (res.) Meir Elran, Brigadier General (res.) Udi Dekel, Colonel (res.) Ephraim Kam, Colonel (res.) Gabriel Siboni, and Colonel (res.) Shmuel Even (see "Experts," at: http://www.inss.org.il/experts.php [Accessed January 12, 2011]). Former staff included Major General (res.) Aharon Yariv, the institute's founder, Brigadier General (res.) Aryeh Shalev, and Brigadier General (res.) Zvi Shtauber.

[47] Its current director is Colonel (res.) Ephraim Lavie (see "Staff," at: http://www.tau.ac.il/peace [Accessed January 12, 2011]).

[48] Its current head is former director of the Mossad and National Security Advisor Efraim Halevy (see "The Shasha Center for Strategic Studies," at: http://public-policy.huji.ac.il/eng/research.asp [Accessed January 12, 2011]).

[49] Staff members include Major General (res.) Emanuel Sakal, Colonel (Res.) Aby Har-Even, Colonel (res.) Danny Shoham, and Lieutenant Colonel (res.) Mordechai Kedar (see: "Research Associates," at: http://www.biu.ac.il/Besa/researchers.html [Accessed January 12, 2011]). In addition, its international advisory committee includes two former IDF major generals, Uri Orr and Daniel Matt. Former staff members include Major General (res.) Avraham Rotem and Zeev Bonen, former director-general and later president of Rafael Advanced Defense Systems (see, respectively, "Maj. Gen. (res.) Avraham Rotem," at: http://www.biu.ac.il/Besa/avraham_rotem.html [Accessed January 12, 2011] and "Dr. Zeev Bonen," at: http://www.biu.ac.il/Besa/zeev_bonen.html [Accessed January 12, 2011]).

for National and Strategic Thought at the Center for Public Management and Policy at Haifa University[50]; the Kinneret Center on Peace, Security and Society[51] at the Kinneret College; and the Institute for Policy and Strategy,[52] the Lauder School of Government, Diplomacy and Strategy,[53] the International Institute for Counter-Terrorism,[54] and the Global Research in International Affairs Center,[55] all at the Interdisciplinary Center in Herzliya (IDC). Many of these institutions as well as others, including some that are located in the United States,[56] conduct research, organize seminars and conferences, author publications, and enjoy considerable media exposure in Israel. However, it seems that at least some of these activities do not always follow academic standards, not least because many of these institutions very often have a more subtle function: to serve as "clubs" or "hubs" for former Israeli security personnel.

   A particular academic field in Israel that has attracted many former security officials, especially from the IDF's Intelligence Branch and the Shabak, is Islamic and Middle Eastern studies. Thus, a recent study has traced the informal networks between Middle East specialists that include former members of the security sector and scholars who teach and do research at Israel's universities,

[50] Its head is former Shabak director, navy commander, MK and minister, Major General (res.) Ami Ayalon. On Ayalon's other position in Haifa University see above.

[51] Current staff members include Colonel (res.) Zeev Drori, who is a former commander of the IDF Radio, Colonel (res.) Reuven Gal, who previously served as head of the Administration for National Civic Service, and Colonel (res.) Amir Bar-Or (see: "The Staff," at: http://www.kinneret.ac.il/SiteFiles/1/663/19795.asp [Accessed May 30, 2011]).

[52] Current staff members include Major General (res.) Danny Rothschild, who is the head of the institute, and Major General (res.) Amos Malka (see "Academic Staff," at: http://www.herzliyaconference.org/Eng/_Articles/Article.asp?ArticleID=146&CategoryID=74 [Accessed: January 12, 2011]). Members of the board of directors include Major General (res.). Ilan Biran, director of Rafael, and Major General (res.) Shlomo Yanai, CEO of Teva Pharmaceutical Industries (see "IPS Directorate," at: http://www.herzliyaconference.org/Eng/_articles/Article.asp?ArticleID=877&CategoryID=149 [Accessed January 12, 2011]). The director of external relations is Colonel (Res.) Michael Altar (see "Administrative Staff," at: http://www.herzliyaconference.org/Eng/_Articles/Article.asp?ArticleID=123&CategoryID=75 [Accessed January 12, 2011]).

[53] Staff members included Uzi Arad, a former Mossad official who was the national security advisor to Prime Minister Benjamin Netanyahu and chairman of Israel's National Security Council, and Colonel (res.) Ruben Erlich-Neeman, who is also the director of the Intelligence and Terrorism Information Center (see "Staff," at: http://portal.idc.ac.il/en/schools/Government/Faculty/Pages/permament.aspx [Accessed January 12, 2011]).

[54] Current staff members include Colonel (res.) Eitan Azani, Colonel (Res.) Lior Lotan, and Colonel (Res.) Jonathan Fighel (see "ICT Team," at: http://www.ict.org.il/AboutICT/ICTStaff/tabid/57/Default.aspx [Accessed January 12, 2011]). On the institute's close connection to Israel's Ministry of Defense, see Eilam (2009: 464).

[55] Current staff members include former Shabak official Reuven Paz (see "About the GLORIA Center," at: http://www.gloria-center.org/about.html [Accessed: May 30, 2011]).

[56] Such as the Washington Institute for Near East Policy in Washington, DC, which hosted former Israeli security officials including Brigadier General (res.) Michael Herzog (see http://www.washingtoninstitute.org/templateC10.php?CID=15 [Accessed January 20, 2011]). The institute also published works by former security officials such as Major General (res.) Giora Eiland and Yoram Cohen, who in 2011 was appointed as director of the Shabak (see Chapter 4).

and discussed their cumulative impact on how Israelis have come to view their Arab neighbors (Eyal 2002).[57]

Finally, several former security officials are active at a number of research centers in Israel that translate and publish material originating from media channels in other Middle Eastern states. These include the Meir Amit Intelligence and Terrorism Information Center in Glilot (ITIC),[58] an organization that sometimes publishes materials collected by the IDF,[59] and the Middle East Media Research Institute (MEMRI).[60]

MECHANISMS FOR RECRUITMENT AND OPERATION

In this section we discuss the notion of an "old boys' network" in Israel (see, e.g., Freilich 2006: 654, 660; Peri 2007: 88). We identify the particular formal as well as informal mechanisms that are at work during the period of service in the security sector, during the retirement process, and after retirement, which ultimately provide Israel's security network with its members.

During Service

First of all, many members of Israel's security network who have a background in the security sector join this network while they are in service in the various

---

[57] An institute that has attracted several former security officials, particularly from the IDF's Intelligence Branch, is the Moshe Dayan Center for Middle Eastern Studies at Tel Aviv University, which was formerly called the Shiloah Center after the first director of the Mossad, Reuven Shiloah.

[58] Its director is Col. (res.) Ruben Erlich-Neeman (see http://www.terrorism-info.org.il/site/home/default.asp [Accessed January 12, 2011]). Erlich-Neeman was deputy to Uri Lubrani, the Coordinator of Israel's Operations in Lebanon (see Chapter 5).

[59] A recent study published by the institute reads as follows: "This study is based on a *vast amount of intelligence information* from the Israeli intelligence community which was made accessible to the team of researchers. It also made extensive use of Palestinian, Arab and international media, and of previous bulletins issued by the Intelligence and Terrorism Information Center (which were used selectively by the Goldstone Mission). In addition, *the intelligence information was supported and complemented* by statements and investigations of *IDF forces* who fought on the ground" [emphases and parentheses in the text] (see "Response to the Goldstone Report," March 2010, at: http://www.terrorism-info.org.il/site/content/t1.asp?Sid=13&Pid=334 [Accessed January 20, 2011]).

[60] Its founder and director is Colonel (res.) Yigal Carmon, a former IDF intelligence officer who also served as counterterrorism adviser to Israeli Prime Ministers Shamir and Rabin. The chairman of its board of advisors is Colonel (res.) Menahem Milson, professor emeritus at The Hebrew University of Jerusalem, who in the period 1976–1978 was a consultant for Arab affairs for the IDF's Judea and Samaria Command and the Coordinator of the Government's Activities in the Territories, and who in 1981–1982 headed the Civil Administration in the West Bank (see "About MEMRI," at: http://www.memri.org/content/en/about.htm [accessed: January 12, 2011; see also "Milson, Menahem," at: http://www.herzliyaconference.org/_Articles/Article.asp?ArticleID=553&CategoryID=58 [Accessed January 12, 2011]). Wedel (2009: 261, n. 86) mentions MEMRI as one of the think tanks with which the neoconservatives in the United States are affiliated.

security agencies, especially those in the IDF. Indeed, in many cases the ties between these individuals go back to their joint military or other security service. When they retire from the security sector and move to the civilian sector, these individuals utilize and ultimately reinforce these connections. For example, some former security officials find it easier to perform when joined by their former colleagues, to whom they remain loyal even after retirement.[61] At the same time, personal and professional rivalries between former security officials, originating in the period of their military or other security service, are sometimes carried on to the civilian sphere.[62]

A second, more formal, factor has to do with the unique position of the IDF's chief of staff, who is the only army officer appointed by the Israeli government based on the recommendation of the minister of defense. The chief of staff, in turn, is authorized to suggest candidates for promotion to the rank of major general to the minister of defense, who can approve or reject these candidates but *cannot* suggest others in their place (State Comptroller 2010a). This state of affairs gives much leeway to the chief of staff to promote officers to the rank of major general and appoint them to the IDF's most senior positions. Indeed, historically this has been a major factor in building the core of Israel's security network, which consists of acting and former IDF officers in the rank of major general and lieutenant general.

The third factor is the politicization of the position of IDF's chief of staff and, to some extent, of other members of the IDF's general staff, influenced by their close ties to civilian policymakers some of whom are their former comrades in the security sector. This phenomenon, which reflects the general lack of separation between the political and military spheres in Israel and the dominating role of the IDF in deciding the state's national security policy, has been exacerbated in recent decades by changes in the nature of the military confrontations waged by Israel (see Peri 2006; Michael 2007).

During the Retirement Process

The retirement process itself is also important. After retirement from the security sector but before entering the political and bureaucratic arenas, the cooling off period for security personnel was always short in Israel. During the last two decades it has become even shorter. Many security officials become government ministers, MKs, and senior functionaries in both the public and private sectors of the Israeli economy, as well as in a host of other civilian spheres,

---

[61] Noted examples are the acquaintance between Israel's current prime minister, Benjamin Netanyahu, and his defense minister, Ehud Barak, which dates to their joint service in *Sayeret Matkal*, the IDF's elite unit; and the acquaintance between Ariel Sharon and Dan Halutz and Meir Dagan, who were appointed as the IDF's chief of staff and the director of the Mossad, respectively, when Sharon served as prime minister.

[62] A noted example is the rivalry between Major General (res.) Matan Vilnai and Major General (res.) Yitzhak Mordechai.

almost immediately after their retirement. An illustration of this policy is a cartoon published in the Israeli daily, *Haaretz*, on November 3, 2002, depicting Lieutenant General (res.) Shaul Mofaz, who had left the position of the IDF's chief of staff in July 2002 and had just been appointed by Prime Minister Ariel Sharon as Israel's minister of defense. As the newly appointed minister enters his old-new office, he smiles and tells his secretaries: "Good morning girls; for me, coffee as usual."

In 2007, and following this and similar cases, the Israeli Knesset approved a new law that stipulated a cooling off period of three years before security officials could run for the Knesset and serve in the government. However, the same year also saw the publication of the interim report of the Winograd Commission, which was appointed to investigate the war between Israel and Hizbullah in 2006, known in Israel as the "Second Lebanon War." The commission report stated that even if situations sometimes arise in which the prime minister and the minister of defense have no security background "because of political considerations, it is desirable that political culture and political conventions will be those that will set experience and knowledge" in security matters "as an essential element, even if not necessary, for the leaders and types of roles they can fill" (Winograd 2007: 134). The significance of this statement was not lost on Amir Oren, a commentator on security affairs in *Haaretz* (April 30, 2007), who wrote:

As in jobs and benefits designed to single out entire sectors of Israeli society, there is a preference here for former members of the general staff of the IDF, at the rank of brigadier general or higher, preferably from the ground forces, with a quota for retirees from the *Mossad* and the *Shabak*. It is a cooling law in reverse.

Indeed, within a few months, in June 2007, Amir Peretz, one of the only two Israeli defense ministers since 1967 who had not been members of the security network, was defeated by Lieutenant General (res.) Ehud Barak in the elections for the leadership of the Labor Party. He resigned his post, which was assumed by Barak.

After Retirement

Finally, factors pertaining to the period after individuals retire from the security sector can also help to explain how members of the security network reach influential positions in the state's civilian spheres and advance their shared interests and goals.

One factor that immediately stands out is Israel's reserves system, which allows security personnel to expand the scope of their acquaintances and thus their social networks. Indeed, according to Senor and Singer (2009: 50), Israel's reserves system "is not just an example of the country's innovation" but also "a catalyst for it." It should be noted, however, that the impact of this factor is not the same for all reservists. It benefits mostly those IDF officers who occupy senior command positions in the reserves and military professionals (e.g., pilots), who are able to maintain close connections to their peers remaining in active service.

A second factor, which seems to have grown in importance in recent years, is the veterans associations of Israel's various security services – especially Tzevet, the IDF Veterans Association. Indeed, as can be clearly inferred from this organization's bulletin, published since 1989 and distributed to some 30,000 members, Tzevet is more than simply a means for former security personnel to associate with one another and find employment in various civilian areas through its regional employment offices. It also functions as a powerful lobby that promotes its members' collective interests in the public sphere, including by directly approaching the IDF's general staff (see, e.g., *Ruach Tzevet* 2009: 2–3; *Ruach Tzevet* 2010a: 2; *Ruach Tzevet* 2010b: 4, 6–7). It is noteworthy that the retirees of the Mossad and the Shabak have similar associations – *Agmon* and *Shoval*, respectively – and that in recent years all three organizations have made considerable efforts to prevent what their spokesmen regard as an attempt by the Israeli treasury to cut down their members' pensions (*Haaretz* February 17, 2010; *The Marker* March 6, 2011). Interestingly, when it approached the IDF and the government, Tzevet, which did not have a formal standing in the issue of its members' pensions, operated behind the scenes, and its members appealed to the shared cultural values between them and the acting security officials. This can be gleaned from an interview with the financial advisor to the IDF's chief of staff, an officer at the rank of brigadier general, who, when asked what lessons can be drawn from this episode, replied that the lesson is "to trust the commanders – in this case the IDF and the Ministry of Defense, the defense minister, and the chief of staff, that they will really do everything for their brothers in arms, not only by virtue of their formal positions but also by virtue of their moral obligation" (*Ruach Tzevet* 2011: 15).

Third, some of the organizations and institutions mentioned previously (i.e., the CPS, the INSS, and the ITIC), as well as others such as the Israeli Missile Defense Association[63] and the Fisher Institute for Air and Space Strategic Studies,[64] not only serve as lodestones for former Israeli security officials, but

[63] On this organization, see "IMDA–Israel Missile Defense Association," at: http://imda.org.il/ ImdaRoot/English/About/about_us.asp (Accessed January 10, 2011). Its board of directors include former air force chief Major General (res.) Herzle Bodinger, Major General (res.) MK Isaac Ben-Israel, and several retired officers at the rank of Brigadier General. Its board of advisors includes Major General (res.) David Ivry and Israel's minister of finance, Yuval Steinitz. A military commentator has likened this organization, which also includes representatives of Israel's military industries, to the military–industrial complex (see: Reuven Pedatzur's article in *Haaretz* July 11, 2008).

[64] Its board of directors includes Major General (Res.) David Ivry, Major General (Res.) Amos Lapidot, Major General (Res.) Herzle Bodinger, Major General (Res.) Eitan Ben-Eliyahu, Major General (Res.) Prof. Issac Ben-Israel, Major General (Res.) Gideon Sheffer, Major General (Res.) Elyezer Shkedy, Brigadier General (Res.) Oded Erez, Brigadier General (Res.) Isaac Gat, Colonel (Res.) Jacob Shporen, and Dr. Eli Levita, former assistant chairman of the National Security

are also meeting venues, or clubs, for members of the security network. Here, they can associate, exchange ideas, and forge connections. Indeed, according to the website of the Fisher Institute, it "was established by the Air Force Association and connects former Air Force personnel to facilitate public discussion in Israel about aviation and space issues."[65] The same function is performed by a host of formal and informal associations and venues in Israel, such as the associations of veterans of particular units in the IDF and of the pre-state military organizations (e.g., the Hagana). These associations play an important role in the commemoration of past events through building museums, holding ceremonies, and authoring publications. But they also serve as informal hubs for their members, and sometimes even attempt to enforce their particular historical narratives on them.[66]

Finally, one can mention more informal gatherings of former security personnel held during Israeli national holidays (e.g., Independence Day) and other occasions that bring together members of Israel's security network. In addition, certain neighborhoods, and even towns, have become popular for former security officials: living next to one another further reinforces their ties.

SHARED PERCEPTIONS AND VALUES

Do members of Israel's security network espouse the same values and perceptions, and if so, what is their nature? It is easy to dismiss this possibility by pointing to the many disagreements among members of the security network, who have often throughout history found themselves on different sides of Israel's political spectrum. However, beyond these political disagreements and quarrels there is ample evidence that members of Israel's security network do express shared values and perceptions, particularly with regard to Israel's national security and its security sector, but also toward one another.

The first of these basic values and perceptions is "securitism," namely, "a situation in which a nation locates security as its major concern and master goal, and as a result, considerations about security become a major determinant of policies and decisions in many spheres of collective life; society members view security as a central issue in societal life with all its implications, and security forces have major determinative power in the society" (Bar-Tal, Magal, and Halperin 2009: 241, n. 1). Indeed, although members of the security network

Council and former deputy-director general of the Israel Atomic Energy Commission. Its managing director is Brigadier General (Res.) Asaf Agmon (see "The Institute's Board of Directors," at: http://www.fisherinstitute.org.il/Eng/?CategoryID=169&ArticleID=6 [Accessed January 12, 2011]).

[65] "Fisher Institute for Air and Space Strategic Studies" at: http://www.fisherinstitute.org.il/ (Accessed May 30, 2011).

[66] A colleague told us he was once invited to "testify" in an informal proceeding held by members of a veterans association of one the pre-state factions against a fellow member who had dared challenge the veterans association's "official" line.

sometimes suggest different ways to promote Israel's national security, they generally do not question the central place of national security in Israel.

A second basic perception shared by many members of Israel's security network is that these members themselves constitute an "epistemic authority" in the realm of national security in Israel. Indeed, the CPS, which, as we have seen, brings together many members of the security network, explicitly states that the motivation for its establishment was "[t]he notion that security is a field requiring experience and professional knowledge" that is enjoyed by "some thousand members [of the organization], each with a solid background in fields associated with security and diplomacy."[67]

The third basic perception of many members of the security network is that Israel's security sector, especially the IDF, stands above criticism. Thus, for example, when the IDF's chief of staff, Lieutenant General Moshe Yaalon, was invited to speak before the CPS in August 2004 and a member of the organization criticized the IDF and its head for what he described as their immoral conduct vis-à-vis the Palestinians, nearly all his colleagues attempted to silence him (*Haaretz* September 14, 2004).

Finally, members of the security network exhibit a high degree of group solidarity and come to one another's help in times of need. This includes attempts to cover up unlawful deeds by members of the security network (e.g., during the Bus 300 Affair in the 1980s); testifying in court on behalf of members of the security network when they stand on trial[68] but refusing to testify against them[69]; holding ceremonies in honor of members of the security network in military facilities *after* they had been convicted in court[70]; and obtaining the release of former security officials from enemy hands despite their involvement in dubious business deals, including drug trafficking, and notwithstanding the high price tag for their release.[71] In addition, members of the security network are very hesitant to reprimand, let alone dismiss, their fellow members when

---

[67] See "About the Council for Peace and Security," at: http://www.peace-security-council.org/about.us.asp (Accessed November 17, 2010).

[68] For example, in the cases of former defense ministers Major General (res.) Ariel Sharon and Major General (res.) Yitzhak Mordechai.

[69] See, for example, an article by Uzi Benziman, a former journalist in *Haaretz* who was involved in a libel suit filed by Major General (res.) Ariel Sharon against Benziman's newspaper, after Benziman had accused Sharon of misleading Prime Minister Menachem Begin and his government during the Lebanon War (*Haaretz* May 13, 2011). Benziman recounts that high-ranking IDF officers who witnessed Sharon's behavior during that war refused to testify against him in court, even when they were confronted with their own public statements on this matter. See, for example, the telling case of Major General (res.) Avigdor Ben-Gal discussed in Chapter 5. Two former IDF officers, Brigadier Generals (res.) Ezriel Nevo and Mordechai Tzipori, who publicly criticized Sharon for his role in Israel's Lebanon War, have done so only recently, after Sharon suffered a coma (see Chapter 5).

[70] For example, retired army colonel and Mossad official Yaacov Nimrodi, who also owns the daily *Maariv*.

[71] This is most notably in the case of Colonel (res.) Elhanan Tenenbaum, who was released in 2004 in a prisoners' swap with Hizbullah.

they are appointed to look into military and other security scandals. An Israeli military correspondent opined that the "general's club seems forever hesitant to dismiss one of its own," noting that for decades there has not been one instance in which an IDF officer at the rank of major general was dismissed on account of his performance (*Haaretz* July 13, 2010).

FACTORS THAT FACILITATE THE SECURITY NETWORK'S PREDOMINANT ROLE IN ISRAEL

In this section we identify four major factors and their interplay that can account for the predominant role of the security network not only in matters of national security in Israel but also in many other spheres, including some that have little to do with security: first, the continuous existential threats facing Israel since its independence; second, the primacy of Israel's national security over all other issues and considerations; third, the process whereby significant parts and spheres in Israel have become securitized; and finally, the status of an epistemic community that members of the security network have managed to acquire in the area of national security and in other spheres.

Since its independence, Israel has faced real or imagined, but in any case perceived, domestic and external existential threats. These threats, in turn, have helped foster Israel's self-image as a small state that is surrounded by hostile enemies bent on destroying it and, at the same time, that it faces an existential threat from its Arab Palestinian community (see, e.g., David 2009; Abulof 2009). As we suggest elsewhere (Barak and Sheffer 2009b), the continuous existential threats facing Israel have stemmed from objective factors, such as the particular circumstances in which the state was established; its contested legitimacy in the eyes of domestic and foreign actors; and the extraordinarily high levels of hostility toward it that has been demonstrated by these actors, especially the latter. At the same time, it is clear that some security officials in Israel have amplified or manipulated the domestic and external threats to the state's national security and presented them as existential for utilitarian reasons, not least of which is the need to increase or preserve the budget allotted to the security agencies.[72] In any case, the continuous real or imagined existential threats facing Israel, have, in time, become inexorably tied to sociocultural

---

[72] According to Major General (res.) Ami Ayalon, who later became chief of the Shabak, an MK, and a government minister, during his thirty-eight years of service in the security sector he "specialized" in amplifying the perceived threats to Israel's national security in order to receive increased funds (quoted in *Haaretz* April 4, 2006). In fact, Ayalon explained, "[t]he level of fear of the Jewish society in Israel ... dictates everything," including the nature of the Shabak (quoted in *Haaretz* November 22, 2006). Charles Freilich, who served as Israel's Deputy National Security Adviser, posits that, in Israel, "Issues of national security are ... commonly argued in highly ideological and partisan terms that exceed their objective weight and arguments are even made in terms of national survival, despite the many cases where this was not truly at stake" (see Freilich 2006: 645).

factors, especially to the collective historical traumas of its dominant Jewish community (Bar-Tal, Magal, and Halperin 2009).

As we have noted previously, this very basic feeling is strongly connected to the cultural-historical background of the Jewish people and the immense history of attacks on Jewish individuals and communities, first and foremost the Holocaust, the enmity of the Arab states and the Palestinians, the wars between Israel and the Arab states, the endless clashes with the Palestinians, and more recently the Iranian nuclear project. All these personal and collective memories played a central role in the process of state formation and development in Israel, especially since the early 1960s (Zertal 2005). Other historical episodes in which the existence of the Jewish people was at stake can also be mentioned in this regard.[73] In sum, what Lake and Rothchild (1998: 7) call "a fear of the future, lived through the past" has become a central component of Israeli identity. In a piece published in the Israeli daily *Haaretz* on December 14, 2007, Doron Rosenblum, an astute observer of Israeli society, wrote:

> Fear, my friend, is the bedrock of our existence. It is the conceptual basis upon which the state was founded: fear of Anti-Semitism, which gave way to fear for security. We might withdraw from territories, we might release prisoners. But we will not let our fear be taken away. Without it – we have no security policy, foreign policy, and public relations policy. Without it we have nothing.

A second factor, interconnected with the previous one, in accounting for the predominant role of Israel's security network is the widely held perception regarding the precedence of national security over all other issues and considerations. Indeed, many Israelis, including civilian leaders and the general public, consider the civilian spheres in Israel, that is the political system, society, the economy, the educational system, and public discourse, not as ends in themselves, but rather in terms of their contribution to Israel's national security. Furthermore, those who deal with matters of national security in Israel have a built-in advantage over other individuals, particularly civilians, who deal with other, "lesser," issues.

The third factor, also related to the two previous ones, is the securitization of many civilian spheres in Israel. Indeed, in view of the continuous existential threats facing Israel and the predominant status of its national security, it seemed only natural that the boundaries between the state's security sector and its various civilian spheres remain extremely porous, and for the security sector, particularly the IDF, to receive the necessary resources for defense purposes. At the same time, civilian issues within the state and in its foreign relations that were seen by Israeli leaders as meaningful for national security were effectively

---

[73] A telling example is the many references made to Iran's current president, Mahmoud Ahmadinejad, as a modern-day "Haman" (see, e.g., Tzippe Barrow, "Purim 2010: Starring Mahmoud Ahmadinejad," *CBN News*, February 28, 2010, at: http://www.cbn.com/cbnnews/insideisrael/2010/February/Purim-2010-Starring-Ahmmoud-Ahmadinejad- [Accessed February 1, 2011]).

securitized and, ultimately, became the exclusive realm of the security sector. Later, we will draw interesting parallels between the situation in Israel and similar processes in other continuously threatened small states, thus situating the Israeli case in a broader comparative perspective.

Finally, the fourth factor that can account for the predominant role of the security network in Israel is the public recognition of acting and retired security officials as an epistemic community in the area of national security. In practice, this means that these security officials not only speak in the name of security in an authoritative manner, but they also fulfill both the individual and collective need for security in Israeli society. Importantly, this need stems not only from the actual threats against the state from its neighbors; it also results from the tragic history of the Jewish people, particularly in the twentieth century, which the institutions of the state – the military, the educational system, and the media – seek to inculcate to its citizens. Idith Zertal (2005: 174) correctly notes that "the transformation of security threats into danger of total annihilation of the state, seem to have characterized the way of speech of Israel's political, social and cultural elites, with very few exceptions."

The privileged status of members of Israel's security network in Israel was further enhanced by three major developments that took place in the state in its early decades. First, Israel experienced a shift to an offensive-defensive military strategy in the early 1950s. Among other things, this stipulated that the security sector, particularly the IDF, would be responsible for identifying the existential threats to the state and thwarting them by launching preemptive strikes. Second, Israel attained a dramatic military victory over its enemies in the 1967 War, which seemed to reaffirm the role of its security sector as its foremost protector while highlighting the "hesitancy" of its civilian leaders. Third, the military debacle in the 1973 War, while dealing a blow to the credibility of the security sector (especially the IDF's command and Intelligence Branch), led to an increase in the power and capabilities of the informal security network, especially of retired security officials such as Rabin, Sharon, Weizman, Yadin, and Amit, in relation to the civilian sector, which, too, was seen as responsible for the blunder (*Mehdal*).

Those who contend that the continuous existential threats facing Israel are indeed real and that they have not changed profoundly since the state's independence in 1948 are also likely to consider Israel's national security to be paramount, to assume that its civilian spheres should buttress its national security, and to accept the status of members of Israel's security network as experts in this critical realm, as well as generally.

Our position, by contrast, is that it is the members of Israel's security network who cast the security threats facing Israel in existential terms, who present Israel's national security as more important than all other issues and considerations, who constantly strive to securitize additional issues and spheres, and who present themselves as experts who are best equipped to preside over security matter and to deal with the threats facing the state.

CONCLUSION

This chapter has identified the various civilian areas in Israel in which members of its security network operate. We also elucidated some of the formal and informal mechanisms (including the cultural ones) that help these individuals formulate their positions and advance their shared interests and goals, the values and perceptions expressed by them, and the factors that can explain their predominant status.

The following are several important general observations based on this discussion: first, to some extent in the early decades of Israel's independence members of the security network had significant impact on policymaking. But, as the "Waiting Period" before the 1967 War so vividly illustrates, the security officials had to contend with a civilian government, which led to mutual tensions.

Israel's military victory in 1967, which seemed to confirm the IDF's, but not the civilians' stance, changed this situation profoundly. As we have shown, more former security officials, especially high-ranking IDF officers, joined the government and the Knesset, a trend that continued following subsequent armed clashes between Israel and its neighbors. Thus, in 1984, Israel's second National Unity Government, which had an unprecedented number of former security officials, succeeded the Likud government. Indeed, in 1967 and in 1984, and to some extent also in 2001, after the outbreak of the second Palestinian Intifada, national unity was deemed a virtue in Israel, and those representing it best were former security officials, who were appointed to key government positions.

In 1992, in the wake of the first Palestinian Intifada and the Gulf War of 1991, a similar process took place. The security sector was not only exempted from its inability to crush the uprising in the occupied Palestinian Territories or deter Iraq from launching some forty missiles at civilian targets in Israel, but Yitzhak Rabin, who as defense minister was the figure most associated with the IDF's predicament in 1987, became Israel's prime minister and defense minister. As we have noted, he was the first former security official to hold both posts. Ariel Sharon's election as prime minister in 2001 and 2003, despite his responsibility for the Lebanon War of 1982–1985, is also indicative of this trend.

The expansion of the security network in the political system, in sum, was not only a function of the success of a particular policy adopted by the security sector, but it rather stemmed from its *relative* power compared to Israel's political parties, institutions, and civilians. Indeed, surveys conducted in Israel show that the IDF enjoys far more credibility than the political and media institutions (Hadar 2009). The growing penetration of former security officials into Israel's political system, in turn, meant that struggles over Israel's security policy, both generally and in specific instances, would occur between competing and even clashing subnetworks *within* the dominant security network and not between civilian and security officials.

But although the integration of former security officials in Israel's political system has continued and expanded since 1967, it also witnessed important changes. In earlier periods, particularly before 1977, there was a close proximity between the political parties and the state's senior security officials, who saw a political role on their part as the continuation of their service in the security agencies. However, in later decades, security officials offered their services to or were approached by several parties before or upon their retirement; moved from one party to another during their political careers; and, at times, even formed parties and political factions by themselves.[74]

A similar and perhaps interconnected pattern can be identified in Israel's economy. Until 1977, former security officials, particularly high-ranking IDF officers affiliated with Mapai, joined economic firms that were run by the state or by the labor union, the *Histadrut*. In later decades, however, senior and junior security personnel joined public and private firms that were interested in their services. But political and socioeconomic factors were not the only ones that determined the expansion of the security network into the Israeli economy. Technological advancements, too, made some security personnel, particularly those who had served in IDF units that used cutting-edge technologies, attractive to local and foreign firms. These individuals began to play an important role, for example, in Israel's emerging high-tech industry. While some of these units, whose names were not even publicized before, became brand names, the code of secrecy that their members had adopted during their military service continued to reinforce the ties between them and to exclude others (Perman 2005: x–xi).

Israel's civil society, including groups operating in the public sphere, the Israeli media, and the educational system, also witnessed a growing penetration of former security officials in recent decades. This has not only contributed to the growing securitization of various civilian spheres in Israel but has also meant that former security officials, who consider themselves as, and are often considered to be, specialists in the field of national security, have better chances to influence policymaking than their civilian counterparts.

---

[74] Examples include Moshe Dayan, Ariel Sharon, Ezer Weizman, Binyamin Ben-Eliezer, Efraim Sneh, Yitzhak Mordechai, Yossi Peled, Uzi Dayan, and Ehud Barak.

4

The Security Network and Israel's Formal Democracy

This chapter discusses the impacts of Israel's security network, and in certain cases the impacts of the subnetworks operating within it, on the domestic arena, which comprises culture, politics, society, and the economy. To this end we highlight some of the manifold ways in which members of the security network, or the subnetworks, influence decisions and actions in these spheres.

In the first part of the chapter, we discuss several cases in which members of the security network have played a decisive role in the appointment and dismissal of both civilian leaders and security officials operating in the area of national security. More specifically, we examine the historical case of the resignation of Minister of Foreign Affairs Moshe Sharett on the eve of the Israeli-Arab War of 1956; the circumstances leading to the appointment of Major General Benny Gantz as the Israel Defense Forces' (IDF's) chief of staff in 2011; and the appointment of Yoram Cohen as director of the Shabak in the same year. We also note the similarities and differences between these cases.

In the second part of the chapter we discuss two telling cases in which members of the security network had a considerable impact on decisions that were related to Israel's national security but that also affected its politics, economy, and society. These include determining Israel's defense budget and the development of a new weapons system.

Finally, in the third part of the chapter, we focus on some of the more indirect effects of the activities of the security network on the domestic arena in Israel. In particular, we show how civilian leaders with a modest background in the security sector have attempted to present themselves as security experts. We then suggest that in recent years, a growing number of civilian issues in Israel have been securitized and illustrate this development by discussing the case of the major forest fire that erupted on Mount Carmel in 2011.

We wish to emphasize that the number of cases in which members of the security network have played a major role is quite large. However, there are several reasons for selecting these particular cases. First of all, we have chosen significant instances in which the pivotal role of Israel's security network in the domestic arena was clear and evident. Second, we have chosen to discuss a very significant historical case that influenced various later processes in this sphere, as well as recent cases that demonstrate that this situation has not changed, and possibly even has become more obvious and influential.

RESIGNATIONS AND APPOINTMENTS IN THE AREA OF NATIONAL SECURITY

As we have noted, the impact of Israel's security network on the political system is evident in the conduct of affairs by the government, the Knesset, and the political parties, especially concerning decisions that are more directly connected to national security issues. One of the most important and indeed sensitive spheres in which this impact can be discerned is the appointment and dismissal of senior government ministers and security officials.

The Resignation of Minister of Foreign Affairs Moshe Sharett

The pressures that several members of the security network applied on former prime minister and minister of foreign affairs, Moshe Sharett, in order to bring about his resignation from the government and thus facilitate the launching of the Israeli-Arab War in 1956, provide an early example of the well-documented impact of Israel's security network on appointments and dismissals even of senior politicians.[1]

During the early months of 1956, with rising tensions between Israel, on the one hand, and Syria and Egypt, on the other hand, and following the supply of weapons to Israel by France, the IDF planned and prepared to launch a preemptive war against Egypt, in accordance with its offensive–defensive military strategy and with the expected active cooperation of British and French forces. The IDF's intensive military clashes with and retaliations against Egypt, Syria, and Jordan and its war preparations, which intensified many months before the escalation of the conflict, exacerbated the tensions between the "activist" and the "moderate" camps in Israel's political system, particularly within its largest and most powerful political party – Mapai. The activist camp was led by Prime Minister and Minister of Defense David Ben-Gurion, who returned to the government in November 1955, whereas the moderate camp was led by Moshe Sharett, who had served as Israel's second prime minister and minister of foreign affairs in the period 1954–1955 and then again held only the latter post (he was Israel's first minister of foreign affairs from 1948 to 1954). It is noteworthy that both senior politicians were leading figures in Mapai (Sheffer 1996a).

---

[1] The discussion of the following case is based on Sheffer (1996a, chapters 27–29).

It was at that point, at a meeting of the government's Subcommittee for Defense and Foreign Affairs, that the IDF's chief of staff, Lieutenant General Moshe Dayan, and his deputy, Major General Chaim Laskov, openly spoke about the IDF's actual preparations for a preemptive war against Egypt. A flabbergasted Sharett replied, "[I am against] this total absorption in planning a war, which is purportedly imminent, or one that we can't escape and is the verdict of fate, or one that we want and [are] determined to bring about out of our will" (Sharett 1978: 1362).

Sharett's view was vindicated by a new political "storm" that erupted in late February 1956 when Ben-Gurion readopted his old position, according to which Israel had an urgent need to occupy the Gaza Strip, then under Egyptian military rule. Firmly adhering to the moderates' line, Sharett deplored "the desire for a preventive war which is obsessing the IDF's elite to the point where they are using every possible pretext to launch an explosive act which will set off the powder keg" (Sharett 1978: 1366). However, by then Sharett's opposition to a war against Egypt had become less accepted, as many of his colleagues in the moderate camp were changing their views concerning Israel's security and joining the ranks of the activists. Consequently, Sharett once again tried in earnest to initiate talks with Egyptian leader Gamal Abdul Nasser in order to avoid the war that the IDF and the activist camp were planning. Despite Sharett's efforts, however, the IDF senior staff and Ben-Gurion and his political supporters, who, at the time, were the prominent members of Israel's security network, continued to push the state toward a war that they had been seeking for so long.

Sharett continuously demanded that the IDF's generals and other members of the security network should exercise restraint and should not make the situation worse by ultimately leading to an Israeli preemptive war against Egypt. Actually, however, the two states' relations only deteriorated further, as did the relationship between, on the one hand, Ben-Gurion and the activists and, on the other hand, Sharett and the remaining moderates, whose number continued to decline. Thus, in response to Sharett's attempts to prevent the war, Ben-Gurion asserted that if it were not for Sharett's rejection of the military logic and intention of launching a preemptive war, most ministers in the government would have supported his position in favor of it. Indeed, because in this period the moderate camp did not disintegrate totally, and given the fact that Sharett, its prominent leader, still had political influence, the activist camp, whose members were also the leading figures in Israel's security network, realized that Sharett himself had become an obstacle to the realization of their plans. They started to demand his actual resignation from the government, and even then attempted to restrict his influence on Israeli politics in general and on Israel's security in particular.

At that point, Chief of Staff Dayan, who despite his formal military position was an active member of Mapai, began in some of the party's meetings to attack Sharett and the Ministry of Foreign Affairs, and what he called its "incompetent ambassadors." Dayan demanded, moreover, that all defense matters should be dealt with by the Ministry of Defense and even more particularly by the IDF (Sharett 1978). When Sharett dispatched an angry letter to Ben-Gurion about Dayan's intervention in political matters, he received the acerbic reply that Ben-Gurion was not interested in "interdepartmental quibbling" but in moving ahead with the preemptive strike against Egypt. The disagreement between Sharett and Ben-Gurion over political authority and responsibility was not settled even during a joint meeting between the activists (including Ben-Gurion, Dayan, and Shimon Peres, the director-general of the Ministry of Defense) and Sharett (Sharett 1978: 1389).

During the following months and despite Sharett's objection, the IDF inflicted heavy casualties on the Egyptian side. In response to these Israeli attacks, Sharett, who due to the worsening security situation continued to lose the support of the moderates in Mapai and in other parties, admonished the activists' appetite for killing (Sharett 1978: 1390). Indeed, despite declining support in his own party, Sharett adopted an increasingly critical position against the security network and its activities. Thus, he was furious when Dayan stated publicly that Israel had only two options – a raid into Sinai or into Gaza. This statement had an impact on the positions of an increasing number of Mapai and other parties' members. Consequently, Sharett was criticized for his moderate and almost pacifist positions by the growing number of activists.

In mid-April 1956, and in what can be seen as an action by Israel's security network, Ben-Gurion formally agreed with the IDF that it should prepare for a war against Egypt. Sharett tried to enlist the support of the remaining moderates to oppose the war. Although Sharett still had some support in the government, its members authorized Ben-Gurion to order a major operation if the Egyptians renewed their attacks on Jewish settlements in the Negev area. Sharett regarded this decision as "a major blow," adding that now he must tell his colleagues in the government to begin searching for a new minister of foreign affairs. Indeed, despite some tactical agreements between Ben-Gurion and Sharett, which are discussed in the next paragraph, the prime minister and his supporters were scheming to oust Sharett from the government in order to gain a majority that would support the war they were planning (Sheffer 1996a: 866–8).

In view of the need to appoint a new secretary general for Mapai, Sharett was pressed to suggest his candidacy for the job. Ben-Gurion saw Sharett's election to this position as an "honorable" way of getting rid of Sharett who, more than anyone else in Mapai, opposed many significant aspects of Ben-Gurion's political views and beliefs and, at that historical point in particular, his designs to launch a preemptive war against Egypt. Accordingly, Ben-Gurion formally proposed Sharett as the only candidate for the position in Mapai. Sharett tried to avoid it, but Ben-Gurion used a forceful tactical campaign to oust Sharett from the government. Since the support for Sharett in his own party and in other coalitional parties substantially declined, and despite his renewed wish of staying in the government, finally, under the pressure of Ben-Gurion and his supporters, especially among the members of the security network, Sharett had no other choice but to resign from his post as minister of foreign affairs on June 18, 1956 (Sheffer 1996a: 869–73).

In his final statement in the government after submitting his resignation, Sharett clearly said that although he greatly feared and opposed Ben-Gurion's proclivity to launch a preemptive war, and although he was aware that his resignation would weaken the position of those who wanted to prevent such a war, he could no longer contribute to the moderate position, as he was a victim of a shift toward greater activism within this camp itself, including in his own party. Sharett closed his resignation by stating "what the government was deprived of [through his resignation] education, culture and experience; the love and the confidence of many people; humane attitude towards everybody; and the belief that there was someone in the government who would not desert the cause of peace under any circumstances" (Sharett 1996a: 884).

This case clearly demonstrates the capacity of members of Israel's security network to influence a major decision in the area of national security, namely, launching a war, by bringing about the resignation of a senior member of Israel's main political party and of the government, based on, but also contributing to the change in, the power relations between moderates and activists within the state's leadership at the time. It also attests to the lack of clear boundaries between the civilian and security spheres in Israel in the early years of its independence, which as mentioned in the previous chapters, would intensify, and not lessen, after the 1967 War.

After discussing this significant historical case, in which Israel's security network still faced opposition from civilian actors and had to neutralize them in order to get its way, let us turn to two contemporary cases, which attest to the clashes within the dominant security network, including between subnetworks within it, but with civilian actors sometimes also playing a discernible role in the events.

The "Galant Affair"

On February 14, 2011, Major General Benny Gantz was promoted to the rank of Lieutenant General and replaced Gabi Ashkenazi as the IDF's chief of staff, thus putting an end to several months in which rival subnetworks within Israel's security network struggled to appoint their preferred candidates to the post.

One of these subnetworks, which was headed by Israel's minister of defense, Lieutenant General (res.) Ehud Barak, sought to appoint Major General Yoav Galant as chief of staff. Galant was a former naval commando officer who had served as the military secretary of the prime minister and as head of the IDF's Southern Command, including during Israel's military operation against Hamas in the Gaza Strip in 2008–2009. However, another subnetwork, which also had members placed in the higher echelons of the security sector, particularly in the IDF (its head was, or so it seems, the chief of staff himself), was resolved to do all that it could to obstruct Galant's appointment.

Importantly, the struggle between these subnetworks over the appointment of the IDF's new chief of staff concerned not only personal issues, especially the rivalry between Barak and Ashkenazi, but also their competing strategic views and those of the three candidates. It was argued, for example, that those opposed to Galant's appointment were also motivated by the fact that until the end of his tenure in 2011, Ashkenazi and his allies in the security network served as a moderating force and attempted to restrain the government's more hawkish tendencies and politics, especially towards the Palestinians, Lebanon and Iran (*NRG* June 6, 2011; *Haaretz* June 29, 2011). Therefore, members of this "pragmatist" subnetwork were worried that as the IDF's new chief of staff, Galant, who in the past expressed hard-line views on these issues (see, e.g., Galant 2007; *Haaretz* January 30, 2011) would reinforce the prevailing "hawkish" tendencies in the security network and, ultimately, in Israel's politics and policies. This would perhaps lead to an unnecessary preemptive attack against Iran's nuclear facilities and Hizbullah in Lebanon and to more hard-line policies vis-à-vis the Palestinians in the West Bank and the Gaza Strip. At the end of the day, it was this pragmatist subnetwork that succeeded in its quest, as another officer, Gantz, was named as Ashkenazi's successor. However, it appears that during the struggle between the two rival subnetworks, the pragmatist subnetwork took drastic and indeed unprecedented measures, including forging documents that were allegedly prepared by the hawkish network but that were actually supposed to tarnish the latter's image and to prevent Galant's appointment (Margalit and Bergman 2011).

Several intertwined elements in this episode need to be mentioned here. First, it is clear that the struggle over Galant's appointment was connected to Israel's policy toward Iran's nuclear project and to the support that Iran extended to radical Islamic armed factions in Lebanon and the Palestinian Territories (see, e.g., *Haaretz* June 29, 2011).[2] Importantly, both hawkish and pragmatist members of Israel's security network see the Iranian nuclear program as the major security threat facing Israel at present, and some have presented it as an existential threat (see, e.g., Freilich 2006: 636). The difference, however, is that whereas the hawks see it as an *imminent* threat that must be dealt with by the IDF, including by launching a preemptive strike against Iran's nuclear facilities, the pragmatists, among them the recently retired chiefs of the Mossad and the Shabak (Meir Dagan and Yuval Diskin, respectively), regard the possible threat

---

[2] Further evidence that the Galant Affair was connected to the Iranian question was revealed later, in June 2012, when it was reported that Defense Minister Barak hinted that after Galant's candidacy for chief of staff was thwarted he refused to extend Ashkenazi's term, even for a short period of time, since he was apprehensive that in this period a large military operation would take place and it would not be possible to appoint a new chief of staff during its course (*Haaretz* June 6, 2012).

to Israel as something that would emerge much further down the line. The latter believe, moreover, that a combination of international diplomacy, including harsh economic sanctions, and a covert campaign is a better way of defusing the Iranian threat, and that an Israeli attack will only push Iran to seek a nuclear capability with even greater determination and, what is more, with international legitimacy.[3] In addition, at least some pragmatists are willing to make concessions to Syria (an ally of Iran) and the Palestinians (some factions, especially in Gaza have received support from Iran) in order to achieve peace agreements on both of these fronts, which, they posit, might remove the Iranian threat to Israel or at least delay it even further (*Haaretz* February 11, 2011).

Then, toward the end of 2010, two pragmatic security officials, Ashkenazi and Diskin, were approaching the end of their tenure as chief of staff and director of the Shabak. This provided Defense Minister Barak and Prime Minister Benjamin Netanyahu, who are the more hawkish politicians, with the opportunity to replace both officials with more hawkish individuals. The first move contemplated was the appointment of Galant as Ashkenazi's successor. However, the pragmatists, who were aware of Barak's and Netanyahu's views, wished to prevent this move lest they be surrounded by hawkish security officials. Hence, and also due to their personal differences with hawkish officials, especially the growing rivalry between Ashkenazi and Barak, they attempted to prevent Galant from succeeding Ashkenazi and supported the candidacy of Gantz instead. But Barak and Netanyahu opposed Gantz and insisted on appointing Galant. This fundamental disagreement, which revolved not only around Galant's appointment but also around its possible military and political results, was at the backdrop of the Galant Affair.

Following are the main facts of and steps that were taken in this episode: In early August 2010, Defense Minister Barak announced that he was beginning to examine possible candidates for the IDF's next chief of staff. Then, on August 6, 2010, Israel's TV Channel 2 revealed the existence of a document, written on the letterhead of a leading public relations firm headed by Eyal Arad, who had been a close associate and adviser for Israeli right-wing prime ministers, which contained a detailed strategy for promoting Galant's appointment and smearing Gantz's and also Ashkenazi's reputation. Galant and Barak quickly stated that they had nothing to do with this document, and both claimed that its main

---

[3] Since his retirement, Dagan made several statements to this effect. In May 2011, for example, he claimed that an Israeli strike on Iran's nuclear facilities would be "a stupid idea," and that military action might not achieve all of its goals and could lead to a long war (see *New York Times* May 8, 2011; see also *Haaretz* June 1, 2011, June 3, 2011). In May 2012, Dagan published an article calling for sanctions but not military action against Iran together with former heads of the intelligence services of Germany and the United States, a former chief of staff of the British armed forces, and two former U.S. ambassadors (see *Wall Street Journal*, May 16, 2012). In April 2012, Yuval Diskin openly criticized the government, and specifically Prime Minister Netanyahu and Defense Minister Barak, and said that he does not trust their policy toward Iran (see *Haaretz* April 27, 2012; *Ynet*, April 28, 2012). See also Chapter 2.

purpose was to prevent Galant's appointment. The police opened an investigation to find out who was behind the document, which was now regarded as forged, and Attorney General Yehuda Weinstein instructed the government to suspend the process of examining candidates to replace Ashkenazi until all the facts were clarified. Toward the end of August 2010, Lieutenant Colonel (res.) Boaz Harpaz, a close friend of Ashkenazi, was arrested by the police as the main suspect of producing the forged document (*Haaretz* November 10, 2010, November 12, 2010; *News1* November 12, 2010. On Harpaz see, especially, Margalit and Bergman 2011). Barak then proceeded with his efforts to appoint Galant as the IDF's chief of staff, and on the basis of his close cooperation with Prime Minister Netanyahu, and with the support of several hawkish members of the government and the Knesset, the defense minister's recommendation to appoint Galant was formally approved by the government.

However, by then Galant's appointment faced a new challenge: the Israel Green Movement, a social-environmental group with moderate political views, launched a campaign against Galant's appointment because of his alleged illegal use of public lands near his home (*NRG* August 13, 2010).[4] This issue, which was also raised by one of the government's civilian members, Michael Eitan, caused a big debate in the Israeli media and public and, consequently, led to a struggle between the two competing subnetworks, that is, between Galant's supporters and their opponents. Israel's State Comptroller, Micha Lindenstrauss, was called upon to examine Galant's alleged illegal use of land and submitted his findings to the government, in which he harshly criticized Galant for his conduct (*Jerusalem Post* January 27, 2011). In view of these findings, Attorney General Weinstein announced that he would not back Galant's candidacy, and Barak and Netanyahu had little choice but to cancel Galant's appointment and appoint Gantz as Ashkenazi's replacement (*Globes* February 1, 2011; *Ynet* February 1, 2011).

The Galant Affair, which elicited much public interest in Israel, prompted several politicians and journalists to argue that this was a critical juncture in the state's history. This, they posited, was not only because rival groups of serving and former security officials tried to influence the government, particularly Netanyahu and Barak, to choose a particular candidate for the IDF's chief of staff (*Haaretz* October 28, 2010, June 29, 2011), but also because of the unprecedented ferocity of the rivalries within Israel's security network. Indeed, these rivalries made their way even to the government table, where two former chiefs of staff of the IDF, Lieutenant Generals Moshe Yaalon and Ehud Barak, openly traded accusations and insults (*Haaretz* February 6, 2011). Fully supporting our main arguments, Amos Harel, the military correspondent of *Haaretz*, wrote:

---

[4] Interestingly, Kalman Liebskind, the journalist who published the story about Galant, was later dismissed from reserve duty at the IDF's Southern Command, the unit commanded by Galant. See *NRG*, February 4, 2011.

The defense establishment in Israel is not made up solely of current office-holders. Its members also include former chiefs of staff and generals in the reserves, former senior officials in the Mossad and Shin Bet [Shabak] security services, executives in the military industries, and here and there, a well-connected journalist. It's not a particularly large group, and many of its members have business dealings with the defense establishment. The connections among its members have been forged over decades and are often quite tense. Last week, the reactions heard among this group were fairly uniform: sorrow (at varying levels) about what happened to Galant, sympathy with the difficult days Ashkenazi has been through, and above all, astonishment at the defense minister's behavior. (*Haaretz* February 11, 2011)

Other observers, however, saw this as a triumph of Israel's civil society, the Comptroller General, the Attorney General, and, ultimately, of Israeli democracy. According to an editorial in *Haaretz*, by bringing about the cancellation of Galant's appointment, "civil society in Israel proved its strength and its ability to stand up to aggressive politicians" and that this was "an achievement for Israeli democracy" (*Haaretz* January 30, 2011).

Yet, it seems that unlike the first case discussed earlier, but much like many of the major decisions on war and peace in Israel since 1967, the Galant Affair was, above all, the product of the rivalry between subnetworks *within* Israel's dominant security network. Moreover, though some civilian actors within the government and outside of it could sometimes exploit these rivalries to their own advantage, they have not been able to "desecuritize" Israel's domestic arena or, moreover, to challenge the security network's hegemonic role. These observations are reinforced by the third case discussed in the text that follows.

The Appointment of Yoram Cohen as Director of the Shabak

Early in 2011, the director of the Shabak, Yuval Diskin, was about to retire after five years of service. Naturally, this raised the question of who would be the next director of this agency, which had become a major actor involved in policymaking in Israel since the 1967 War, especially with regard to the occupied Palestinian Territories.

Defense Minister Barak and many other politicians, security officials (including of the Shabak), and journalists who were familiar with the efforts to find a suitable replacement for Diskin, were absolutely sure that his deputy, a man that due to the sensitivity of his position is known only by the first Hebrew letter of his surname – "Yud" – would be appointed. This expectation was based on the premise that Yud was considered to be a very experienced official with distinctive capabilities and achievements, and, moreover, that the outgoing director of the Shabak clearly preferred him over other candidates (*Ynet* October 22, 2010; *Haaretz* March 29, 2011).

However, and to the surprise of many observers, Prime Minister Netanyahu announced, on March 28, 2011, that rather than Yud, another deputy director of the Shabak, Yoram Cohen, would be the agency's new director. It is important to note that the new appointee was born to a religious family in Jerusalem, studied in a *Yeshiva*, and then served in the IDF. Immediately after completing his military service, he joined the Shabak, and during thirty years of service there he gradually moved up to the position of deputy director of the agency. It is also significant to note that one of his positions at the Shabak had been head of the department responsible for dealing with Palestinian armed activities in the occupied West Bank, adding to his close relationships with the Israeli settlers in the area. Though Cohen's political views are relatively unknown, a recent publication that he coauthored at a pro-Israeli think tank in Washington, which has become a lodestone for acting and former security officials, does suggest that he is an "activist" member of Israel's security network (Cohen and White 2009; see also *Ynet* March 29, 2011).

What is more clear, however, is that senior members of the Religious Zionist Movement in Israel, many of whom adhere to right-wing positions, had conducted a vigorous campaign against the appointment of Yud as director of the Shabak, including attempts to form a strong lobby and sending delegates to Prime Minister Netanyahu. To these actors, Yud was anathema to the Religious Zionist Movement on account of the actions taken by the Shabak against the Israeli settlers who protested against the government, actions that were allegedly initiated and conducted under Yud's command (*Ynet* March 28, 2011; *News1* March 28, 2011; *Haaretz* March 29, 2011). It is also noteworthy that the leaders of the campaign against Yud, which had begun as early as 2009, knew Shabak personnel and other leading figures in Israel's security sector very well. Among other things, rabbis affiliated with the Religious Zionist Movement initiated and had a great number of meetings with senior officials in the Shabak, including Yud himself and several of his subordinates. The rabbis' impression, based on these meetings, was that Yud was hostile to them and to the settlers in the occupied Palestinian Territories. Moreover, these leaders concluded that Yud may negatively influence the delicate relations and cooperation between the Religious Zionist Movement and the government (*Haaretz* March 29, 2011; *NRG* March 30, 2011).

At a certain point, these religious figures learned that Diskin had strongly recommended to Prime Minister Netanyahu and the government that they appoint Yud as Diskin's successor. The fact that these religious leaders were immediately informed about such a sensitive appointment, and their ability to lobby on behalf of their candidate for the job, testifies to the existence of a subnetwork made up of Religious Zionist leaders with vast connections to Israel's security network, most notably to senior officials in the Shabak, and to civilian politicians involved in national security issues in Israel. Since that point, the campaign of this Religious Zionist subnetwork intensified and was soon revealed by the Israeli media (*NRG* March 30, 2011). The intention to appoint Yud apparently became known to Yoram Cohen himself, who had connections with the Religious Zionist network, prompting him to start his own campaign to become of the next director of the Shabak.

Interestingly, the Religious Zionist actors, who were supported by their allies in the security network, lobbied not only the most senior Israeli politicians but also in the Knesset and government, with the result that government ministers, too, started to lobby Prime Minister Netanyahu himself for their candidate. Evidence of the efficiency of these actions can be seen in the fact that Netanyahu finally appointed Yoram Cohen rather than Yud as the as the next director of the Shabak (*Haaretz* June 3, 2011). There is evidence that suggest, moreover, that Netanyahu, who consulted with Barak and other senior security officials supporting Yud, was also influenced by a number of his Religious Zionist assistants, by the aforementioned lobbyists, by activist settlers, by some ministers in his government, by officials in the security sector, and by coalitional calculations (*Haaretz* June 3, 2011). In any case, claims regarding political involvement in the appointment were not denied in an official manner, and this caused resentment within the security sector, where some regarded this as a negative signal toward those serving in the Shabak (*Israel Defense* May 15, 2011).

Interestingly, the campaign for Yoram Cohen's appointment continued also *after* the appointment, this time by the Prime Minister's Office (which is in charge of the Shabak). According to one report, by a newspaper close to Netanyahu, the Prime Minister's Office gave journalists the names of potential interviewees on the appointment who included two former Shabak officials, Members of the Knesset (MKs) Avi Dichter, its former director, and Israel Hason, its former deputy director and Yoram Cohen's former superior, who, in their turn, spoke very highly of the appointee and his merits: that he had "risen from below," was a "field expert," a "professional," a "creative person," an "Arabist," and an "expert on Iran and Lebanon." They did not, however, mention the campaign for his appointment (*Israel Hayom* April 1, 2011).

In sum, this third case also demonstrates very clearly not only the existence of a security network in Israel whose members influence major decisions and actions taken by politicians and bureaucrats, particularly in the area of national security, but also the ability of other actors in Israel – in this case Religious Zionist leaders – to tap into the hegemonic security network in order to achieve their particular goals, thereby acknowledging its hegemonic role in the area of national security.

DECISIONS ABOUT ISRAEL'S NATIONAL SECURITY

This section discusses two cases in which members of Israel's security network have had a significant impact on major political decisions related to Israel's national security that also had a considerable effect on its politics, economy, society, and culture: first, determining the defense budget, which is not only the largest item in the state's budget and expenditures but also has significant implications for Israel's economy; second, the decision to develop the "Iron Dome" antiballistic defense system.

It should be noted here that we have chosen only two cases from many other relevant ones. This is for similar reasons that we mentioned previously concerning the general rationale of the choice of cases for analysis in this book.

Determining Israel's Defense Budget

Israel's Accountant General, Shuki Oren, recently complained, "It is difficult if not impossible to supervise the defense budget ... the security sector does everything it can so that it will not be subject to true supervision ... [and] the civilian sector that funds them [the security agencies] does not supervise them" (quoted in *The Marker* July 14, 2010). Indeed, a close examination of the process whereby Israel's defense budget is determined suggests that the civilian agencies involved in this process, namely, the government and the Knesset, are effectively short-circuited by members of Israel's security network.

According to data published in 2005, the actual budget of Israel's Ministry of Defense in the period 1999–2004 has exceeded the budget officially approved by the government by 10 to 15 percent (*The Marker* September 1, 2005). Interestingly, this occurred without the government, the Knesset, or the Israeli public being informed. In order to understand how and why this was the case, let us examine how the defense budget for one of these years – 2004 – was determined (for a useful discussion of the defense budget, see Shiffer 2007).

For several months in 2003, Israel's Ministry of Finance, then headed by Benjamin Netanyahu (the former and future prime minister), had been announcing its intention to make a deep cut in the security allocations for 2004. This was a part of Netanyahu's overall plan to cut governmental expenditures. For a number of reasons it appeared that at this time such a cut would succeed. First, while the overall economic situation in Israel was grave and seemed to require drastic cuttings, the security situation, which had deteriorated since 2000, improved somewhat. Second, the Ministry of Finance managed to make substantial cuts in other areas, most notably in health, social security, wages for public officials, and education. In this context, the security sector too, it was argued, must contribute its share. Third, the destruction of the Iraqi army in the wake of the U.S.-led invasion of Iraq in 2003 significantly reduced the perceived existential threats to Israel, potentially allowing for deep cuts in the IDF's ground forces. Fourth, a media virtuoso, Netanyahu, who was regarded then as the probable heir to Prime Minister Ariel Sharon, led the campaign. Finally, several security experts, economists, and journalists supported the Treasury in its quest to cut the defense budget, and the Israeli media was flooded with reports on the excessive privileges of military personnel, including op-eds urging the government to introduce long-awaited reforms in the security sector (see, e.g., *Haaretz* March 14, 2003, May 27, 2003, July 24, 2003, August 28, 2003).

The original allocation for security purposes for 2003 had been 33.6 billion NIS (new Israeli shekels),[5] but the security sector later was granted "supplements" that increased it to 36.5 billion NIS. The Treasury had hoped to reduce the base budget for 2004 by 3 billion NIS (i.e., to 30.6 billion NIS), whereas the IDF required an allocation similar to the one it received for 2003. But the security sector proved to be a formidable opponent. In what has become an annual ritual in Israel,[6] the IDF command, supported by other members of Israel's security network, underscored the major threats to Israel's security and argued that responsibility for cuts in security allocations in such perilous times should rest on the civilians' shoulders (see, e.g., *Haaretz* June 16, 2003, August 4, 2003, September 1, 2003. For criticism, see *Haaretz* September 9, 2001, January 20, 2002).

Thus, for example, the IDF's chief of staff, Lieutenant General Moshe Yaalon, equated the negotiations with the Ministry of Finance to a "Turkish bazaar," adding that the latter was not authorized (!) to make decisions on cuts in the defense budget since it would not be responsible for their disastrous consequences. The Treasury's behavior, he stated, was "on the threshold of irresponsibility" (*Haaretz* September 10, 2003; see also *Haaretz* June 9, 2003, September 3, 2003). Instead of reprimanding him, the defense minister, Lieutenant General (res.) Shaul Mofaz, himself a former chief of staff of the IDF and a member of the security network, accused the Ministry of Finance of stabbing the security sector in the back, adding that the proposed budgetary cut would place Israel's security under an "unreasonable threat" (*Ynet* September 14, 2003; *Haaretz* September 15, 2003).

Another security official playing a role in this period was the aforementioned Major General Yoav Galant, then the military secretary of Prime Minister Ariel Sharon. According to a recent book, during his tenure (2002–2005), Galant was able to prevent cuts of billions of NIS in Israel's defense budget by placing lookouts who informed him when the prime minister was meeting the director-general of his office and making sure that Galant himself was also present in these critical meetings. In addition, Galant would call up "reinforcements" in the form of the director-general of the Ministry of Defense, Major General (res.) Amos Yaron, and Chief of Staff Yaalon (Margalit and Bergman 2011: 143).

Other members of the security network, who operated in various civilian spheres in Israel, also joined the struggle. Several former security officials published a newspaper advertisement that explicitly warned the government not to "shatter our security" by opening an "internal front" against the security forces "who are fighting day by day and hour by hour for the security and future of the state of Israel" *(Haaretz* September 14, 2003). Others, who after

---

[5] In early January 2003, one US dollar was equal to 4.785 NIS.

[6] Freilich writes, "Each year, the Mod [Ministry of Defense] and IDF mount a public relations campaign, which at times borders on scare tactics, to generate public support for their budget request" (2006: 650).

retirement from the security sector became integrated in various civilian spheres but remained members of the security network, utilized their new positions to strongly promote the IDF's case. A telling example is the military-affairs correspondent of Israel's TV Channel 2, who is a lieutenant colonel in the IDF's reserves, and who argued that the proposed budgetary cut would "destroy" the security sector (*Israel Channel Two News* September 12, 2003). He did not disclose to his viewers, however, that his own pension, too, was liable to be affected by the proposed budgetary cuts.

Another example is MK Brigadier-General (res.) Ephraim Sneh, who at that time chaired the Subcommittee for Defense Preparedness of the Knesset's Committee of Foreign Affairs and Security. Alluding to the trauma of the 1973 War, Sneh warned against an additional cut in security allocations, arguing, in a press conference that he convened for this purpose on October 2, 2003 – a few days before the 30th anniversary of that war – that "30 years ago there was a conception that led to a disaster, and now again there is a conception and a lack of preparedness. The Middle East in our time has not become friendlier," he declared (*Ynet* October 2, 2003; see also: *Haaretz* August 4, 2003, September 8, 2003). Since his was one of the only civilian institutions acquainted to a certain degree with the details of the security budget, this position was of particular significance.

Thus, and despite certain public support for the moves of the Ministry of Finance, the security network managed to reduce the proposed cut in the defense budget, especially after Prime Minister Sharon, yet another long-time member of the security network, personally intervened in the matter and ruled against a drastic cut. Initially, Sharon ruled that the allocation for security for 2004 would be 32.85 billion NIS – 0.75 billion NIS less than the base budget for 2003 and 3.65 billion NS less than the overall budget for 2003. However, the next day he increased the cut to 1.07 billion NIS, leaving the base budget at 31.78 billion NIS. In late 2003, the Knesset approved a budget of 29.9 billion NIS for security purposes. This was after its Committee for the Security Budget, which is made up of members of the Knesset's Finance and Foreign Affairs and Security Committees, refused to vote on the proposed military budget (of 32.4 billion NIS), after Mofaz, Yaalon, and his deputy appeared before the committee and criticized the plan (*Haaretz* December 19, 2003).

Finally, however, in April 2004, the Knesset's Finance Committee decided to raise the security budget to 35 billion NIS, only slightly less than the 36.4 billion NIS demanded by the security sector in late 2003. With other resources, especially the U.S. annual military aid to Israel, the security budget then stood at 47.13 billion NIS. The Treasury's initiative was, thus, all but reversed (*Haaretz* September 15, 2003, September 16, 2003, January 4, 2004, May 5, 2004).

This case demonstrates the extent to which members of Israel's security network influence major policymaking processes in Israel, even when the objective circumstances are, ostensibly, unfavorable to them. Indeed, by joining hands together in order to promote their collective goal, and by employing an "existential" discourse with regard to Israel's national security, including an attempt to equate the challenges of the present with the traumas of the past, these members, who were situated in the government, the Knesset, the media and society, managed to overcome their civilian counterparts and get their way in the end. In later years, and especially after the war between Israel and Hizbullah in 2006, which led to a 30% increase in the defense budget in the next five years (*Haaretz* December 27, 2010), members of the security network have found it even easier to get their way. Thus, although such struggles over the defense budget continue until the present time, the security network generally has the upper hand in these decision-making processes.

The Development of the "Iron Dome" System

The planning, development, and production of the Iron Dome, an Israeli antiballistic defense system that was deployed for the first time in 2011, is yet another telling example of how a subnetwork of Israel's security network, which is composed of officials in the Ministry of Defense, Israel's military industries, and business tycoons, makes joint decisions and acts behind the scenes without effective control by the state's civilian institutions, particularly by the government and the Knesset. Moreover, under the cover of the military censorship that prevails in Israel, these actors manage to misrepresent their actions to the general public.[7]

For many years, the Ministry of Defense, the IDF in general, and the air force in particular, refused to develop an antiballistic defense system. This refusal was based on their traditional preference for offensive weapons systems and on their belief that an antiballistic defense system would not be effective and is hence not worth funding (*Haaretz*, December 16, 2010). However, after the War between Israel and Hizbullah in 2006, in which many cities and villages in northern Israel were hit by rockets launched by Hizbullah from Lebanon, civilian pressures to develop such defense systems increased dramatically. It was then that Minister of Defense Amir Peretz, a civilian politician without a significant military background, managed to overcome the objection of the officials in his ministry and in the IDF and imposed the development of such a defensive system on the security sector (*Haaretz*, December 16, 2010).

The decision made in this period was, reportedly, to entrust several Israeli arms producing firms, including Rafael and Elta, a firm connected to the air force, with the development of the new antiballistic defense system. A third firm, mPrest Systems, which is owned by a former IDF colonel, was to develop the system's electronic components. The main purpose of giving this project to Rafael was to compensate it for not taking part in the development of a much larger ballistic project – the *Arrow* weapon system, which was placed in the

---

[7] On this episode, see especially a piece by Yossi Melman, the correspondent for security affairs of the daily *Haaretz* (*Haaretz* December 16, 2010).

hands of another Israeli arms manufacturer, the Israel Aerospace Industries (*Haaretz* December 16, 2010).

However, and not untypically in Israel, in fact, the Iron Dome project had started to take shape before the initiative of Minister of Defense Peretz and before the government made any decision on the matter (*Haaretz*, December 16, 2010). In his Report, Israel's State Comptroller, Michael Lindenstrauss, strongly criticized the flawed process of decision making that led to the development of the Iron Dome system, the cost of which was estimated at several billions NIS in late 2007 (State Comptroller 2009: 5). More specifically, the report mentions the following steps that were taken in the decision-making process: Already on August 3, 2005, Brigadier General Dr. Danny Gold, head of the Research and Development Unit at the Research and Development Directorate (RDD) at the Ministry of Defense, which is responsible for the development of new weapon systems for the IDF, decided on his own to start the planning, the development in full scale, and the production of the antiballistic defense system. Gold then allocated funds for this project on his own without any decision by the prime minister, the defense minister, or the IDF (State Comptroller 2009: 8). An Israeli reporter, Yossi Melman, adds that "at the same time Rafael secretly approached Singapore and persuaded the country to share the costs of development or promise to buy the system. This information was withheld from the [Israeli] public" (*Haaretz* December 16, 2010).

It was about a year later, on August 27, 2006, that Minister of Defense Peretz stated that "the Iron Dome is the most important project at the moment and therefore we should consider defining it as an 'emergency plan' and expedite it as soon as possible" (State Comptroller 2009: 12). On November 12, 2006, the RDD formally instructed Rafael to begin the project, and, as mentioned previously, on December 1, 2006, Peretz decided that since Iron Dome was essential for the defense of the Israeli cities and villages there was a need for external financing for the project (State Comptroller 2009: 12). Apparently, that decision led to a major financial deal with Singapore, which was also interested in an antiballistic defense system. It was only then that Prime Minister Ehud Olmert approved the defense minister's decision. This means that the Iron Dome project was, above all, the brainchild of members of Israel's security network, and was moreover initially developed without the government's approval.

However, after the initial stages of the project, and apparently as a result of a more accurate and critical examination of it, the IDF's chief of staff decided at the beginning of June 2007 not to approve the further development of the project. Yet about a month later, Minister of Defense Ehud Barak, known for his close connections to several Israeli business tycoons, approved it. Finally, on December 23, 2007, the ministerial committee for defense approved the project (State Comptroller 2009: 12).

In view of the need for additional funds for the Iron Dome project, on May 13, 2010, U.S. President Barack Obama announced that his country would grant $205 million to the project (*Reuters* May 13, 2010). However, a former

IDF officer, Brigadier General (res.) Meir Elran, argued that this sum would be insufficient for protecting all population centers and military and national infrastructures against attacks (*Haaretz* April 10, 2011).

In any case, in March 2011, and following an escalation in Israel's ongoing tense relationship with Hamas in the Gaza Strip, the first Iron Dome system was deployed in Israel's south for what Defense Minister Barak described as an "operational test" (*Haaretz* March 23, 2011). However, Barak and high-ranking officers in the IDF made it quite clear that the Iron Dome's capability to intercept rockets coming from the Gaza strip was quite limited and very costly. According to Barak, Iron Dome "is a system that can already shoot if fired in its direction, but we need to understand that apart from the fact that this is an extraordinary achievement of our defense industries, which is unprecedented anywhere else, it eventually does not give 100 percent coverage" (*Ynet* March 25, 2011).

According to Melman, India, the United States, and other states have also been interested in the Iron Dome project, invested quite substantive sums in it, and were ready to provide it with more funding. Thus, it seems that one of the project's major goals was to increase the activities and profits of Rafael (*Haaretz* December 16, 2010). Moreover, it eventually turned out that the Iron Dome project's main objective is not to protect civilian settlements at all, especially those that are close to the border with the Gaza Strip, but rather to protect military bases in that area. Hence, the decision to develop and produce the Iron Dome project instead of other, much cheaper systems (e.g., the Vulcan-Phalanx short-range antimissile defense system) was made to avoid a situation in which Rafael would not be able to produce the Iron Dome and benefit from it (*Haaretz* December 16, 2010).

In April 2011, after the first system of Iron Dome managed to intercept several rockets fired by Hamas from the Gaza Strip, acting and former security officials in Israel praised not only the project itself but also the decision-making process that led to its development. Uzi Rubin, who had served as head of Israel's Missile Defense Organization and who oversaw the development of Israel's *Arrow* antimissile defense system, observed:

In the Austro-Hungarian Empire before the First World War there was a special award for officers who violated a command and thereby saved the state. It would be appropriate to give such an award to Brigadier General (res.) Danny Gold, who was severely criticized by the state comptroller for starting the Iron Dome project without waiting for long months until all the bureaucratic steps were completed. (*Haaretz* April 17, 2011)

However, the attempt made by members of the security network to justify the flawed policymaking process described above in "existential" terms, which, as shown in this book, is not untypical in the area of Israel's national security, was not very convincing. Melman, who investigated the origins of the Iron Dome project, concludes:

The behavior of the army and the defense system in this affair is shamelessly cynical, proof of the contempt of bureaucrats and decision-makers for the public and its money… [They] have the feeling that they can make fools of the public without being asked to give explanations and without taking responsibility for their actions. (*Haaretz* December 16, 2010)

SECURITIZATION IN ISRAEL

In the previous sections we demonstrated how members of Israel's security network have joined hands to influence civilian decision-making processes in the area of Israel's national security. But to realize the full impact of the security network on the domestic sphere in Israel, we also must consider more indirect and informal – including cultural and discursive – forms of influence.

In this section, we provide several examples for how Israeli political leaders with a "modest" background in the security sector have tried to present themselves as security experts. We suggest that this behavior stems not only from a militaristic culture in Israel. Rather, the expectation of these civilian actors is that this would place them on par with members of the dominant security network, including some of their political opponents, and moreover earn them the same public support accorded to the security experts in Israel, that is, serving and former security officials. We then provide several examples for civilian issues that have been securitized in recent years.

Civilian Politicians as Security Experts

In recent decades, but particularly since 1967, a growing number of Israeli politicians, including some who had not held senior positions in the IDF or in other security agencies, have presented themselves as security experts in order to join, or tap into, Israel's dominant security network. This behavior is obviously related to the widespread perception in Israel that it faces continuous existential threats and the expectation of many Israelis that their leaders should be capable of responding to their individual and collective feelings of insecurity. Indeed, members of the security network often argue that the fact that they are security experts makes them better equipped to be Israel's leaders than their civilian counterparts. Former prime minister and defense minister, Lieutenant General (res.) Ehud Barak, who was one of the contenders in Israel's general elections in 2009, posited:

If there's a storm at sea, you take an experienced captain. As long as it looks like a game and not like the real thing, this is one kind of judgment. But when the test comes and [the people] need to ask who do we want to raise the phone at 3 am, the people will know to choose the man with life experience, with the understanding of the things themselves. This is not a reality show. You do not choose a new moderator for "Survivor" or a new participant in "Dancing with the Stars." (Quoted in *Haaretz* August 8, 2008)

By presenting themselves as notified security experts, then, Israeli civilian politicians are trying to do two things, both of which attest to the considerable impact of the security network in the domestic arena. First, they attempt to show that they are on par with those who have "the understanding of the things themselves," that is, members of the security network. But it seems that these civilian leaders also try to tap into the security network, which, as argued several times in this book, enjoys a hegemonic status in the area of national security in Israel but also generally. Let us consider several cases that illustrate these points.

The first example is Israel's president, Shimon Peres, who throughout his long political career has emphasized his previous positions as director-general of the Ministry of Defense, as deputy defense minister, and as minister of defense. In addition, Peres and his supporters have repeatedly mentioned the fact that he was the initiator of the Dimona nuclear reactor and the driving force in building Israel's nuclear capabilities (Ministry of Foreign Affairs 2001; Peres Center for Peace n.d.) Among other visible expressions of his position, Peres, who became prime minister following the assassination of Prime Minister Yitzhak Rabin in November 1995, wore a military jacket at the time of Israel's military operation against Hizbullah in 1996, right before the general elections scheduled for that year. By doing so, Peres attempted to show to the Israeli public but also to other members of the security network that, like his predecessor, he was also a security expert worthy of support.

Peres did not, however, become Israel's next prime minister, but was defeated by another civilian politician who also presented himself as a security expert: Benjamin Netanyahu. During his military service, Netanyahu served in the IDF's primary elite unit, *Sayeret Matkal*, and after the 1973 War, when he joined the IDF reserves, he was promoted to the rank of captain (Prime Minister's Office n.d.). However, compared to other former security officials-turned-politicians in his party, the Likud, and in other parties, especially the Labor Party, this was a rather modest security background, which could turn into a political liability. Therefore, Netanyahu continuously sought to present himself as a security expert, on the one hand, and as a leader surrounded by other security experts, on the other hand. The first strategy can be gleaned from Prime Minister Netanyahu's official biography, which appears on the website of the Prime Minister's Office:

In 1979 and 1984 Mr. Netanyahu organized two international conferences that emphasized the need to fight terror groups and the regimes supporting them. US Secretary of State George Schultz has written that Mr. Netanyahu's public advocacy and books had a decisive influence in shaping American policy toward fighting terrorism. (Prime Minister's Office n.d.)

Other security-related issues dealt with by Netanyahu include Iran's nuclear program and the existential threats emanating from it not only to Israel but also to the West, and the Palestinian threat to Israel, which he claimed was connected to Nazism (Zertal 2005: 175–6). On the "positive" side, Netanyahu espoused the "democratic peace" theory which, according to him, should be applied to Israel's relations with its neighbors (Ish-Shalom 2006: 582–4).

Netanyahu's second strategy was clearly manifested in 1996, when he became Israel's prime minister for the first time and immediately named a former high-ranking IDF officer, Major General (res.) Yitzhak Mordechai, as his defense minister. In 2009, when Netanyahu reoccupied the post of prime minister, he also appointed a former high-ranking IDF officer, Lieutenant General (res.) Ehud Barak, who was his former commander in the IDF, for this post. In 2012, following a fierce attack by former director of the Shabak, Yuval Diskin, on the security policy of Netanyahu and Barak, another senior IDF officer, Lieutenant General (res.) Shaul Mofaz, joined the government, thus increasing its security credentials.

Another telling case is Ehud Olmert, an Israeli politician who during his compulsory service was a military correspondent and underwent an officers' course only when he served in the IDF reserves (*Yedioth Ahronoth* April 14, 2006). Like Peres in 1996, Olmert became a candidate for prime minister only after his predecessor, Ariel Sharon, leader of the newly founded Kadima party, abruptly left the scene after suffering a hemorrhagic stroke. But unlike Netanyahu, who could choose his defense minister in 1996, Olmert, because of the coalition structure, had to accept a civilian, Amir Peretz, the leader of the Labor Party, as his defense minister.

Without security credentials, both Olmert and Peretz were at a considerable disadvantage, not only within their own parties, both of which included several former officers and security officials, but also vis-à-vis other political parties (especially the Likud), in their dealings with the IDF and the other security services, and, of course, in their attempts to gain public support for their policies. It is not surprising, then, that throughout their term these two leaders continuously sought to demonstrate that they, too, cared much for Israel's security. This was evident, for instance, during the outbreak of the war between Israel and Hizbullah in July 2006, when Olmert told the IDF commanders:

The government does not limit you in any significant way ... The government just sets the space in which much can be done ... You have a prime minister and a defense minister who are willing to take responsibility for tough decisions. Take advantage of it; don't make us your concern. Think as far as you can ... leave it to us to make decisions. (Quoted in Levy 2010b: 796)

Indeed, as late as September 2010, a year and a half after he left office, Olmert still blamed Barak, who in 2007 succeeded Peretz as defense minister, for trying to prevent the government under Olmert from taking "daring steps" in the area of Israel national security, alluding to the attack that was allegedly launched by Israel against the Syrian nuclear reactor in September 2007 (*Jerusalem Post* September 20, 2010).

In what can be regarded as the epitome of this process of assimilation to Israel's hegemonic security network, Peretz, who was always despised by the IDF's top brass,[8] was photographed looking through a pair of binoculars whose cap was still on. An Israeli journalist commented:

The ridicule by the top IDF brass is infuriating: Before slandering the defense minister, the generals should first complete the reforms needed in the IDF. He "does not understand security"? And what about their ongoing failures? Peretz is certainly not responsible for the army's situation. (*Haaretz* February 25, 2007)

Civilian Issues as Security Challenges

Securitization in Israel has not been limited to the country's civilian politicians but is also widely practiced with regard to civilian issues. Indeed, in recent years various individuals and groups in Israel have sought to present quite a number of civilian issues as security-related matters, regardless of whether these issues had anything to do with security. These civilian issues include, among others, anti-drug campaigns that portrayed pot smokers as collaborators with Hizbullah[9]; efforts to integrate more ultrareligious Jews into the Israeli economy by recruiting them to the IDF[10]; calls made by Israeli MKs[11] and former security officials[12] to quickly exploit the large reserves of natural gas discovered off the shores of Israel lest they fall into the hands of Israel's enemies, Iran and Hizbullah; and an attempt by leading Israeli business tycoons, members of the Ofer family, to justify their business ties with Iran by arguing that these ties assisted "official Israeli actors" – that is, the security sector – for "national purposes."[13]

---

[8] Personal conversation with an advisor to Amir Peretz, May 2007.

[9] See Yonatan Almaliah, "At the End of Every Joint Sits Nasrallah," April 2, 2008, at: http://www.mouse.co.il/CM.articles_item,778,209,21490,.aspx (Accessed April 24, 2011) [Hebrew].

[10] See, for example, the interim report of a team of the Knesset's Foreign Affairs and Defense Committee, at: http://www.news1.co.il/ShowCurrentFile.aspx?FileID=3516, January 16, 2011 (Accessed: April 24, 2011) [Hebrew].

[11] See, especially, the protocol of the Knesset's Economic Affairs Committee from October 5, 2010, at: http://www.knesset.gov.il/protocols/data/html/kalkala/2010-10-05.html (Accessed: April 24, 2011) [Hebrew]. The protocol later served as the base for a satirical play. See: http://cafe.mouse.co.il/post/1997932 (Accessed: April 24, 2011).

[12] For example, the statements made by Major Generals (res.) Yossi Peled and Giora Eilend in the Knesset's Economic Affairs Committee in its meetings on October 5, 2010 and March 10, 2011 (on the former, see: http://www.knesset.gov.il/protocols/data/html/kalkala/2010-10-05.html [Accessed April 24, 2011] [Hebrew]; on the latter, see: *Ynet* March 10, 2011).

[13] See an article by Yossi Melman in *Haaretz*, June 1, 2011. In addition to Major General (res.) Yom-Tov Samia (see above), former security officials employed by the Ofer family include Major General (res.) Yaacov Amidror, who in 2011 was appointed as security advisor to Israel's prime minister, Benjamin Netanyahu; Brigadier General (res.) Pinhas Buchris, the former commander of the IDF's Unit 8200 and director general of the Defense Ministry; Yaacov Peri, former director of the Shabak; Major General (res.) Ami Sagis; and Major General (res.) Chaim Erez.

One illustrative case elucidates this phenomenon: the forest fire in Mount Carmel in Israel in late 2010. As we will suggest, this event, which actually had very little to do with Israel's security, was almost immediately presented by civilian politicians and by media commentators as a security threat. This not only served to mobilize the domestic and foreign support that was deemed necessary to put out the forest fire, but also enhanced the status of Israel's civilian leaders as security experts.

Although in recent decades Israel has dispatched relief missions to other countries following earthquakes and other national disasters, the Israel Fire and Rescue Services (IFRS) have, in recent years, been neglected by consecutive Israeli governments.[14] According to a report by Israel's State Comptroller from December 2010, the IFRS is the "weakest Link" in Israel's emergency rescue apparatus and faces a danger of collapse during a national emergency. Indeed, even after the war between Israel and Hizbullah in 2006, which exposed the weakness of Israel's home front, this situation has not improved (State Comptroller 2010b).

In view of this state of affairs, it is not surprising that the IFRS could do little in response to the huge forest fire that erupted in Mount Carmel on December 2, 2010. The fire spread very quickly and consumed much of the Mediterranean forest covering a substantial western part of the mountain. The fire, which lasted for four days, claimed 44 lives, making it the deadliest in Israel's history. Eventually, more than 17,000 people were evacuated from their homes, including from several villages in the vicinity of the fire. In addition, considerable damage, estimated at 240–270 million NIS,[15] was inflicted on civilian property, infrastructures, and the environment (*Haaretz* December 5, 2010).

At first, the police suggested that the Mount Carmel fire was caused by a bonfire that was not extinguished properly and arrested two adolescent brothers from the Druze town of Usfiya as suspects in this matter; they were later released from custody. Despite the fact that most members of Israel's Druze community identify with the state and there is mandatory conscription for Druze males, official statements and media reports concerning the fire immediately suggested, or insinuated, that in fact the Mount Carmel fire was an act of terror. The issue became even more controversial when a Druze MK, Ayoob Kara, a resident of Usfiya, said on the evening of December 2 that he had received information that the fire was an act of terror. Two other MKs, Yaakov Katz and Michael Ben-Ari, also raised this possibility and called for a major investigation.

The securitization of the Mount Carmel fire became even more pronounced following an apparent wave of arson throughout Israel and the occupied West Bank. Indeed, although these additional fires were all extinguished within a

---

[14] It should be noted that unlike other states, such as the United States, where the public image of fire fighters is very positive, in Israel this is generally not the case.

[15] In early December 2010, one US dollar was equal to 3.665 NIS.

few hours, they created considerable confusion in Israel not only over the identity of those responsible for this wave but also about the source of the Mount Carmel blaze. The fact that the police referred to some of these fires as arson, and that both the Israeli public and the security forces regarded them as an actual and potential serious threat to the Israelis in those areas, added to this perception of an imminent security threat. Indeed, it can be argued that a sort of a national consensus emerged in Israel in this period that all of these fires, as well as the difficulties in dealing with them, constituted part of the security threats Israel encounters, and that they exposed the fragility of its home front, especially in face of missile and rocket attacks.

This perception of a security threat to Israel on account of the fires was further enhanced when actors hostile to Israel referred to them as detrimental blows to its security. A leading Israeli news website reported that many Arab media outlets had been taking advantage of Israel's fire disaster to disparage the Jewish state and rejoice over its misfortune. Based on a survey of comments from readers on Arabic websites, the *Jerusalem Post* reported that many Arabs called on Israel's enemies, particularly Iran, Hamas, and Hizbullah, to use the opportunity presented by the disaster to wipe Israel off the face of earth (*Jerusalem Post* December 10, 2010). Other Arabs condemned Egypt and Jordan for agreeing to help Israel put out the fire. Prime Minister Ismail Haniyeh of Hamas told Reuters: "These are plagues from God. Allah is punishing [the Israelis] from a place they did not expect." In the same vein, a Palestinian official identified with the Islamic Jihad criticized those "whose hearts fill with compassion for the Zionist disaster," adding: "Let the fire consume this spider state". In this he referred to a well-known speech by Hassan Nasrallah, leader of the Lebanese group Hizbullah, in 2000, in which he argued that "Israel may own nuclear weapons and heavy weaponry, but, by God, it is weaker than a spider's web" (quoted in Cordesman and Sullivan 2007: 33). Hizbullah-run *Al-Manar* also stated that the fire signaled Israel's vulnerability: "The great Carmel fire has embarrassed Israel's firefighting capabilities and proved its almost complete incompetence. The enormous blaze that broke out on the Carmel proved that Israel is not prepared for war or a mass terrorist strike that would cause many casualties in the home front."

There is little doubt that the securitization of the Mount Carmel fire helped Israel's civilian politicians deal with it more quickly, especially in view of the weakness of the relevant civilian agencies, particularly the IFRS. Indeed, senior government members, including Prime Minister Benjamin Netanyahu and Minister of Foreign Affairs Avigdor Lieberman, quickly enlisted Israel's security agencies to deal with the fires and called on other countries, including some with close security ties with Israel, to assist it in its efforts. Israel's security agencies, which mobilized their members for this purpose, included not only the IFRS but also the police and the IDF, which dispatched two battalions to assist in fire-fighting and evacuating residents from the area. The IDF also sent heavy equipment such as fire trucks, water tanks, cranes, and bulldozers, and the air force used its unmanned aerial vehicles for reconnaissance and intelligence collection concerning the fire. It is noteworthy that the use of other military aircrafts was prohibited due to a decade-old decision that prohibits these aircrafts from being used in such instances, spurring a demand to change this rule and involve the IDF more in these events. The fact that the casualties of the Mount Carmel fire were mostly officer cadets from the Israel Prison Service, as well as three senior police officers, among them the chief of Haifa's police, further underscored the link between the event and Israel's security.

On the external level, too, Israel requested and received help from various countries, including the United States, Turkey, and Greece. In view of Greece's developing military cooperation with Israel, it is perhaps not surprising that it was the first state to respond to Israel's call for help. Later that year, Greece assisted Israel in preventing a pro-Palestinian flotilla from sailing from Greece to the Gaza Strip. Turkey's assistance was more surprising, however, due to the strained Turkish–Israeli relationship since Israel's raid on the Gaza Flotilla earlier that year, in which several Turkish citizens were killed by the IDF. Indeed, at a meeting of Israel's Security Cabinet, Prime Minister Netanyahu thanked Turkish Prime Minister Erdoğan for his help, saying that he hoped this would be the beginning of better relations between the two countries (*Ynet* December 3, 2010). However, despite some help from other countries (including the Netherlands, Belgium, Germany, Finland, Norway, and Russia) and even from the Palestinian Authority, the main help came from the United States, where Israel rented a huge Evergreen's Boeing Supertanker to help extinguish the fire.

By presenting nearly all matters related to the Mount Carmel fire as security-related, Israel's civilian leaders sought to invest them with the kind of importance and urgency generally accorded to "pure" security matters in Israel. However, in view of the predominant status of the security network, these actors may have hoped that its members would help them advance these goals. Indeed, in addressing these securitized issues, former security officials sometimes employed the same terminology that they used when dealing with genuine security threats (see, e.g., Elran 2010). Moreover, by transferring the fire from the civilian to the security realm, Israeli politicians, and especially Netanyahu, may have hoped to prevent hard questions about their performance before the fire and, perhaps, boost their public image as those who are safeguarding Israel's security.

In May 2011, several months after the Mount Carmel fire, Israel's first firefighter squadron, the *Elad* Squadron,[16] was launched not under the auspices of the IFRS but as part of the Israeli air force. Prime Minister Netanyahu, who attended the ceremony, thus put paid to the previous arrangement, according to which civilian aircraft used to spray agricultural crops were employed for

---

[16] Reuven Pedatzur suggested that the contract for the supply of airplanes to this squadron was "tailored" to its two providers – Elbit and Chimnir (*Haaretz* April 24, 2011).

fire-fighting purposes, transferring the responsibility for airborne fire fighting to the security realm. Leading commentators on security affairs, who criticized this blatant act of securitization, noted that under pressure from Netanyahu, the air force was now entering an area that did not belong to it (*Haaretz* April 24, 2001, June 13, 2011). One commentator even suggested that this was an attempt by the prime minister to prevent additional criticism of his government by the State Comptroller. The air force, the commentator added, was prepared to make this small concession in return for more say in more serious matters, such as war-making (*Haaretz* June 13, 2011).

Securitization of a civilian sphere, fire fighting, thus opened the door for an even more accentuated role of Israel's security sector and, ultimately, for members of the security network, in decisions of war and peace in Israel.

CONCLUSION

The preceding discussion of the impact of the security network on the domestic arena in Israel allows us to draw a number of conclusions.

First, the various cases clearly demonstrate the overriding power and influence of the security network and, occasionally, the subnetworks within it, in critical areas of Israeli politics and society. Moreover, the power and influence of Israel's security network has superseded that of other state institutions that are entrusted with making political decisions, especially the government, the Knesset, and the political parties. Indeed, the considerable weakening of all of these institutions, as well as a host of other social actors in Israel, such as the labor union, the *Histadrut*, and the Kibbutz and *Moshav* movements, particularly since the 1967 War, occurred parallel to the strengthening of Israel's security network, and was, perhaps, exacerbated by this process.

A second conclusion, which follows directly from the previous, is that Israel's political parties and civil society groups can hope to achieve only limited goals in the domestic arena, for example, influencing only few of the government's policies and decisions, distributing government positions among the coalitional participants, and allocating funds to those societal sectors that have powerful political patrons. It is the security network that influences major policies in Israel, especially in the area of national security but sometimes in other spheres as well. Indeed, although arguments sometimes exist between members of the security network, or struggles between subnetworks within it, and despite the fact that these divisions can be exploited by determined civilian actors, the latter are incapable of challenging the predominant status of the security network in Israel. Struggles between civilian actors and the security network, which occurred before 1967 and sometimes led to the removal of civilian leaders from office (e.g., Moshe Sharett before the 1956 War) or taking away some of their prerogatives (e.g., Levi Eshkol and the other civilian members of his government before the 1967 War), were thus replaced with struggles within a dominant security network.

The third conclusion, which additional research can help substantiate, is that the growing power and influence of the security network in Israel was reinforced and perhaps also accelerated by more general political and socio-economic processes that have taken place in the country in recent decades, such as the decline of collectivism and the rise of individualization, liberalization, and privatization (see, e.g., Migdal 2001: 149–71).

In sum, this chapter has suggested that one of the main reasons why Israel is still a formal democracy and not an effective democracy, even after more than six decades of independence, is the persistence and strength of Israel's security network and its considerable impacts on the state's various civilian spheres. In the concluding chapter, we discuss the interplay between this critical factor and other major weak points of Israeli democracy, particularly its "ethnic" or "ethnocratic" character (cf. Smooha 2002; Yiftachel 2006).

5

The Network at Work

Shaping Israel's Foreign and Security Policies

Several years ago, the authors of this book participated in a workshop titled *The Future of Israel's Ministry of Foreign Affairs* at the Leonard Davis Institute for International Relations at The Hebrew University of Jerusalem in Israel. In addition to several academics, those attending were about a dozen of former officials in Israel's Ministry of Foreign Affairs (MFA), including nine who had served as its director general and deputy directors general, as well as a representative of the MFA at the rank of head of division.[1]

A major issue that was raised by many participants in this informal gathering was the pivotal role played by Israel's security sector, especially the Israel Defense Forces (IDF), in shaping Israel's foreign policy. The MFA officials posited, for example, that whenever a particular state or topic that fell under the responsibility of the MFA became relevant to Israel's national security, the decisive influence with regard to it was immediately passed to the security sector. This pattern, they emphasized, was not limited to Israel's close relations with the United States, which were run mostly by the Prime Minister's Office, the Ministry of Defense, and the IDF, but also to Israel's relations with other states.

In addition, the MFA officials maintained that Israeli security officials not only refused to share sensitive information with the MFA, but they also enjoyed far greater access to Israel's most senior politicians. One participant mentioned, for example, that during Israel's Annual Intelligence Assessment, when both security and civilian relevant state agencies present their views to the government, most of the time allotted to these presentations is taken by the IDF's Intelligence Branch whereas other agencies, including the MFA, have very limited time to present their views. "What can I do in such a short time?" he complained, "tell the ministers that all of the things that the IDF's officers had said to them are wrong?"

---

[1] For a summary, see Barak and Cohen (2006). Cf. Freilich (2006: 652, 657–8).

Accounts by former ministers in the Israeli government, especially those without a significant background in the security sector, tell a similar tale. These ministers, who were on the receiving end of the assessments and policy recommendations of the security sector, again, especially the IDF, and particularly its powerful Intelligence Branch, have testified that when they served in the government they did not have the means with which to analyze the security officials' opinion, verify the materials that the latter presented to them, and set alternative policies to those suggested by the security officials (Peri 2006: 69; see also Freilich 2006: 649–50). Dan Meridor, who has been a minister in several Israeli governments of different stripes and also served as secretary of the government and chairman of the Knesset's Foreign Affairs and Defense Committee, explained this predicament:

Meetings with military personnel have a fixed scenario. The military representatives present three options: the first could be very effective, but bears many risks and has a low chance to succeed; the second might succeed and bears no danger, but is of marginal effectiveness; and the third, which was the one they preferred from the start. It got to the point where I would just say to them – "start from the third option." (Quoted in Peri 2006: 52)[2]

But the decisive role of Israel's security sector has not been limited to policy making. It has also related to carrying out the government's decisions. Shlomo Ben-Ami, who served as Israel's minister of foreign affairs in the early stage of the second Palestinian Intifada, later recounted that when it came to implementing the government's decisions with regard to the Palestinians in that period, the IDF sometimes acted like a state within a state, and that its chief of staff, Lieutenant General Shaul Mofaz, "did whatever he wanted" (Peri 2006: 106–7). Indeed, according to a recent study, Mofaz, who considered the Palestinian attacks against Israel as an existential threat, gained the upper hand over the political echelon in shaping Israel's security policy (Bar-Or and Haltiner 2009: 166–8).

As these Israeli diplomats and politicians suggest, the security sector, particularly the IDF, has for some time enjoyed an unparalleled role in shaping Israel's foreign policy, especially in the realm of national security but also on issues such as the import and export of items and economic deals with other governments.[3] At the same time, government ministers, who were supposed to participate in and in fact dominate policymaking and

[2] Others suggest that, in fact, IDF officials present only two options, which are stated in such a way that the politicians have no other way but to accept the IDF's view.

[3] A recent report by Israel's State Comptroller (2012) provides several examples of how the Ministry of Defense effectively by-passed the Ministry of Foreign Affairs (MFA) with regard to defense exports. According to the report, "the director general of the Ministry of Defense [Major General (res.) Udi Shani] made decisions that ran contrary to the security export policy or that ran contrary to the position of the Ministry of Foreign Affairs, without consulting the defense minister" (ibid., 1553).

implementation in the external realm, have often found themselves sidelined by the security agencies.[4]

This chapter asks why the security sector, especially the IDF, has exercised such an overriding influence over Israel's foreign policy, making three inter-related arguments. The first is that it is not so much the security sector itself that has been so influential in shaping Israel's foreign policy as it has been the members of Israel's security network, and, on certain occasions, one or more of its subnetworks. Second, we argue that the impact of the security network on Israel's foreign policy has been so pronounced not simply because Israel's civilian sector, especially the government and the Knesset, is weak and has failed to provide the security sector with a clear directive, which is a claim made by former security officials and some scholars (see, e.g., Ayalon 2003: 7; Peri 2006: 13, 30–1; Freilich 2006; Michael 2007). Rather, it is due to the fact that the security network has managed to effectively short-circuit these institutions. Our third argument in this context is that the predominant role of the security network in shaping Israel's foreign policy has been facilitated by a set of factors that include the real or imagined continuous existential threats to the state, the primacy accorded to national security over all other considerations, the securitization of major aspects of Israel's foreign and domestic policies and the failed attempts to desecuritize them, and the recognition of members of the security network as specialists in the area of national security.

Previously, we traced the development of Israel's security network and how its members have come to monopolize the realm of national security in Israel, including issues pertaining to war and peace, particularly since the 1967 War. We now focus on two concrete cases in which the role of the security network in shaping and executing Israel's foreign policy has been pronounced, that is, Israel's policy in and vis-à-vis the Palestinian Territories occupied in 1967; and Israel's policy toward Lebanon in the period 1975–2000.

There are several reasons to focus on these two cases. First, in recent decades these two issues have been regarded as posing existential threats and therefore these are critical for Israel, and they subsequently became major policy areas for the state and in which its civilian and security institutions have invested considerable efforts. Second, these Israeli policies were sustained for long periods of time despite the significant changes that took place in Israel itself (especially in its government), in the Middle East, and in the international arena, in particular the decline of the existential threats to Israel. Finally, these two policies were sustained even as their human, material, and moral costs became apparent to many Israelis, who found it extremely difficult to change them fundamentally.

---

[4] Rulings of Israel's Supreme Court have also been ignored by the IDF. In 2008, for example, it was reported that the IDF resorted to "targeted assassinations" or "preventive killings" of Palestinian activists even when the arrest of these individuals was possible, in an apparent violation of the Supreme Court's rulings (see: *Haaretz* November 28, 2008). It is noteworthy that Uri Blau, the journalist that published this report, was later indicted for his alleged holding of secret documents (see: *Jerusalem Post* May 30, 2012).

ISRAEL'S POLICY TOWARD THE PALESTINIAN TERRITORIES

Since the end of the 1967 War, the major political question Israel has grappled with is what to do with the Palestinian Territories that it occupied during that conflict: the West Bank, including East Jerusalem, which had formerly been under Jordanian rule, and the Gaza Strip, which had been under Egyptian military rule. During four and a half decades of Israeli occupation of the West Bank, Israelis have built about 130 settlements there in which some 350,000 Israeli settlers live at the time of writing, and to these one can add 190,000 Israelis who live in the Jewish and to a lesser extent in the Palestinian Arab neighborhoods of East Jerusalem. During the period 1967–2005, Israel also controlled the Gaza Strip, where it built about twenty Israeli settlements, but as part of the Disengagement Plan of the government of Prime Minister Ariel Sharon, Israel withdrew from that area and evacuated the 9,500 Israelis who had settled there.

As noted by several authors (see, e.g., Yiftachel 2006; Benvenisti 2007), however, the settlements that Israel has built in the Palestinian Territories since 1967 are only one part of the state's massive involvement in these areas. Indeed, during the last forty-four years, Israel has invested an estimated 2.5 billion NIS per annum in the Palestinian Territories, where among other things it constructed civilian settlements, built numerous military bases and other installations, paved hundreds of kilometers of roads, and constructed water and electricity systems. Moreover, since the outbreak of the second Palestinian Intifada (or, the al-Aqsa Intifada) in 2000, Israel began constructing a massive 700-kilometer-long Separation Barrier in the West Bank, including in East Jerusalem.[5]

Despite Israel's involvement in the Palestinian Territories, which has had a considerable impact not only on Israeli politics but also on its society, culture, economy, and of course on the relationship between the state's civilian and security sectors, the origins of Israel's policy toward these areas have only recently begun to be explored in a systematic way (Pedatzur 1996; Gazit 2003; Zertal and Eldar 2004; Gorenberg 2006; Segev 2007). Drawing on these works, especially those that employ declassified official Israeli documents from the first decade after the 1967 War, this section highlights the pivotal role of

---

[5] See the following sources: Peace Now, "Full Settlement List," at: http://peacenow.org.il/eng/sites/default/files/settlements_database_1.xls (Accessed March 11, 2011); Peace Now, "East Jerusalem," at: http://peacenow.org.il/eng/content/east-jerusalem (Accessed March 11, 2011); Peace Now, "West Bank and Jerusalem Map–2011," at http://peacenow.org.il/eng/content/west-bank-and-jerusalem-map-2011 (Accessed March 11, 2011); Hagit Ofran, "The Price of Maintaining the Territories–Data from 2011–2012 Budget," December 26, 2010, at: http://peacenow.org.il/eng/content/price-maintaining-territories-data-2011–2012-budget (Accessed March 11, 2011); B'Tselem, "Separation Barrier Statistics," at: http://www.btselem.org/english/Separation_Barrier/Statistics.asp (Accessed: March 11, 2011).
In December 2010, one US dollar was equal to 3.665 NIS.

members of Israel's security network in shaping Israel's policy toward the Palestinian Territories.

The Origins of Israel's Policy toward the Palestinian Territories

Israel's policy toward the Palestinian Territories was initially marked by considerable hesitancy on the part of Israel's senior politicians (Pedatzur 1996; Gorenberg 2006). On the one hand, the Government of National Unity, which had been established on the eve of the 1967 War, did not offer to concede the occupied Palestinian Territories in return for peace with the Arabs, as it did, at least initially, with regard to the Sinai, which was occupied from Egypt, and the Golan, which was occupied from Syria (Pedatzur 1996: 47–57; Segev 2007: 500–6). On the other hand, Israeli leaders refrained from formally annexing the Palestinian Territories; the notable exception to this was East Jerusalem, which was "unified" with the city's western part soon after the war. Later, in 1981, the Golan was also brought under Israel's jurisdiction.[6]

This hesitation, or as Prime Minister Levi Eshkol put it in a conversation with U.S. President Lyndon B. Johnson, a decision "not to decide" (Gorenberg 2006: 127), stemmed from the disagreements within the Israeli government regarding the future of the Palestinian Territories, which precluded a positive decision on its part. Some government members, especially Deputy Prime Minister and Labor Minister, Yigal Allon, and Minister of Defense, Moshe Dayan, believed that Israel should keep at least part of the Palestinian Territories, as well as parts of the other occupied Arab territories, which they claimed were crucial for Israel's security. Others, such as Minister of Justice Yaacov Shimshon Shapira, Minister of Foreign Affairs Abba Eban, and Minister of Education Zalman Aran, expressed fear that incorporating so many Arabs into Israel would lead to the destruction of the Jewish State (Pedatzur 1996: 144–5; Segev 2007, 501–3). Still other government ministers were, at least initially, indecisive on this matter. These included, first and foremost Prime Minister Eshkol, who wished to keep parts of the Palestinian Territories under Israeli control. Eshkol himself would later play an active role in settling these areas, but at the same time did not know how Israel could rule these areas without controlling their Arab Palestinian inhabitants (Gorenberg 2006: 46, 118).

But for some Israeli ministers, especially Allon and Dayan, the lack of a formal government decision regarding the Palestinian Territories after 1967 did not mean that Israel should refrain from shaping the future of the Territories. Indeed, it was these two ministers, both former senior IDF officers, together with other members of Israel's security network, especially Israel Galili, a

---

[6] Interestingly, several senior IDF officers – such as Major General Uzi Narkis, commander of the IDF's Central Command, and Rehavam Zeevi – played a pivotal role in this episode. Together with the Jewish National Fund, Narkis also played an important role in deporting the Palestinian villages in the Latroun enclave (see Pedatzur 1996: 118, 106).

minister without portfolio who until 1948 had served as the chief of staff of the Hagana, who were the driving force in transforming Israel's policy toward the Palestinians from one characterized by hesitancy to an activist policy clouded by ambiguity on both the domestic and external levels.

There were several reasons why Israeli politicians resorted to ambiguity when dealing with the Palestinian Territories in this period and also later. First, an ambiguous policy could help alleviate tensions within the government and the ruling coalition, which, as we have seen, included ministers with quite divergent views regarding the future of the Palestinian Territories. Second, such a policy could make it easier for Mapai, then Israel's leading party, to reunite with *Rafi* and *Ahdut Ha'avodah* and, later, to keep the Labor Party from falling apart (Gorenberg 2006: 50, 127–8, 199). Third, this policy could win the support of, on the one hand, influential center-right political groups that claimed that Israel should continue to rule the "Liberated Territories," and, on the other hand, center-left and leftist movements that warned of the dangers inherent in Israel's "colonialist" project. Ira Sharkansky writes that "[t]he tactics of accommodation, indirection, improvisation, avoidance, and ambiguity are ways of keeping together a polity easily split by contending demands and loyalties" (Sharkansky 1999: 9). Indeed, the available written materials suggest that in the formative period this was one of the major causes of Israel's ambiguous policy toward the Palestinian Territories.

But on the external level, too, Israel's politicians saw the benefits of an ambiguous policy toward the Palestinian Territories, and later, toward other Arab territories occupied in 1967. This is because an ambiguous policy should help to avert external pressures for a quick withdrawal from these areas, especially on the part of the United States, Israel's closest ally. But this scenario was based on the precedent of Israel's withdrawal from the Sinai in the wake of the Arab–Israeli War of 1956, which came after international pressures, and it did not repeat itself after 1967. This was due not only to Israel's intended ambiguous policy but also to the fact that during that period the United States was not ready to propose its own solutions to the conflict between Israel and the Arabs or to pressure the former to withdraw to the pre-1967 borders.

The ambiguous policy that Israel adopted toward the Palestinian Territories in the wake of the 1967 War has indeed helped keep together its divided political system and avert external pressures.[7] At the same time, it provided ample opportunities for other actors, especially members of Israel's security network but also the Israeli settlers in the Palestinian Territories, who were motivated by national religious and sometimes materialist values, to promote their personal and collective agendas. Indeed, both actors soon came to the conclusion that if they coordinated their activities they would be able to influence Israel's

[7] A telling example is Freedom House, which, despite 45 years of Israeli occupation of the Palestinian Territories, considers pre-1967 Israel to be "free" (i.e., democratic) and gauges the Palestinian Territories in a separate list of "Disputed Territories" (see Freedom House 2011)

policy toward these areas by creating "facts on the ground" there that no one, including the government, would be able to ignore (Gorenberg 2006: 71).

The pivotal role played by members of Israel's security network in shaping Israel's policy toward the Palestinian Territories after the 1967 War, especially by Dayan, Allon and Israel Galili, was largely due to the fact that this entire issue became securitized. Indeed, the government's ministers agreed from the outset that every policy with regard to the future of the Palestinian Territories, which they considered as a "security deposit," would have to respond to Israel's security needs. This would allow Israel to solve a considerable portion of its national security problems and physical distress, which stemmed from its existence in the pre-1967 Green Line (Pedatzur 1996: 28).

In securitizing the Palestinian issue, Israel's political leaders thus responded to the perceived existential threat that beleaguered the state since its independence. But it was the period after the war too that seemed to necessitate such a move: despite Israel's military victory in the conflict, Israeli politicians, including the IDF's senior officers, believed that the Arabs had not given up their desire to destroy Israel and that Israel's continued occupation of the West Bank would prevent the threat of annihilation. The anxiety that had gripped so many Israelis before the war, when they faced a perceived existential threat, now served as an argument against withdrawing from the territories (Segev 2007: 544).

Importantly, these positions were shared by many political, social, and cultural groups in Israel that were made up of leading writers, poets and artists, journalists, religious leaders, as well as young national religious activists who perceived Israel's military victory in the 1967 War as a divine action on the Jewish people's behalf. Many of these actors openly called upon the government not to withdraw from the Palestinian Territories, an action they claimed would be tantamount to being pushed back into a "ghetto" (Pedatzur 1996: 173–4; Segev 2007: 545). Thus, and also since Israel's leaders did not feel they had a serious Arab partner for peace, the Palestinian Territories and the other Arab territories occupied in 1967 were to remain under Israel's control but without changing their formal status.

It should be emphasized, however, that the securitization of the Palestinian Territories in this period, like Israel's ambiguous policy regarding these areas, also had practical motives. Israeli leaders, including first and foremost Prime Minister Eshkol, were informed by their legal advisers that confiscating Palestinian lands and building Israeli settlements in the Palestinian Territories contravened international law, particularly the Fourth Geneva Convention of 1949. Hence, Israel's actions in these areas, particularly building Israeli settlements, needed to be justified on security grounds (Pedatzur 1996: 151, 194–7, 215; Gorenberg 2006: 99–100, 114; Segev 2007: 376). Indeed, Allon later explained that in the city of Hebron, for example, the Israeli authorities "did not confiscate land, but 'seized' [it] for a military base as a sort of a 'trick', namely, as if they were building for the IDF" (Pedatzur 1996: 166). On another occasion, and alluding to the period before 1948, Allon stated, "Once we built an army camouflaged as settlements ... Now we'll build settlements camouflaged as an army" (Gorenberg 2006: 121; see also Pedatzur 1996: 194). Moreover, by securitizing the Palestinian Territories, the government also ensured that its own discussions and decisions relating to building new Israeli settlements and the many concessions that it made to the Israeli settlers would remain a state secret.

Whatever the definitive causes for the securitization of the Palestinian Territories in this formative period may be, the result was that these areas became the exclusive domain of the security network and, of course, of the settlers. Indeed, the civilian ministers, who did not consider themselves experts in national security, passed on to the security experts the decision regarding the principles of future agreements with the Arabs, including the Palestinians. All matters related to the occupied Arab territories soon began to be discussed in "forums that ... emphasize secrecy, which are appropriate for a sensitive security issue" (Pedatzur 1996: 29). Consequently, the government was effectively short-circuited from day-to-day Israeli policymaking on the Palestinian Territories, which was taken over by more informal policymaking bodies. In these informal bodies, the members of the security network – in this period these were mainly Allon, Dayan, and Galili, but later others such as Peres and Rabin – played the most important role.

In addition, members of Israel's security network took it upon themselves to govern the daily life of the million and a half inhabitants of the Palestinian Territories. Minister of Defense Dayan, for example, "ruled the occupied land directly, personally, with minimal oversight from cabinet or parliament" (Gorenberg 2006: 130). Officially, this was done through a new body called the Military Administration, which was "tossed together in a hurry after the unplanned conquests" in 1967 and was headed by a high-ranking IDF officer that held the title of the Coordinator of the Government's Activities in the Territories. This practice would later be repeated in Lebanon. Indeed, Dayan quickly "transformed himself into the sultan of the occupied territories," short-circuiting not only the government but even the members of the IDF's general staff (Gorenberg 2006: 131, 222; see also Segev 2007: 473).

But other IDF officers, too, regarded the regions that they commanded after 1967 as their personal "kingdoms." Thus, for example, they invited celebrities, including media persons and actors, to these areas, and were later rewarded with positive media coverage. Some of these officers with militant views, such as Major General Rehavam Zeevi, who was in charge of the IDF's Central Command that controlled the Jordan Rift area (the main road in this area, Route No. 90, is named after him), expressed enthusiastic support for the expansion of Israeli settlements in the areas under their control (Eilam 2009: 135, 143–4). Others, such as Ariel Sharon, then in charge of the Southern Command, were involved in removing the Bedouins from the Rafiah Plain, possibly under Dayan's instructions, but without notifying the Coordinator of the Government's Activities in the Territories and even without notifying the IDF's chief of staff, Lieutenant General David Elazar (Gorenberg 2006: 222–3). Other security officials, such as Lieutenant General (res.) Tsvi Tsur, assistant to Minister of Defense Dayan, channeled generous sums of money from the defense budget for Jewish settlement purposes (Eilam 2009: 143–4). It is noteworthy that some of these security officials, especially Zeevi and Sharon, continued to support the settlement project after they left the IDF, carrying with them friendships with and commitments to the settlers.

It should be noted, however, that although Allon, Dayan, and other members of Israel's security network played a decisive role in shaping the state's policy toward the Palestinian Territories after 1967, these actors themselves disagreed on the best way to promote Israel's interests there. Indeed, Dayan and Allon, who at the time belonged to different and indeed rival parties, held quite divergent views on this issue. Through their partners in their security subnetworks, each tried to promote his own plan for settling the parts of the Palestinian Territories deemed crucial for Israel's security. Allon, for example, claimed that the Jordan River should be Israel's security border, a position he persuaded the government to adopt in 1968, and called for settling the Jordan Rift. Dayan attached greater importance to the mountainous areas of the West Bank and promoted the building of settlements there. In addition, Dayan worked to deepen the economic integration between the Palestinian Territories and Israel in order to make separation between them more difficult (Pedatzur 1996: 102–4, 159; Gorenberg 2006: 173–5). To this policy, which received domestic support not only on ideological grounds but also because of the new economic opportunities it offered, was soon added an Open Bridges Policy, which allowed goods, especially agricultural products and people, to move from the Palestinian Territories to Jordan and other Arab states. In this respect, the "direct and straightforward contact between the territories and the Arab world ... nurtured the hope that the occupation would facilitate a 'reality of peace,' and strengthened the illusion that that there was no need to rush to find a political settlement" (Segev 2007: 469; see also Gorenberg 2006: 131).

In a penetrating essay on the 1948 Generation in Israel, Dan Horowitz, a leading Israeli political sociologist, asserts that Dayan was a man "ridden with contradictions [who] finds it difficult to make unequivocal decisions from which there is no way of return, and yet is attracted as if by magic to situations in which such decisions are unavoidable." Accordingly, Dayan adopted an ambiguous policy regarding the Palestinian Territories after 1967: "On the one hand, a policy of the institutionalization of the temporary that was anchored in the premise that it is possible that the situation of continuous temporariness in the Territories will continue for many years, and as opposed to this undermining the status quo with his own hands through the policy of settlement in the mountainous areas" (Horowitz 1993: 122; cf. Pedatzur 1996: 81; Segev 2007: 470–3, 548).

The disagreements among them notwithstanding, Allon, Dayan, and Galili, with the active cooperation of other actors (such as senior IDF officers, officials in the Settlement Department of the Jewish Agency, some leaders of Israel's agricultural sector, and, of course, the settlers), became so effective in promoting their own policy in and vis-à-vis the Palestinian Territories that Prime Minister Eshkol came to feel "that there is the one government and there is the security government" (Pedatzur 1996: 67).[8] Indeed, in this formative period of Israel's policy toward the Palestinian Territories, Israeli settlements were built according to both Allon's plan in the Jordan Rift and according to Dayan's plan in the mountainous areas, thus creating facts on the ground that would have a considerable impact in later periods.

In sum, the lack of a clear and decisive civilian Israeli policy toward the Palestinian Territories in the wake of the 1967 War soon gave way to an activist policy that was clouded by ambiguity in order to preserve domestic consensus and fend off international criticism. This policy, together with the securitization of the Palestinian Territories, which was seen as a response to the pre-1967 existential threat to Israel, but also had practical reasons, provided ample opportunities for members of Israel's security network and the main two subnetworks within it at the time, one led by Dayan and the other led by Allon, to operate, especially when they were considered as experts on national security. Indeed, since 1967 these actors worked to promote their own personal and collective interests with regard to the Palestinian Territories, which they claimed would enhance Israel's security. These plans, which were sometimes contradictory, were carried out with the help of other members of the security network (whether in the IDF, in other security services[9] or in various civilian spheres) and with the active cooperation of the Israeli settlers. Not always conforming to the government's decisions, these plans were sometimes presented as spontaneous actions by the settlers, despite the fact that these plans were very often supported by government ministers, mainly by the IDF. And sometimes the government's approval for these actions was sought only after the fact (Pedatzur 1996: 75–6).

Allon, who, among other things, encouraged and endorsed the Israeli settlers in Hebron, including the provision of weapons to protect their safety, later explained his role in the following way, thus offering a glimpse into the workings of Israel's security network in this period: "It is true that I took upon myself an authority I did not formally have, but as a minister, and as a general in reserve duty, I thought I could not leave the area [Hebron] without promising something [to the settlers]" (quoted in Segev 2007: 579).

---

[8] Allon had close ties with members of the Kibbutzim in this region, and these ties played a role in Israel's settlement activities in the Golan.

[9] The Shabak, especially, witnessed a significant growth in its size and scope of activities in this period (see Gorenberg 2006: 129–30).

Developments in Later Periods

On the whole, Israel's policy toward the Palestinian Territories in later periods remained basically unchanged: successive Israeli governments did not annex these areas, either because they were worried that Israel would lose its Jewish majority or because they were fearful of a domestic and external backlash. At the same time, however, Israel maintained its control over most of these areas, claiming that they were crucial for its security, and continued to build settlements and other installations there.

This policy, which acting and former security officials in Israel helped perpetuate, remained an important source of power for Israel's security network. Indeed, following in the footsteps of Dayan and Allon, other prominent members of the security network and of subnetworks within it who served as Israel's prime ministers and defense ministers,[10] as well as other members of the security network who served in other ministries,[11] continued to stress the importance of the Palestinian Territories for Israel's security. At the same time, these actors presented themselves to Israel's civilian leaders and to the general public, especially those who were fearful for Israel's existence, as the only ones capable of dealing with this question, which they often cast in existential terms.

In addition, members of Israel's security network continued to play a dominant role in policymaking and implementation with regard to the Palestinian Territories, particularly in the various informal bodies that dealt with this issue. Many of these individuals were instrumental in building Israeli settlements, military bases and installations, and roads in the Palestinian Territories, making separation between Israel and these areas more and more difficult. Moreover, they cooperated with Israeli settlers in the Palestinian Territories both during and in the wake of Israel's settlement activities (Peri 2006: 168; cf. Pedatzur 1996: 232). Indeed, it was recently observed that "behind every settlement action there is a planning and thinking mind that has access to the state's database and maps, and help from sympathetic officers serving in key positions in the IDF and the Civil Administration" and that "the story is not in the settlers' uncontrolled behavior, though there is evidence of this on some of the hilltops, but rather in conscious choices by the state to enforce very little of the law" (*Haaretz* July 9, 2009).

Since 1987, Israel's ongoing occupation of the Palestinian Territories has faced three major challenges: first, the Palestinian Intifada in 1987, a popular uprising of the Palestinians in the West Bank and the Gaza Strip; second, the Oslo process between Israel and the Palestine Liberation Organization (PLO) in the 1990s, which included the transfer of parts of these areas to Palestinian

---

[10] Examples include Yitzhak Rabin, Shimon Peres, Ariel Sharon, Ehud Barak, Moshe Arens, Binyamin Ben-Eliezer, and Shaul Mofaz.

[11] Examples include Raphael Eitan, Rehavam Zeevi, Ephraim Sneh, Matan Vilnai, and Moshe Yaalon.

control but without establishing an independent Palestinian state; and third, the second Palestinian Intifada, which resulted, among other things, in the Disengagement Plan, an Israeli withdrawal from the Gaza Strip and a small area in the West Bank in 2005.

The First Palestinian Intifada

In 1987, the then Israel's defense minister, Yitzhak Rabin, who believed that the Intifada would be a passing phase, instructed the IDF to use force to suppress it (Rabin 1996: 243). This was despite the advice of civil society actors, including several Middle East specialists in Israeli universities, that this was an authentic Palestinian uprising and that Israeli military action against the Palestinians in the Territories would only alienate them. This attempt by Rabin and the IDF to securitize the Intifada can be read as an attempt to place it and the entire question of the Palestinian Territories within the exclusive purview of the specialists on national security (that is, members of Israel's security network). However, it was largely unsuccessful, and a number of acting and former security officials, including Rabin himself, later came to realize that the Intifada "could not be quashed militarily" (Horovitz 1996: 117–18).

Oslo Process

In 1993, civil society actors in Israel made the first attempt to desecuritize Israeli–Palestinian Relations[12] by engaging in secret talks with Palestinians who were connected to the PLO (Hirschfeld 2000). As these talks progressed, additional civilian actors, including Deputy Minister of Foreign Affairs Yossi Beilin, who would also play a role in Israel's withdrawal from Lebanon in 2000, were brought in, and, eventually, Minister of Foreign Affairs Shimon Peres. But the attempt to "desecuritize" Israel's policy toward the Palestinians was short lived. Yitzhak Rabin, who since 1992 served as both prime minister and as defense minister, believed that the IDF's professional expertise was crucial for gaining political and public support for the Oslo Agreement of 1993. Thus, he brought the IDF and the Shabak into the negotiations with the Palestinians, and, consequently, helped resecuritize Israeli Palestinian Relations (Peri 2006: 65; Michael 2007: 530). This can be inferred not only from the negotiations themselves, which were dominated by security officials mainly from the IDF, but also from the lengthy parts devoted to security issues in subsequent Palestinian–Israeli agreements and the prominent role of the IDF in their implementation (Sela 2009: 115). Indeed, some writers identify the overriding influence of an "issue net" composed of acting and former security officials in Israel in this period, which, they posit, was characterized by the lack of effective, as opposed to formal, civilian control of the military. Major General (res.) Matan Vilnai, who served as head of the IDF's Southern Command and later joined the Knesset and the government, even argued that "There is no

---

[12] On desecuritization, see, especially, Wæver (2009).

political level. The army decides the conception. There is no political level. Believe me, the army decides everything" (quoted in Michael 2007: 534 and see also 524). In 1994, for example, when an Israeli settler massacred scores of Palestinians in Hebron, it was the IDF that prevented the removal of the Jewish settlers from the city (Peri 2006: 66).

The Second Palestinian Intifada

As mentioned earlier, the IDF, under Chief of Staff Mofaz, played a critical role in the escalation between Israelis and Palestinians that led to the second Palestinian Intifada, when it used massive military force to suppress it, often disregarding the government's pleas for moderation. Mofaz and his successor, Lieutenant General Moshe Yaalon, presented the Palestinian challenge to Israel in existential terms, a view that was persuasive to many Israelis (Freilich 2006: 636). Yaalon even argued that this confrontation was, in fact, the continuation of Israel's War of Independence. It is noteworthy that this and similar statements by other Israeli leaders elicited fear among the Palestinians, who see the 1948 War as the *Nakba* – their national Catastrophe (Ayalon 2003: 11–12). At the same time, cooperation between the IDF and the Israeli settlers intensified, and "both camps saw in one another a partner in the struggle" (*Haaretz* July 9, 2009). This was manifested in the IDF's encouragement to build even more new settlements in the Palestinian Territories – referred to as "outposts" – and enlarge existing ones. Indeed, some observers speak of an IDF-settlers "symbiosis" during this period (*Haaretz* July 9, 2009). Furthermore, the IDF sought to incorporate the settlers into its security apparatus in the Palestinian Territories through various organizational devices, such as the armed "Territorial Defense" units (composed of settlers) and, more recently, the *Kfir* Brigade and the infantry and armored units deployed in the Territories, which also include a considerable number of settlers. The IDF also decided to decrease the use of reservists in the Palestinian Territories and to give a preference for conscripts (Peri 2006: 195; Levy 2009). As we will see, a similar pattern can be seen in Israel's involvement in Lebanon.

Prime Minister Ehud Barak and other members of the security network blamed the Palestinian side, and especially PLO leader Yasser Arafat, for the failure of the Camp David summit in 2000 and the outbreak of the Second Palestinian Intifada (Bar-Siman-Tov 2003; Peri 2006: 100). Indeed, although other former security officials later presented different opinions in this matter,[13] this was, above all, a debate within the security network that was based on the premise that Israeli–Palestinian Relations were, essentially, a security issue and that assessing the Palestinians' intensions, but without referring to Israel's actions in the Palestinian Territories since 1993, was the prerogative of the specialists.[14]

[13] See, e.g., an interview by Colonel (res.) Ephraim Lavie in *Haaretz* June 13, 2004. See also an article by Brigadier General (res.) Yossi Ben-Ari in *Haaretz* April 4, 2006.
[14] A notable exception is Brigadier General (res.) Tzvi Fogel. See his interview in *Haaretz* December 27, 2007.

ISRAEL'S POLICY TOWARD LEBANON

Kibbutz Hanita was founded in 1938 on the northern edge of British-ruled Palestine. The stones that marked the border between Palestine and Lebanon, then under French rule, "originally cut across the hilltop chosen for the kibbutz." This bothered Yigal Allon, then a senior officer in the Palmach, "because it wasn't ... symmetrical or aesthetic, so I rounded up my guys and we moved the border stones a few hundred meters northward." Allon emerges from this story as "carefree, in command, unconcerned with rules, happy to redraw an international border to fit his imagination" (Gorenberg 2006: 30). As we will see, this description fits as well other members of Israel's security network who helped shape Israel's policy toward Lebanon in the period 1975–2000.

Israel's involvement in Lebanon from the latter's "failure" in 1975, when its decade-and-a-half-long civil war began and the state's institutions became paralyzed, until Israel's withdrawal from its self-declared "Security Zone" in South Lebanon in 2000, is seen by many authors as an attempt to address Israel's broader "security dilemma" in the Middle East (Yaniv 1987; Evron 1987; Sobleman 2004; Zisser 2009). However, what is often overlooked is the marked continuity in Israel's policy toward Lebanon despite significant developments in both states, in the Middle East and beyond, and notwithstanding the considerable human, material, and moral costs of Israel's policy. In Lebanon, these developments included the removal of most Palestinian fighters from Beirut in 1982, following Israel's invasion of Lebanon; the subsequent rise in the power of the Shi'i community and its two major and rival militias, Amal and Hizbullah; and the end of the civil war in 1990, which opened the way for Lebanon's reconstruction. More broadly speaking, one can mention the weakening of Syria in the early 1990s, after the end of the Cold War and the disintegration of the Soviet Union, and the launching of the Middle East peace process following the Madrid Conference in 1991.

As far as Israel is concerned, during the period from June 1985 to September 1997, its major Lebanese client, the South Lebanon Army (SLA), sustained 358 fatalities and 1,210 injuries, and in the same period, the IDF lost 212 soldiers with 677 others injured, as well as 6 killed and 170 injured civilians. This in addition to 73 Israeli soldiers killed in a helicopter crash on their way to Lebanon in February 1997. In comparison, during the 12 years that preceded the Lebanon War, the IDF lost 54 soldiers at the Lebanese front with 297 injuries compared to 40 killed and 380 injured civilians (Sela 2007: 64–5).

But there were other costs: Israel not only failed to defeat, let alone obliterate, Hizbullah, Israel's major rival in Lebanon since 1985, but Israel's actions provided the Shi'i party-militia with an ample opportunity to improve its fighting capacities and, no less important, to increase its political and socioeconomic power in Lebanon. Brigadier General Moshe Tamir, who served in Israel's self-declared Security Zone in South Lebanon for several years, observes that "Hizbullah transformed from a rejected terrorist organization, which acts against the wish of the central government in Lebanon, into a legitimate resistance movement of the Lebanese people to the Israeli occupation" (Tamir 2005: 65). In addition, Israel's involvement in Lebanon tarnished Israel's image since it occupied Lebanese territory, committed violations of human rights, and allowed its proxy, the SLA, to do the same. In addition, Israel turned a blind eye to illegal activities in the Security Zone, including smuggling and drug trafficking that was sometimes directed at Israel itself.

As we will demonstrate in the text that follows, this marked continuity in Israel's policy toward Lebanon can be attributed, to a large extent, to the role of members of Israel's security network involved in shaping Israel's policy toward Lebanon and in implementing it through the years. After briefly surveying Israel's policy toward Lebanon before the outbreak of the Lebanese civil war in 1975, we will turn to discuss the role of members of Israel's security network in shaping this policy until 2000, the result of which was the expansion of Israel's involvement in Lebanon first on the Israeli–Lebanese border area and then in other regions of the country and, ultimately, in Israel's self-declared Security Zone in South Lebanon.

The Origins of Israel's Policy in Lebanon

During the period from the signing of the Armistice Agreement between Israel and Lebanon in 1949, following the First Israeli–Arab War, until the late 1960s and early 1970s, when Israeli–Lebanese relations began to deteriorate, Lebanon was not a major concern for Israeli policymakers, both civilian and military. Israel's relations with Lebanon were managed mainly by the Israeli–Lebanese Mixed Armistice Commission (ILMAC), which included representatives of the Israeli and Lebanese militaries and a UN observer. This is not to say that in this period some Israeli politicians did not consider a radical change in the two states' relationship: thus, for example, in 1955, Israeli Prime Minister Moshe Sharett argued that Lebanon would be the first candidate to be the second Arab state to sign a peace treaty with Israel. At about the same time, former Prime Minister and Minister of Defense David Ben-Gurion and the IDF's chief of staff, Moshe Dayan, toyed with the idea of conquering South Lebanon up to the Litani River and installing a pro-Israel Lebanese officer as the area's ruler (Sharett 1978, 2:377, 4:996). However, both of these visions, particularly the second one, which is sometimes claimed to be at the root of Israel's massive involvement in Lebanon in later periods, did not materialize at the time and, moreover, were proved to be erroneous in later decades (Randal 1983: 189–95; Shlaim 1988; Sheffer, 1996a).

In the late 1960s and early 1970s, the situation in the Israeli–Lebanese border zone began to deteriorate after Palestinian armed factions, especially Fatah, began to entrench themselves on the Lebanese side of the border, as they did also in Jordan, and carried out attacks against Israel from Lebanon's territory. Following the 1967 War, these attacks intensified, as did Israel's forceful reprisals. Thus, in late 1968, after Palestinian activists hijacked and attacked Israeli civilian airplanes, the IDF launched a retaliatory raid against the Beirut international airport. Dayan, then in his capacity as minister of defense, claimed that since the Palestinian factions were engaged in military training in Lebanon and launched their operations from its territory, Lebanon, too, would be held responsible for their actions (Dayan 1976: 544). However, Palestinian attacks on Israel's territory continued, and these and Israel's counterattacks led to the gradual deterioration of Lebanon's control over its side of the border. This process was further enhanced after the signing of the Cairo Agreement of 1969 between Lebanon and the PLO, which accorded legitimacy to the Palestinian factions' armed presence in Lebanon, and following the events of Black September in Jordan in 1970–1971, which resulted in a fresh influx of Palestinian armed activists into Lebanon.[15]

In 1975, the Lebanese civil war began and the state's institutions quickly became paralyzed. These included, first and foremost, the Lebanese Army, which experienced a rebellion led by a junior Sunni Muslim officer who took over parts of South Lebanon (Barak 2009). This development, together with the continued presence of armed opposition members and Palestinian fighters in the Israeli–Lebanese border area, led Lebanese officers and noncommissioned officers (NCOs) who served there, as well as local militiamen, mainly Maronite Christians, to initiate ties with Israeli officers who served on the Israeli side of the border (Hamizrachi 1988; Barakat 2011).

The Israeli officers who set up the relations with these Lebanese military personnel and militiamen, in particular Lieutenant Colonel Yoram Hamizrachi, who became known as the "King of the North," were low-ranking. However, they enjoyed direct access to Major General Raphael Eitan, who was in charge of the IDF's Northern Command and later became the IDF's chief of staff, and who was sympathetic to their cause. This modus operandi, which is reminiscent of the informal support that local IDF commanders extended to the Israeli settlers in the Palestinian Territories, discussed earlier, was manifested, among other things, in a special communications code between Hamizrachi and Eitan (Hamizrachi n.d.; see also Eitan 1985: 148–62).

Other members of Israel's security network, including Minister of Defense Shimon Peres, soon embraced the idea of providing military and humanitarian support to the Christian militias on the Lebanese side of the border. This policy, which Israel called the "Good Fence" (Peres 1978: 85–8), signaled that for Israeli policymakers permeable borders with Israel's northern neighbor were good borders. In conceptual terms, the Israeli–Lebanese border area thus became a "frontier" (Ron 2003) that afforded Israel's security sector and members of Israel's security network freedom of action. At the

---

[15] Interestingly, in this period Israel did not construct a sophisticated fence in the Lebanese–Israeli border despite the recommendations made by the head of the IDF's Armament Department (see Eilam 2009: 150–1).

same time, and reminiscent of Dayan's aforementioned Open Bridges Policy toward the Palestinian Territories, Israel's policy toward Lebanon encouraged greater economic integration between the Lebanese–Israeli border area and northern Israel.

By 1976, members of Israel's security network had established the "South Lebanon Area" (known by its Hebrew acronym, *ADAL*) in the territory adjacent to the Israeli–Lebanese border. It consisted of several enclaves that, with Israeli assistance, were brought under the control of Israel's local clients, the Christian militias commanded by a junior Lebanese officer, Major Saad Haddad (Hamizrachi 1988). The Litani Operation in 1978, which Israel launched as a response to a Palestinian attack against Israel, consolidated the Haddad's effective control over the South Lebanon Area. Hostile forces that attempted to deploy their troops there, including both the Syrian and the Lebanese armies, were prevented from doing so.

It should be emphasized, however, that there were differences of opinion among members of the security network concerning Israel's policy toward Lebanon. Prime Minister Rabin, for example, held the view that Israel should allow Syria to pacify Lebanon, but that Syrian forces must not approach the Israeli–Lebanese border area. He also believed that Israel should "help the Christians help themselves" in Lebanon but without getting embroiled there. In 1976, Rabin's policy resulted in the "red lines" agreement between Israel and Syria, attained through Jordanian and U.S. mediation, which facilitated Syria's military intervention in Lebanon (Evron 1987: 45–56).[16] But by 1977, when Rabin left office, the relationship between Israel and the Christians (especially Maronites in South Lebanon, as well as with some of the Maronite-led militias in other parts of Lebanon (most notably the Phalanges Party and its militia, the Lebanese Forces), was already well developed, not least because of the efforts of members of Israel's security network (Schiff and Yaari 1984).

Developments in Later Periods

In the late 1970s and early 1980s, especially after the appointment of Ariel Sharon as defense minister in 1981, members of the security network began to advocate a full-fledged Israeli invasion of Lebanon with the goal of removing the Palestinian armed factions and, possibly, also the Syrian Army, which they saw as a threat to Israel's security. To achieve this end, these members obtained the support of Israel's civilian leaders, in particular Prime Minister Menachem Begin. Begin not only perceived the Palestinian threat to Israel from Lebanon in existential terms, but was also very attentive to the claims made by some Maronite Christian leaders in Lebanon that they, too, were facing an existential threat.

In June 1982, the IDF invaded Lebanon with the declared goal of removing the Palestinian military threat to Israel. However, it soon turned out that

---

[16] Another example is Yoram Hamizrachi, who resigned from the IDF and left Israel for Canada.

Israel's military operation had three broader aims: to remove the Syrian Army from Lebanon, to assist Israel's major local ally, Bashir Gemayel, leader of Lebanese Forces militia, in becoming Lebanon's next president and signing a peace agreement with Israel, and to crush the PLO, and the Palestinian national movement in general, politically and militarily, thus facilitating Israel's continued occupation of the Palestinian Territories. The fact of the matter is that the Lebanon War represented a change only in the scope of Israel's policy toward Lebanon but not in its essential components, which were laid down by members of Israel's security network.

First of all, Israeli–Lebanese relations had already been securitized, that is, perceived primarily through the lens of security, for some time, particularly since the mid-1970s. Toward 1982 this process was expanded to include other parts of Lebanon that were also seen as critical for Israel's security. Second, the Palestinian threat to Israel from Lebanon, first from South Lebanon and then from Beirut, was presented in existential terms long before the outbreak of the war. Third, bypassing the Israeli government with regard to Israel's policy in Lebanon did not begin in 1982 but occurred in earlier periods as well. Finally, many members of the security network themselves did not regard the Lebanon War as an aberration in Israel's policy in Lebanon and cooperated with its leading figures. The Labor Party, under the leadership of Peres, supported the war, and Rabin even served as an unofficial advisor to Sharon, who had been Rabin's advisor in the 1970s. Indeed, even members of the security network who criticized Sharon's conduct in the war later denied their claims.[17] A telling example is Major General (res.) Avigdor Ben-Gal, who in 1982 was a corps commander in the IDF and later became a private businessman and a director in the Israel Aerospace Industries. In 1987, four years after he left the IDF, Ben-Gal stated that one of the problems of the Lebanon War was "the covert and non-authorized plan of the defense minister [Sharon] and the chief of staff [Eitan] who led the government step-by-step to its approval." But twelve years later, in 1999, Ben-Gal renounced his earlier claims, allegedly because Sharon, who in 1999 served as Israel's minister of infrastructure and foreign affairs, offered that Ben-Gal should join him in an official visit to Russia, which would be beneficial to Ben-Gal's business (Attorney General 2001; see also *Globes* May 2, 1999).[18]

In 1985, Israel's National Unity Government, in which Peres, Rabin, and a number of other former security officials were members, decided to withdraw the IDF from Lebanon.[19] At the same time it was decided that Israel would

---

[17] This is not to say that there were no dissenting views of the war in the IDF in this period.

[18] Some of the claims against Sharon were recently confirmed by Brigadier General (res.) Ezriel Nevo, who in 1982 was the military secretary of Prime Minister Begin, and by Brigadier General (res.) Mordechai Tzipori, who in 1982 served as minister of communication. See their interviews, respectively, in *Maariv* May 8, 2011 and in *Maariv* June 8, 2011. See also Chapter 3.

[19] According to Gorenberg (2006: 369), the number of Israeli settlers in the West Bank, not including East Jerusalem, rose by 80% in the period 1984–1988.

establish a "Security Zone" in the Israeli–Lebanese border area, to be maintained by the local militia with the IDF's support. This ambiguous decision, stemmed, among other things, from the commitments that some members of the security network had made to the Lebanese militias in earlier periods.[20] It enabled members of Israel's security network and their Lebanese clients, now reorganized and renamed the South Lebanon Army (SLA), to control the Lebanese–Israeli border area for another decade and a half, until Israel's final withdrawal from Lebanon.[21]

During the period 1985–2000, Israel's self-declared Security Zone in South Lebanon was managed almost exclusively by two bodies: the Office of the Coordinator of Israel's Operations in Lebanon[22] and the IDF's Liaison Unit to Lebanon, which by 2000 included 1,500 soldiers commanded by an IDF officer at the rank of brigadier-general (*Ynet* June 11, 2000).[23] Because in this period the IDF's reserves did not serve in South Lebanon, and since Israeli media reporters who entered the area mostly engaged in embedded journalism, it is easy to comprehend why the Israeli public knew very little about the Security Zone up to the late 1990s (Tamir 2005: 10). In any case, most Israeli journalists who covered the area identified with the IDF's mission there and many had close ties to acting and former security officials. Finally, some former security officials, including at least one former chief of the Liaison Unit to Lebanon, served as media commentators on military affairs, and in this capacity continued to present the position of the army and, ultimately, of the security network, in a positive light.[24]

But other factors also played a role during this time. In the period 1986–2000, there were about 2,500 Lebanese militiamen on Israel's payroll (Erlich

---

[20] Interview with Brigadier General (res.) Shlomo Iliya, who served as the intelligence officer of the IDF's Northern Command since 1977 and later commanded the Liaison Unit to Lebanon, at: http://www.yadlashiryon.com/show_item.asp?levelId=64566&itemId=2073&itemType=0 (Accessed February 5, 2011) [Hebrew].

[21] A recent study that provides more details on the role of members of the security network in South Lebanon and their close relationship with the SLA, is Gazit (2011).

[22] The head of the office was Uri Lubrani, who, among other things, was Israel's ambassador to Ethiopia and Iran. His deputy was Colonel (res.) Reuben Erlich-Neeman (see Yochi Erlich, "Uri Lubrani: Man of Secrets, Advice, and Action," *Mabat Malam* 54 (2009): 16–19 [Hebrew]).

[23] The unit, which was under the command of the IDF's Northern Command, was headed by an officer at the rank of Brigadier General. Its commanders were Ephraim Sneh, Meir Dagan, Shlomo Iliya, Daniel Rothschild, David Agmon, Zeev Zacharin, Micha Tamir, Gabi Ashkenazi, Giora Inbar, Elie Amitai, Erez Gershtein, Elie Amitai (after Gershtein was killed by Hizbullah), and Benny Gantz, the IDF's current chief of staff.

[24] See, e.g., articles by Brigadier General (res.) David Agmon, former head of the Liaison Unit in Lebanon, and Brigadier General (res.) Amos Gilboa, former head of Israel's negotiation team with Lebanon in 1984–1985: *Maariv* October 20, 1995; October 26, 1995; March 20, 1996; April 11, 1996; February 18, 1997; January 4, 1998. This practice continued after Israel's withdrawal from Lebanon in 2000. See, for example, a sympathetic review of the Hebrew version of the memoirs of ex-SLA chief Antoine Lahad by Eliezer Tsafrir, a former Mossad and Shabak official who had been involved in establishing Israel's ties with Lahad: *Maariv* August 13, 2004.

1997: 15) and each earned $400–500 per month, reaching a total of about $17 million for the entire period. SLA officials enjoyed an additional income from various "taxes" imposed on commodities entering the Security Zone (*Maariv* October 17, 1997; *Haaretz* January 29, 1999, April 20, 1999; see also Tamir 2005: 107). Several thousand Lebanese workers were employed in construction, agriculture, industry, and the hotel sector in northern Israel. Although these laborers earned more than five times what their counterparts earned in other parts of Lebanon, they were dependent on the SLA: They could enter Israel only if sponsored by the SLA's fighters (in most cases, these were their relatives), and had to pay their sponsor about $50 per month, as well as an additional 10%, which went to the SLA command (*Haaretz* February 21, 1997, April 11, 1997). Israeli employers, who were encouraged to hire Lebanese workers, also benefited from this arrangement since these workers did manual labor jobs and were not represented by Israel's labor union, the *Histadrut*.

For some of Israel's northern settlements, especially those near the border checkpoints, this situation was particularly advantageous. Metula, for example, became a popular tourist resort for Israelis and Lebanese, as well as an unofficial hub for all those who mattered regarding the Security Zone, including politicians, reporters, and IDF and SLA officers. Israeli firms, in their turn, sold soft drinks, alcoholic beverages, clothing, medicine, and fruit and vegetables to Lebanon, reaching an annual volume of $1–2 million via the border crossing near Metula only. Israeli construction firms, too, profited from building massive fortifications in and around the Security Zone, as well as from the continuous efforts of the Liaison Unit to Lebanon and its Civilian Assistance Unit (whose annual budget was $8 million) to improve the infrastructure there as a counterweight to the enticements and pressures of the government in Beirut and Hizbullah (*Haaretz* January 30, 1995, October 27, 1995, April 11, 1997, April 10, 1998, May 25, 2001).

Finally, one can mention the Lebanese networks of smugglers and drug traffickers, who capitalized on the virtually open border between the two states, and who, sometimes, were assisted by Israeli officials. According to a former commander of the of IDF's Liaison Unit to Lebanon, "In Lebanon ... there were many systems of connections, including drug smuggling networks, and some of them apparently paid ... for their work with drug networks in Israel by supplying information to Israel, and by that their transfer of the drugs to Israel was, perhaps, made more easy" (*TV Channel 2 News* November 19, 2009).

In the latter half of the 1990s, and especially after two Israeli helicopters collided in February 1997, leaving 73 Israeli soldiers dead, the public debate in Israel over its "presence" in Lebanon intensified, ultimately prompting its prominent politicians to outbid one another over who would get Israel out of there first. One way to consider Israel's withdrawal from Lebanon in 2000 is to regard it as a triumph of the country's civil society, which managed to overcome the resistance of the security sector to any change in Israel's Lebanese policy. Another explanation, which seems much more convincing in light of the above, is to view it as an internal dispute within the security network that was triggered by civilian actors but that did not lead to a desecuritization of Israel's Lebanese policy. Indeed, Prime Minister and Defense Minister Barak, who initiated and carried out the withdrawal, was himself a member of the security network. As a senior IDF officer in particular in his capacity of chief of the Intelligence Branch (1983–1986) and Chief of Staff (1991–1995), he had been closely involved in the formulation of Israel's policy toward Lebanon. This enabled Barak to disregard the apocalyptic warnings of the IDF's general staff, as well as the opposition of other members of the security network (e.g., the Coordinator of Israel's Operations in Lebanon, Uri Lubrani, and some media correspondents), and to carry out his plan. Though civil society groups in Israel, especially the "Four Mothers" movement, were active in campaigning for an Israeli withdrawal from Lebanon, they were ultimately successful not because they offered a *civil* alternative to Israel's current policy, but because they managed to prove, by embracing the hegemonic discourse of national security in Israel and by recruiting specialists, who were mostly former security officials, that the *security* logic of this policy was flawed. Further support for this conclusion can be deduced from the fact that Israel's relationship with Lebanon has not been desecuritized after 2000.

At any rate, even the creation of a rift within Israel's security network was no easy task. Several ministers in Barak's government, such as Brigadier Generals (res.) Binyamin Ben-Eliezer and Ephraim Sneh, had laid the groundwork for the "South Lebanon Area" during their military service and they continued to feel that they were personally committed to the SLA despite the fact that they now served as government ministers (Sela 2007). Indeed, the IDF had to sustain several major blows in Lebanon, as well as two unsuccessful large-scale military operations against Hizbullah in 1993 ("Accountability") and in 1996 ("Grapes of Wrath") and the aforementioned helicopter crash to tilt the scale.

In the wake of Israel's withdrawal from Lebanon in 2000, members of the security network continued to monopolize Israel's policy toward Lebanon, and most of them supported the "containment policy," which left the unsettled matters between the two states, and especially the disputed Shebaa Farms area, unresolved (Kaufman 2002; Barak 2010). This gave Hizbullah the justification it needed to continue its "resistance" against Israel, this time with the goal of deterring Israel from attacking Lebanon and not only liberating Lebanon's occupied territory.

Later, in July 2006, members of Israel's security network, especially the IDF's chief of staff, Lieutenant General Dan Halutz, suggested to the then prime minister, Ehud Olmert, and to the defense minister, Amir Peretz – both civilian politicians, a rare case in Israel since 1967 – that a massive military operation was needed in order to "rehabilitate" Israel's deterrence vis-à-vis Hizbullah and possibly vis-à-vis Hamas in the Gaza Strip. But in this they did not consider the difference between states, which can be deterred by the use of military force, and nonstate actors, which require a more complex approach. The result was yet another Israeli military debacle in Lebanon which led, among other things, to the removal of Peretz from the Ministry of Defense and the appointment of his main rival, Barak, in his place.

CONCLUSIONS

Several conclusions can be drawn from the foregoing discussion of the role of Israel's security network in shaping Israel's foreign and defense policies both generally and in the two cases discussed in more depth.

First of all, Israel's foreign and defense policies evince a considerable measure of continuity. Basic policies in major areas persist for years and even decades, and are carried on from one government to another, despite significant political changes in Israel itself, in its regional environment, and in the international arena. Israel's policy towards the Palestinian Territories since 1967 and its policy toward Lebanon in the period 1975–2000 demonstrate this well.

Second, some external policies in Israel persist despite their material and moral costs: in the Palestinian Territories, particularly in the West Bank, Israel has become so entrenched since 1967 that a de facto "one-state" has become a reality. According to Moshe Halbertal, if this happens "the only question will be what will be the nature of this one state – it will either be apartheid or Lebanon … We will be confronted by two horrors" (*New York Times* December 11, 2010). In Lebanon, the PLO was expelled in 1982 but Hizbullah, the Lebanese Shi'i party-militia, took its place, and through its "resistance" became "a significant political factor in the Lebanese arena and in the Muslim world that also enjoys wide international legitimacy" (Tamir 2005: 273).

Third, members of Israel's security network have played a critical role in formulating, implementing, and sustaining these Israeli policies. This is manifested in their securitizing of issues by claiming that they are relevant and indeed critical for Israel's security; in legitimizing Israel's policy in these spheres by using existential terms; and in forging informal ties with nonstate actors such as the Israeli settlers in the Palestinian Territories and the Christian militias in South Lebanon, which resulted in long-term commitments to these actors. At the same time, both cases suggest that Israel's informal security network is neither fixed nor static: some members joined it while others left, and the emphasis of its members changed with regard to various policy areas. Moreover, sub-networks within it sometimes clashed among themselves, such as Dayan and Allon and their supporters with regard to the Palestinian Territories in the period 1967–1977, Rabin and other security officials with regard to Lebanon in 1975–1977, and Barak and the opponents of his plan to withdraw from Lebanon in 1999–2000. However, the general policy supported by most of these members has persisted over time.

Fourth, Israel's foreign and defense policies have been characterized by considerable ambiguity, which, in the course of time, has become an instrument of foreign policy. In addition to the Palestinian Territories and South Lebanon, discussed in the preceding text, ambiguity has also been adopted in the realm of Israeli nuclear capability, and there, too, it has helped preserve domestic consensus and preclude international, especially U.S., pressure and, ultimately, provided additional room to maneuver for members of Israel's security network (see, especially, Cohen 1998).

Finally, civilian challenges to policies formulated and implemented by members of the security network in the external realm have had mixed results: With regard to the Palestinian Territories, civil society actors and MFA officials launched the Oslo Process but Israeli–Palestinian Relations were soon securitized and dominated by the security network even before the second Palestinian Intifada. Concerning Lebanon, civilian efforts managed to create a fissure within the security network and weaken its members' resistance to an Israeli withdrawal. But they did not desecuritize Israeli–Lebanese relations, as demonstrated by later events, especially the war between Israel and Hizbullah in 2006. It is interesting to note that these civilian efforts, as well as others that were more successful, such as with regard to Israel's relations with South Africa (see Liel 1999), were joined by only a few Israeli academics and did not involve major civil society groups (e.g., "Peace Now"). This fact attests to the considerable weakness of Israel's civil society compared to the strength of Israel's security network, not only in shaping Israel's foreign and defense policies but also in general

6

Israel in a Comparative Perspective

In this chapter we place the discussion of Israel's security network and its domestic and external impacts in a broader perspective by discussing several other "small states" that face, or faced in the past, real or imagined, but in any case perceived, continuous existential threats, and by drawing comparisons between these other states and Israel. As we stated at the beginning of this book, the purpose of these comparisons is to assist in providing some analytical and theoretical insights regarding the Israeli case but also generally. The most relevant cases in this context are Taiwan, South Korea, and South Africa in the period of Apartheid, which are three non-Western states that have democratized in recent decades, and a fourth non-Western case, Singapore, which has remained partially democratic since its independence.

After discussing some of the attributes of this general category of "continuously existentially threatened small states," we focus on each of the other four cases and its main characteristics. We then discuss some of the similarities and differences between these additional cases and the Israeli case.

CONTINUOUSLY THREATENED SMALL STATES: MAIN CHARACTERISTICS

As we noted, most studies that examine Israel's civil–security relationship from a comparative perspective have chosen Western cases as their point of reference, particularly the United States, United Kingdom, France, and Switzerland. However, because we see Israel as a partially Western or even a non-Western small state in which the process of state formation and development is still underway, and because Israel has faced real or imagined, but in any case perceived, continuous existential threats since its independence, our view is that Israel ought to be compared to similar cases from these perspectives. Future investigators in this field might find it useful to compare the five states discussed here to some Western small states that have or are still encountering similar developments.

Like Israel, the cases of Taiwan, South Korea, South Africa, and Singapore represent relatively new states that are also small states in terms of their size and material and human resources. These characteristics have had considerable implications for their position, power, and influence in the international system. Indeed, since their independence, these states could expect to be the allies, protégées, or clients of more powerful states, especially the great powers, and moreover to be affected by such powers' behavior more than they can influence it. At the same time, these states could cooperate among themselves, or with other small states, to address their security predicaments.

There are additional features of these five states that set them apart from other small states and, ultimately, make them a distinct analytical category. These include the particular circumstances in which these states were established; their contested legitimacy in the eyes of domestic actors, foreign actors (including states and international organizations), or both; and the unusually high levels of hostility toward them expressed by such actors. These factors led the political and security elites in these states, as well as significant portions of their publics, to regard themselves as facing domestic and/or external continuous existential threats. As a result, the boundaries between these states' civilian and security sectors have become blurred, a factor that affected their domestic and external policies, including the perception of a continuous existential threat to the state.

Most works that discuss the cases of Israel, Taiwan, South Korea, and South Africa, and to a lesser extent Singapore, in the same context focus on these states' position and role in the international system, particularly on their "pariah" status (Harkavy 1977) and, more recently, on their international isolation (Gledenhuys 1990). It is argued, moreover, that the precarious position of these states in the international system has rendered some policy options, such as neutrality and membership in international organizations, highly unrealistic. This leaves these states with the choice of allying with other pariahs or with the great powers or going it alone to ensure their continuous existence (Cohen 1995; Inbar and Sheffer 1997).

A second feature of these states that has elicited attention is their development of significant military capabilities, which effectively transformed them into "middle powers" or "regional powers" (Handel 1981; Tan 1999, 2012; Chang 2003). Some of these states, including Israel, Singapore, and South Africa, later adopted an offensive–defensive military strategy, which their political and military leaders saw as a better way to respond to the continuous existential threats facing them than their previously adopted defensive–offensive military strategy.[1] The shift in these states' military strategy had quite different

---

[1] Lee (2007: 212) observes that "In the past, Taiwan has cautiously avoided declarations of pre-emptive strike or the acquisition of a significant force as a deterrent to China," but suggests that the government has shifted from the former to the latter strategy in recent years.

implications for each: Whereas Israel and South Africa used massive military force against their neighbors, Singapore maintained peaceful relations with its external environment (Yew 2007; Tan 2012). In addition, some of these states, including Israel and South Africa, sought to buttress their sovereignty by developing a clandestine nuclear weapons programs with the tacit consent of the superpowers and the active assistance of other international players (Harkavy 1981; Cohen 1998; Gonzalez 2002; Polakow-Suransky 2010).[2]

The militarization of these five small states in response to the continuous existential threats facing them sets them apart from other small states that have sought to address their security predicament since 1945 by acquiring formal or informal neutral status in the international system (e.g., Sweden and Switzerland) or reaching political and security arrangements with the great powers (e.g., the Czech Republic and Finland) and/or with their neighbors (e.g., Lebanon and Jordan). This does not mean that at least some of these other small states, especially Switzerland and Finland, did not develop their own military capabilities, but rather that this factor was not regarded as the main guarantee for these states' security.

Our focus in this chapter is on the domestic implications and, to an extent, the external ones of building a powerful security sector in these five continuously threatened small states, and the complex relationships that emerged between their security sectors and civilian sectors, which, as demonstrated later, are best described in terms of a security network. Indeed, although the exact nature of these security networks differs from case to case, we posit that this phenomenon is markedly different from the patterns of civil–security relations that emerged not only in Western states but also in many other small states in the contemporary world.[3]

THE FOUR CASES

In our short and focused examination of the four cases of South Africa, South Korea, Taiwan, and Singapore, we do not elaborate on the history and development of these states, but mainly focus on the existential threat to each state; the relationship that emerged between its civilian and security sectors; and the

---

[2] Other small states later emulated this behavior when they faced similar circumstances (see Henriksen 2001). In 2002, following the attacks of 9/11, U.S. president George W. Bush labeled Iraq, Iran, and North Korea as an "Axis of Evil" and accused them of supporting terrorism and seeking weapons of mass destruction. In 2003, following the U.S.-led invasion of Iraq, the two remaining members of this Axis, North Korea and Iran, accelerated their nuclear programs, and Syria, which was also harshly criticized by the United States in this period, acquired a nuclear facility, possibly from North Korea, that Israel destroyed in 2007. At the same time, Libya, another state that was criticized by the United States, agreed to trade its nuclear program for a rapprochement with the West.

[3] As mentioned in Chapter 1, two additional cases that witnessed phenomena comparable to Israel's security network are Lebanon in the period 1958–1970 and since 1990, and Turkey.

long-term impact of this factor on the main aspects of the regime and on the state's foreign relations. As we shall see, there are marked similarities but also important differences between these cases and these will be discussed here and in the concluding chapter.

South Africa

From the rise to power of the National Party in 1948 until the challenging transition to democracy in the early 1990s, South Africa's white population, which includes Afrikaners and English, dominated the state's political system, the economy, and the security sector according to the official policy of Apartheid. Since the 1960s, South Africa faced growing political pressures from its African community, and its relations with the rapidly changing regional environment also became tense. At the same time, its position in the international system deteriorated and became contested: sanctions were imposed on it and most international actors regarded it as a pariah state. Furthermore, the presence and involvement of the Soviet Union in the region posed a major threat to its national security.

The continuous existential threats facing South Africa during that period were represented in the concept of "total onslaught," which referred to the combined domestic and external threat to the state's security. To counter these continuous existential threats, the government in Pretoria devised an official policy termed "total strategy," which called for mobilizing the state's military and economic resources. At the same time, South Africa adopted a policy of military intervention in its regional environment (e.g., in Namibia) and forged close ties with other pariah states such as Israel and Taiwan.[4] Like Israel, during the 1970s South Africa also developed a clandestine nuclear weapons program" (Liberman 2001; Purkitt and Burgess 2005).

The "total strategy" devised by South Africa's leaders, in particular by President P. W. Botha, accorded a pivotal role to the South African Defence Forces (SADF) and to the other security agencies, prompting many observers to speak of the state's militarization (Frankel 1984; Grundy 1988; Cock and Nathan 1989). Indeed, this factor, together with the intimate ties forged between South Africa's political and military leaders, led to the considerable blurring of the boundaries between the state's civilian and security sectors and, ultimately, to the security sector's significant impact on policymaking (Griffiths 1991). Communication and cooperation between the SADF and the private business sector, which was seen as a crucial part of the state's security, was also enhanced, resulting in a state-sponsored "highly complex and articulated tripartite network supporting a wide variety of war-type military-private-sector transactions" (Frankel 1984: 80). Indeed, it was suggested that "[a]s the

---

[4] On South Africa's relations with Israel and the pivotal role of Israel's security network in initiating and sustaining it, see Liel (1999); Polakow-Suransky (2010).

garrison state has taken a hold on the psychology and organization of local society, so we find today many of the ingredients of ... the 'military-industrial complex' in the South African context" (Frankel 1984: 79).

It should be emphasized in this context that, like Apartheid itself, South Africa's militarization was highly institutionalized. In addition to the official ideology of total strategy, the growing impact of South Africa's security sector on policymaking was felt in the State Security Council (SSC), established in 1972. Despite its civilian nature, the SSC included a large number of military officers and was highly influenced by the SADF. In addition, there emerged close ties between civilian bureaucrats and military officials, who served together in the National Security Management System (NSMS), the official body of the SSC, which was in charge of policymaking in the area of national security. These relationships amounted to a security network of businessmen, senior military officials, and politicians (Frankel 1984; Rotberg 1988; Seegers 1991; Griffiths 1991). Indeed, a member of the parliamentary defense committee later remarked that during this period there were no civil–military relations to speak of in South Africa, and no strict civilian oversight over the military existed (Griffiths 2010: 588).

Following the international arms embargo imposed on South Africa, its military industry expanded considerably and, among other things, a body called Armaments Development and Manufacturing Corporation (ARMSCOR) was created. It was in charge of manufacturing, purchasing, and distributing arms. This body, too, included members of the military, governmental, and business elites, and some of its functionaries later became independent industrialists, thus enhancing the aforementioned military–industrial complex, or rather, the security network. It should also be noted that the impact of the SADF and of military values on the educational system, the media, and society at large in South Africa in that period was considerable (see, especially, Frankel 1984).

In the 1990s, significant changes took place both in the continuous existential threats facing South Africa and the relationship between its civilian and security sectors. Domestically, more and more South Africans, including many Afrikaners, reached the conclusion that Apartheid was untenable, opening the way for negotiations with the African community and, ultimately, for democratization. At the same time, significant changes took place in the state's regional and international environments, especially the decline of the Soviet threat, leading to the decline of both the total onslaught and total strategy concepts (Cawthra 2003).

The security sector in South Africa was divided with regard to the democratic reforms and its own character after Apartheid. Although President Frederick de Klerk bypassed the SADF and the defense ministry by appointing the participants to the talks on political transition, the military did exercise influence on policymaking in this period, and retired SADF officials maintained contacts with officials in the African National Congress (ANC).

One of the most important processes during South Africa's retreat from Apartheid and transition to a democratic regime was the integration of the country's various armed formations into its new military institution – the South African National Defence Force (SANDF) – which became more representative (Griffiths 2010: 590–2). Even though the old SADF did not initiate the creation of SANDF, moderate military officials took part in the unofficial meetings leading to its establishment. But the creation of SANDF had mixed results: Although the integration of the various armed formations was completed by 1996 without violence, the process encountered numerous problems. These included disproportional representation and influence of the former armed bodies, particularly former SADF personnel, in SANDF, and the retirement of many former members of the opposition forces; internal tensions, sometimes of a racial basis, between former SADF personnel and ex-members of the other formations; the growth of trade-unionism within SANDF; and problems of discipline and professionalism (Wood 1996; Cawthra 2003).

At the same time, with the growing possibility that both Apartheid and the external continuous existential threats facing South Africa would come to an end, consecutive South African governments, first and foremost the transitional government led by de Klerk and then the ANC-led government, adopted several important measures to establish democratic control over the security sector. First, structural changes in the SSC reduced the ability of military officials to influence policymaking. The influential NSMS was changed to National Coordination Mechanisms (NCM) and its emphasis was to be responsible for socioeconomic and not security matters. In addition, only politicians, and not bureaucrats or military officials, could be members of the SSC, and a new ministerial committee on security affairs was created. The result of these changes was the decline of the military's influence on national security policies (Seegers 1996; Griffiths 2010). Second, the new 1996 constitution emphasized democratic control over the military and the police, including sections specifying the role of the president as commander-in-chief of the armed forces. Moreover, the secretariats for both the military and the police were to be civilian, and national security would need to comply with national and international laws. Third, parliamentary control of all security services was introduced: the Joint Standing Committee on Defence (JSCD), a multiparty joint committee of the two houses of parliament, was established to supervise the activities of the department of defense, including its budget, and to make policy recommendations on defense management. This and other parliamentary committees were indeed very active in the first two years of the new parliament, but their involvement and influence declined somewhat later (Cawthra 2003). Fourth, inside the defense secretariat a balanced model specifying the roles and responsibilities of the chief of the SANDF, the secretary of defense, and the minister of defense, was adopted.

These were the formal changes. In reality, however, the lack of civilian professional knowledge in most aspects of the defense policymaking process, and the reluctance of some military officers to accept civilian supervision, was an obstacle to the full implementation of civilian control over the military through the defense secretariat (Cawthra 2003). However, these early tensions between the SANDF and the parliamentary committee have later given way to greater cooperation and, ultimately, to greater civilian oversight (Griffiths 2010: 589–90). It should be noted that although SANDF did retain its influence in the ministry of defense, the military's budget was decreased by 40% in the period 1989–1994, the status and power of the military industry decreased, and ARMSCOR elicited growing public criticism and demands to make it more accountable. Still, it remained an important part of South Africa's industrial sector (Mills 1993). Finally, the Police Service Act of 1995 established the Secretariat for Safety and Security, aiming to establish civilian supervision over the police. But the result was not very successful: Tension between the secretariat and the police was apparent and many programs devised by the secretariat were not implemented by police officers (Cawthra 2003).

In sum, South Africa witnessed a successful transition from an authoritarian regime to a formal democracy in the 1990s not only because both the domestic and external continuous existential threats facing the state had declined but interconnectedly due to the fact that the state's pattern of civil–military relations, and especially its formal aspects, was transformed, largely without violence (Cawthra 2003; Griffiths 2010). Still, the security sector in South Africa has retained some of its status and influence, not least because of the weakness of the civilian institutions which are supposed to oversee it, and among other internal developments this factor is one of the reasons why South Africa remains a formal and not an effective democracy.

South Korea

Like other cases examined in this chapter, an analysis of the current relationship between South Korea's civilian and security sectors must include consideration of the impact of historical and more recent relevant developments, including the nature of the continuous existential threats facing the state and the social–cultural sphere (Cha 2001; Bechtol 2005; Woo 2011; Moon and Rhyu 2011). From such a perspective, the character of South Korea's social and political systems has indeed been substantially influenced by the existence of a "formidable coercive apparatus in which the military and the police constituted the primary forces" (Jinsok 2001: 122).

Despite the democratization that took place in South Korea in the late 1980s, and the imposition of increased civilian control over its military, its society is still characterized by a strong and persistent urge for conformity and order. Thus, the "glue" for the state's social and political systems has been a rigid hierarchy. Although this hierarchy is rooted in Confucianism, it was formed, concentrated, and magnified by the military-style discipline enforced on the state after its establishment and especially since 1961.

Rather than by the members of its semidemocratic political parties, South Korea has been ruled by a few powerful individuals, many of whom had previously served in the military or elsewhere in the security sector. In other words, there has been an ingrained military influence on South Korea's political culture and on the political system that is manifested, for example, in powerful personal relations revolving around extended families, the security sector and the elite schools, along with essentially formal democratic patterns (Clifford 1994; Moon and Rhyu 2011). As in the other cases discussed in this chapter, this state of affairs is best described in terms of the existence of a powerful security network.

This state of affairs can be attributed to several factors: first, long-term historical legacies, including the impact of Confucianism and the old authoritarian ideologies and values of the Chosun Dynasty (1392–1910); second, the impact of the Japanese colonial period; third, the Korean War; fourth, later regional and local wars; and finally, other threatening external developments, most notably the development of North Korea's military and nuclear capabilities in the 1990s (Jinsok 2001). Thus, the continuous existential threats facing South Korea, which are mostly external, have played a significant role in shaping various aspects of its political and social systems, including the relations between its civilian and security sectors.

Focusing, however, on developments during the post–World War II period, the division of the Korean peninsula into two separate states and the Soviet control of its northern part marked an increase in the continuous existential threats facing South Korea. The Korean War (1950–1953), which was viewed as a clash between the "free world" and the Communist bloc, especially affected South Korea, where the consequent dependence on the United States only added to the feelings of fear and insecurity (Bechtol 2005). The Vietnam War, in which hundreds of thousands of South Korean soldiers took part alongside U.S. soldiers, also aggravated these perceptions, which were further enhanced by the continuous failure of peacemaking in the Korean peninsula and recurring U.S. plans to pull out its troops.

With regard to its historical background and the continuous existential threats facing it, immediately after the establishment of South Korea a civilian-led authoritarian regime emerged in which President Syngman Rhee (1948–1960) controlled the military through his own charisma and by exploiting factional struggles within it. This pattern continued through the days of the Second Republic (1960–1961), but changed after a military coup in 1961, which resulted in the clear domination by the military of the political system. Although the military regime was terminated after two years, military involvement and intervention in almost every sphere of public life and politics continued. During the quasi-military rule of Park Chung-hee (1961–1979), a former army general who was backed by active and retired military officers, the latter penetrated and controlled civilian politics and government, and civil society was mobilized and reorganized to achieve "total security" (Moon and Rhyu

2011: 252). Thus, the South Korean military and the various informal networks that its high-ranking officers belonged to became involved in almost all domestic political and economic affairs. This pattern continued under the government of Chun Doo-hwan (1980–1988), another former army general. However, unlike Park, Chun restricted the number of retired officers in the Korean government, creating a new civil–military symbiosis (Jinsok 2001; Woo 2011).

South Korea's third (1963–1972), fourth (1973–1979), and fifth (1979–) republics were not pure military regimes. Rather, these were semicivilian regimes heavily supported by the military, whose involvement in society and politics was mainly through the presence of retired officers on all governmental levels, starting with the prime ministers, through cabinet and parliament members, the bureaucracy, and the public sector (Croissant 2004). Since the 1961 coup, moreover, the military virtually monopolized policy and decision making in the sphere of national security. Civilian participation and public debates on these issues were not tolerated. This privilege was justified by an anti-Communist ideology and, later, by other national security considerations (Jinsok 2001; Woo 2011).

The power and influence of the security sector in South Korea were also significant concerning social issues and the economy (Graham 1991; Croissant 2004). The military contributed to modernization and socioeconomic development of the state and to building its infrastructure. Under the influence of U.S. advisers, one could find "many officers leaving the Korean military and going into management of private companies, in large numbers, so a lot of management skills that were learned in the military were then transferred to the civilian economy" (Clifford 1994: 304–5). In addition, young people gained various forms of military education and the military became one of the state's main socializing and educational institutions. The military's budget was increased, and it became a major agent of social mobility due to the many posts provided to retired security officials in the bureaucracy and economy. Thus, the security sector became a powerful actor that neither the government nor civil society could ignore (Croissant 2004). One observer concluded: "The formal differentiation between the military establishment and civil polity was weak ... The physical and psychological presence of the military in Korean society is now unavoidable" (Cha 2001: 116).

In the late 1980s, the Chun government suffered a crisis of legitimacy that led to the introduction of semiparticipatory elements to the political system. At first, senior members of the security sector were concerned about their ability to maintain their privileged and influential positions and debated among themselves the steps that could be taken to overcome the crisis. But the moderate group of officers, who were opposed to military intervention in politics, ultimately gained the upper hand, mainly because of the long-standing practice of profound informal influence on the government. Eventually it turned out that the public protest was not directed against the security sector, and the subsequent victory in the presidential elections of yet another former army general, Roh Tae-woo, convinced the military that its position and privileges would be maintained. In fact, during Roh's presidency (1988–1993), the security sector maintained its influence over the civilian sector. Public opinion surveys conducted in the late 1990s showed that though certain groups were interested in limiting the power of the security sector, most citizens appreciated its contribution to the state's security (Croissant 2004; Bechtol 2005).

The collapse of the Soviet Union, the end of the Cold War, the changes in the positions and policies of China, North Korea's main supporter, and the 1991 agreement between the two Koreas concerning negotiations about the resolution of conflicts between them – all of these factors contributed to a temporary relaxation of the continuous existential threats facing South Korea. After 1993, however, when the development of nuclear weapons by North Korea became imminent, the continuous existential threat facing South Korea was reawakened and still exists at the time of writing. This was enhanced after 9/11 by the U.S. inclusion of North Korea in the "Axis of Evil." South Korea, for its part, adopted a dual policy toward its northern neighbor: On the one hand, it prescribed nontolerance toward Pyongyang's aggressive policies and actions; on the other hand, it decided not to attempt to undermine North Korea's government or unite the two states by force, and to welcome cooperation with North Korea. This meant that although it was less threatened than before essentially the continuous existential threats facing South Korea remained intact (Saxer 2004; cf. Woo 2011).

To a certain degree like South Africa, an institutional change in South Korea's civilian–security interface has begun in 1998, with the onset of Kim Dae-jung's presidency. A National Security Council was established under the president's control, the legislative branch became more involved in determining national security policy, civil society actors, including nongovernmental organizations (NGOs) and the media, emerged as more influential actors, and active military officers were placed under civilian control in the process of managing national security policy. However, the increase in formal civilian control of the military did not mean the imposition of effective civil control over the military and national security policy, where the military still played an influential role.[5] In any case, South Korea's formal democracy, the new political deterrents to military intervention in politics, the expansion of civil society, the changing political calculus in the military, and punishment of politicized officers all encouraged a certain degree of political neutrality of the military, which became unified and professionalized (Jinsok 2001; Im 2004; Woo 2011; Moon and Rhyu 2011).

---

[5] Moon and Ryuh (2011: 259) note the lack of professional expertise among South Korea's civilian leaders, which forces them to rely on active or retired military officers for defense policymaking, and the monopolization of the position of defense minister by retired army generals and of important decision-making posts in the ministry by uniformed or retired military officers.

Interconnectedly, although the number of retired officers in governmental positions in South Korea has declined in subsequent years, and especially during the presidency of Kim Young-sam (1993–1998), the first civilian president in thirty years, the security sector still served as a vital source for recruitment of personnel for senior political and bureaucratic positions (Croissant 2004; Saxer 2004; Croissant and Kuehn 2009; Moon and Rhyu 2011). This is not surprising in view of the importance of security in the divided peninsula and consequently in view of the military's significant social and economic position. In any case, it is pretty clear that military-turned-civilians have controlled politics in South Korea through a quasi-military format even after democratization (Jinsok 2001; Bechtol 2005).

Although the trend in recent years is toward greater civilian control over the military in South Korea (Croissant and Kuehn 2009; Moon and Rhyu 2011; Woo 2011), further political development, and especially a transition from a formal democracy to an effective democracy where the civilian leaders have effective control over the security sector, remains conditional on the threats facing the state, the power exercised by the security sector and the informal security networks in the domestic arena, and the interplay between these two factors.

Taiwan

Since its establishment in the late 1940s, Taiwan, too, faced continuous existential threats, mainly from China. As it is well known, the Kuomintang party and its leader, Chiang Kai-Chek, were forced to leave mainland China and move to the island of Taiwan, some 180 kilometers off the southeastern coast of China, where they established a base from which they hoped to return and regain hold on the mainland that was controlled by the Communist party and its leader Mao Tse Tung. Communist China never recognized Taiwan and has not concealed its goal to annex it. The continuous existential threat facing independent Taiwan thus stems from a possible Chinese invasion and annexation of the island. The United States has supported Taiwan in order to deter China from invading it. But the termination of the U.S.–Taiwanese agreement in the 1970s, and, later, the U.S.–Chinese rapprochement, added to Taiwan's perception of a continuous existential threat (Clough 1998; Hickey 2001; Lee 2007). Recently, the tension between China and Taiwan has somewhat been reduced, but not entirely: There are occasional clashes between the two states' navies, as well as threatening military exercises, especially by China.

After Taiwan's establishment, the ruling Kuomintang party, which sought to secure its control over the state, the security sector, and society in view of the Chinese threat, regarded the military as the party's main tool for this purpose. An overlapping between the party and the state's agencies, and thus the predominance of the security sector, was thus established. The military, in turn, penetrated deeply into Taiwanese society in a variety of ways. First, it played an important role in domestic security, economic life, the mass media, and electoral politics. In addition, active-duty or retired personnel easily occupied positions in the judicial and administrative systems. A compulsory military service also reinforced the integration of the army and society in Taiwan (Lo 2001; Kuehn 2008). The control exercised by Taiwan's security sector over the media, universities and social organizations helped the Kuomintang party to secure its predominant position in the state and vis-à-vis society and fulfill its goals. Indeed, during that period the party and the military penetrated one another and old boys' networks existed within them (Lee 2007: 217; see also Tzeng 2009: 24–7). As far as the military was concerned, it was granted a key role in the state's development, including its economy, and the lion's share of the national budget was allocated to it (Lo 2001; Woo 2011).

However, in the late 1970s circumstances and forces emerged that eventually pressed the Taiwanese president and government to start a careful and slow process of democratization. This new policy was supported by the emerging Détente in the 1980s that contributed to a decline in the perception of the imminent threats from the Soviet bloc and China. On the domestic level, democratization was enhanced by Taiwan's economic development, by the consequent growing and strengthening of its middle class, and by the return of Taiwanese émigrés from the West (Lo 2001; Fravel 2002).

Taiwan's demand to rejoin the UN in the early 1990s once again spurred the toughening of the Taiwanese government position vis-à-vis mainland China. After a visit of Taiwanese President Lee Teng Hui to the United States in June 1995, which was interpreted by China as another step toward permanent independence for Taiwan, China conducted tests of its missiles not far from Taiwan and launched a campaign against President Lee. In 1996, on the eve of the presidential elections, the Chinese military conducted large military maneuvers to deter the Taiwanese from electing Lee, but he won nonetheless. All these developments renewed Taiwan's perception that it faced an existential threat from China and contributed to an increase in military budgets. Yet, slow democratization continued with the election of Taiwan's first non-Kuomintang president, Chen Shui-bian, in 2000. He was reelected in 2004 (Fravel 2002).

When Taiwan turned toward democratization in 1987, difficulties arose regarding civilian control over the military, and it seemed as if the latter's political influence was increasing (Croissant and Keuhn 2009). According to most observers, one of the major problems was a lack of clear boundaries between the civilian and military sectors, that is, the existence of a security network in Taiwan. The Taiwanese constitution mentions the principle of greater civilian control over the military. However, in practice, additional laws were needed in order to advance this goal. Thus, until 2002, when the National Defense Act and the Organization Act of the Ministry of National Defense came into effect, the latter ministry consisted mainly of military personnel. After this reform, the number of civilians in the ministry increased, the command structures were reorganized, and policymaking in the area of national defense was made more accountable (Croissant and Keuhn 2009; Kuehn 2008; Tzeng 2009).

Another example is that although the National Defense Act stipulated that the number of military personnel should not exceed one third of the total staff working in the National Security Council (NSC), which shapes Taiwan's national security policy, both the general secretary of the Council and the director of the National Security Bureau were military officers (Lo 2001). However, in the period 2003–2008, "the NSC ultimately became the primary defense decisionmaking agency with the effect of reducing the role of the military and even the civilian defense bureaucracy to one of bystanders when it comes to real influence in defense policy-making" (Croissant and Keuhn 2009: 199).

Taiwan's democratization has also led to a growing demand for checks and balances to reinforce the legislature's role in monitoring the military establishment and defense policymaking. Indeed, "democratization has produced an impetus for legislative oversight and therefore civilian control of the military. In this regard there is a discernible trend toward greater transparency and accountability of defense decisions and the military establishment" (Lo 2001: 149. See also Croissant and Keuhn 2009). Thus, every two years the military has to report on its position and expenditures, and parliament officially approves the defense budget, which has become more transparent to the general public.

Still, several writers note that the parliament in Taiwan is not powerful enough to control the security sector due to the asymmetry of access to intelligence information and the almost total lack of control over the defense budget itself (Philips 2006; Tzeng 2009).

The military's gradual withdrawal from Taiwan's political system is evident in the military's changing relationship with the former ruling party, the Kuomintang. As noted above, before the lifting of martial law in Taiwan in 1987, the party and the military were two sides of the same coin. Thus, the military participated in the decision-making process and the party penetrated the military. But democratization changed this pattern: The defense minister was the only military representative to hold a seat in the Central Standing Committee of the Kuomintang, and all active-duty military personnel have been removed from the party's major decision organs.

Thus, in tandem with the relaxation of the continuous existential threats facing it, Taiwan too has witnessed a gradual adjustment of its pattern of civil–security relations. Spheres of interests long monopolized by the military were challenged in the early 1990s by opposition parties and by various actors outside the security sector, and as a result of criticism and public pressure, the military had to give up some of its powers and interests. Several factors underlie this change: First, negotiations between civilian and military leaders, during which Taiwan's first civilian president skillfully exploited crises, manipulated support, reorganized the military leadership, and expanded civilian control over the military; second, the changing international setting as a result of the ebbing of external threats; and third, the changing domestic setting and the rise of a civil society due to liberalization.

However, although Taiwan's constitution stipulates civilian control over the military, and despite the fact that the latter "is neither able to single-handedly dominate defense policy nor bypass oversight and direction by the president and the parliament" (Croissant and Keuhn 2009: 198. See also Lo 2001; McVadon 2003; Woo 2011), a Western-type civil–military relationship, where the civilian leaders have effective control over the military, particularly over military internal affairs and defense policymaking, still needs to be established (Croissant and Keuhn 2009; Tzeng 2009).

In sum, the relationship between Taiwan's civilian and security sectors has been connected to the external continuous existential threats facing the state. Major changes in the international system, especially in the triangular relations between the United States, China, and Taiwan, have lessened these threats somewhat and facilitated democratization. These changes brought about competition between Taiwan's political parties, greater respect for individual and civilian groups' rights, and more separation between the various branches of the government, including between the civilian institutions and the security sector. Still, the security sector continues to play a major role in many public spheres and is well connected to the civilian circles (Diamond 2001), and the lack of effective (and not just formal) civilian control of the security sector prevents Taiwan from becoming an effective, rather than a formal, democracy.

Singapore

Like the other cases discussed here, Singapore has been preoccupied with its national security since its independence in 1965. In 1942, when it was still under British rule, Singapore was invaded by Japan, and later, when it was part of the Malaysian Federation, it was the subject of constant meddling in its affairs by Malaysia, and vice versa. Even after its separation from Malaysia, Singapore, which lacks natural resources, remained dependent on its larger Muslim neighbor for water and food. Another challenge to Singapore's security, which is closely connected to this external continuous existential threat, has to do with the tensions between its Chinese majority and its Malay minority.[6] In the eyes of Singapore's leaders, and especially its first prime minister, Lee Kwan Yew (1959–1990), "Singapore's status as a nation-state was not only uncertain

---

[6] Rahim (2012: 70) speaks of an "essentialist crisis discourse," in Singapore, which is "centred on reminding Singaporeans of the vulnerabilities associated with being a resource-poor and largely Chinese city state surrounded by larger, more densely populated, resource-rich and potentially hostile Muslim states to the immediate north and south." According to this source, this discourse "has reinforced the stature of the long-serving People's Action Party (PAP) government as guardians of the predominantly Chinese populace" and "serves as an effective means of rallying the masses behind an ethno-nationalist rhetoric that rationalises draconian legislation, high defence spending and compulsory national service."

but, more significantly, contested and challenged by others," and its "claim to nationhood could not ... be taken for granted, [and had to be] reiterated, assertively if necessary" (da Cunha 2002: 112, see also Leifer 2000).

To protect itself against these continuous existential threats, Singapore conducted its affairs according to a defense policy based on "twin pillars": diplomacy and deterrence. On the one hand, Singapore forged strong commercial ties and defense links with other states in Southeast Asia and beyond, and actively participated in international organizations on the regional and global levels (Narayanan 1997; Tan 1999, 2012; Huxley 2000; Leifer 2000; da Cunha 2002: 140–1). At the same time, Singapore adopted defense strategies designed to deter would-be aggressors. Initially, it sought to make the cost of its invasion so high as to prevent such an option. According to PM Lee, "In a world where the big fish eats small fish and the small fish eats shrimps, Singapore must become a poisonous shrimp" (Narayanan 1997: 12).

But by the mid-1970s, and in view of the growing military buildup in Singapore itself and in Southeast Asia, this defensive–offensive military strategy was deemed insufficient. It was replaced by an offensive–defensive military strategy that sought to deter would-be aggressors by building a preemptive conventional capability that emphasized air-power, armor, and mobility (Peled 1998; Tan 1999; da Cunha 2002; Chang 2003). In 1984, a comprehensive new defense strategy for Singapore called "Total Defense" was unveiled. It focused not only on the military but also spoke of "psychological defense, social defense, economic defense, and civil defense" (da Cunha 1999: 460). This policy, which according to some observers exemplifies Singapore's "siege mentality" (da Cunha 1999), was reaffirmed in 2000 (Chang 2003). These facts are the background for the unique position of the military and the security sector in Singapore's affairs.

The Singapore Armed Forces (SAF), whose structure and military doctrines were inspired by Israel (in fact they were designed with Israeli military assistance), had three major components: first, a permanent core of military professionals; second, conscripts recruited by compulsory military service of two years; third, reservists who could be mobilized during emergencies. At the same time, and in order to provide Singapore with a qualitative edge over its potential enemies, emphasis was placed on manufacturing and acquiring sophisticated military technology and weapons for the SAF. As a result of Singapore's remarkable military buildup in the late 1980s, the SAF became the most credible armed force in Southeast Asia (Narayanan 1997; Tan 1999, 2012; da Cunha 1999).

Despite the official statements in Singapore, which focused on the need to foster an all-engulfing national identity, members of its ethnic Malay minority, whose loyalty was questioned by the Chinese majority, were systematically excluded from the SAF, where they formerly constituted between 50 and 80 percent (Peled 1998, 104; see also Walsh 2007, Rahim 2012: 92). To make up for the deficiency in Chinese officers in the SAF, "trustworthy" civil servants,

most of them Chinese, were appointed as military officers, despite their minimal military experience. This process, which involved an intended porosity of
the boundaries between the state's civilian and military sectors, was justified by
the desire of Singapore's leaders to build a "civil service in uniform," namely, an
officer corps characterized by unquestionable loyalty, ideological affinity, and
non-Malay racial background (Peled 1998: 116–17).

By the early 1980s, however, the SAF was called upon to supply talented
personnel to Singapore's bureaucracy and political system (Yong 2001). A
change in the government's policy allowed "scholars-officers," who are talented young people that received scholarships for academic studies before their
enlistment to the SAF, to choose between joining the civil service and pursuing
a military career. As a consequence, middle-ranking and senior SAF officers
began to be appointed to positions in the state's bureaucracy and commercial
firms and were involved in policymaking in the Ministry of Defense (Huxley
1993, 2000; da Cunha 1999). In addition, SAF officers became increasingly
involved in Singapore's political system, including the government, and began
to assume a significant degree of influence over governmental decision making
in a wide variety of spheres. For example, in 1999, serving SAF officers were
even appointed ambassadors to China, South Korea, and Myanmar (Huxley
1993, 2000).

This development has been interpreted in different ways. Some observers
emphasize civilian control over the military in Singapore, which has been preserved through the years despite the continuous existential threats facing the
state. According to them, the process whereby SAF officers have moved to
civilian spheres in fact suggests that a part of the SAF officer corps has become
civilianized (da Cunha 1999; Mauzy and Milne 2002). Despite the pervasive
presence of SAF reserve officers in almost every government and quasi-govern-
ment organization in Singapore, the SAF is firmly subordinated to the political
elite and does not appear to have any influence on the political process (da
Cunha 1999). Noting the lack of a "clear-cut distinction between a professional armed force and its civilian clientele" in Singapore, one author has suggested a different model, "civil-military fusion," which holds that "the military,
rather than functioning as an independent or dysfunctional component outside
the civilian polity, is for all intents and purposes an integral part of the administrative structure, playing an essentially complementary role in the social and
economic functions of the state" (Yong 2001: 278).

But other observers have argued that since the late 1980s civilian control
over Singapore's Ministry of Defense and the SAF may have been significantly
eroded, not least because of the appointment of high-ranking reservist officers
to critical policymaking positions (Huxley 1993). If this practice persists, they
suggested, there is a danger of a military mind-set coming to dominate governmental decision making in the area of defense and wider security considerations assuming an unwarranted priority in official policies. Another possible
consequence is that government ministers with military background would

maintain their loyalty to the SAF even when serving in the government (Huxley 2000). Some authors even suggested that Singapore's quest for maintaining its military edge over its neighbors could encourage a regional arms race and, ultimately, push Singapore into acquiring a strategic strike capability, which is like the situation in other continuously threatened small states such as Israel (Tan 1999). Finally, some noted the linkage between the presence of former senior SAF officers, all of whom are Chinese, in the Singaporean cabinet and the continued exclusion of minorities from strategic and sensitive posts in the SAF (Huxley 1993; Mutalib 2002).

Singapore, in sum, has responded to the perceived and actual continuous existential threats that it faced not only by building a powerful security sector that has provided the political system and the bureaucracy with skilled manpower, but also by pursuing an active foreign policy that is commensurate with the country's role as a commercial hub. The flip side of the same coin, however, is the gradual penetration of Singapore's security sector, especially the SAF, into various civilian spheres, leading one to speak of civilian–security fusion and, possibly, also of a security network, though one in which the civilian actors are dominant. Like the other cases discussed in this chapter, it seems that a democratic transition in Singapore would depend not only on the decline of the continuous existential threats facing the state, which, as we have seen, are both external and domestic in nature, but also on the imposition of effective civilian control of its security sector and the dismantling of its security network, or civil–military fusion.

CONCLUSION

This chapter has situated the discussion of the Israeli case, and particularly the existence of informal security networks and their impact on the Israeli regime, in a broad, comparative and theoretical perspective. More specifically, we compared Israel to several other small states that, like Israel, have faced continuous existential threats since their establishment and early development. These imagined and real existential threats affected, but, in turn, were also influenced by, the relationship between their civilian and security sectors. In addition, we discussed the impact of these factors on the political development of these states. We have noted in this context that three of these additional states have been democratizing, and a fourth state, Singapore, is still considered to be partially democratic. Hence all of these states, like Israel, are not effective democracies.

Based on this discussion, our main conclusions are the following. First, in all of these states the security sector has accumulated great power and influence over policymaking in security matters as well as in civilian spheres, such as the political system, society, the economy, and public discourse. Second, this power and influence has been exercised not only by the security sectors in these states but also by informal security networks composed of acting and former security officials and actors in various civilian spheres. Third, despite the changes in the continuous existential threats facing these states and the simultaneous tendencies toward democratization in some of them, which contributed to a certain reduction in the power of the security sector and security network, these actors have retained much of their influence. This is particularly apparent in policymaking in the area of national security, including, first and foremost, determining the state's defense budget and national security policies. Fourth, the continuation of this state of affairs over a long period of time seems to be one of the factors preventing the formal democracies and the democratizing regimes in Israel, South Korea, Taiwan, and South Africa from becoming effective democracies and might explain the robustness of the only partially democratic regime in Singapore. This is because the security sector and the security networks in these states have managed to eschew effective civilian control by the political system and civil society, and also because the strength and impact of their security sectors and security networks have worked against the emergence of robust political parties, an informed legislature, a professional bureaucracy, and a vibrant civil society that are effectively involved in policymaking. Lastly, the persistence over time of significant spheres of public life characterized by secrecy, ambiguity, and a lack of accountability prevents democratic norms from becoming more ingrained and influential in these states.

Conclusion

In recent years, one major issue has captured most of the attention of leading politicians, security officials, and large segments of the public in Israel: the possible threat to Israel's security, and maybe even to its existence, stemming from Iran's nuclear program. Indeed, it would not be an exaggeration to argue that the "Iranian Question" has become the Archimedean point from which Israel's politics and actual external and domestic policies can be viewed. Earlier in this book we discussed the circumstances whereby the Israel Defense Forces' (IDF's) chief of staff, Benny Gantz, was appointed in 2011, and the prevailing view among many in Israel and beyond that the "Galant Affair" was closely connected to the Iranian Question. But there are numerous other examples that can be mentioned in this context. It is too early to tell what Israel might or might not do with regard to the Iranian Question – would Israeli leaders continue to support and encourage an assertive international policy toward Iran to prevent it from acquiring nuclear weapons, or would they follow Israel's offensive–defensive military strategy and order an attack on Iran's nuclear facilities, as Israel did with regard to Iraq in 1981 and probably also with respect to Syria in 2007? But our discussion thus far does provide some insights regarding this issue, and these will serve as an introduction to this concluding chapter.

First, there is no doubt that the Iranian Question, like many other policy areas in Israel, has been securitized. This means that political, social, economic, and cultural factors that may also be relevant to the discussion of this issue, such as Iran's international position, its economy, society, and culture receive far less attention than they deserve. In addition, other policy issues, such as Israel's relations with Lebanon and with the Palestinian Hamas in the Gaza Strip, and even the natural gas reservoirs off the shores of Israel, have been securitized, and their relationship to the Iranian Question has been highlighted. This is not to say, of course, that Iran is not involved in Lebanon (mainly through its local client, Hizbullah), and perhaps also in the Palestinian Territories, but that issues such as Israeli–Lebanese and Israeli–Palestinian relations, which are highly complex and involve many actors and considerations, cannot and should not be viewed only through the Iranian "lens."

Second, policymaking with regard to the Iranian Question in Israel has become the near-exclusive domain of members of Israel's security network, and especially retired and acting security officials. These include, first and foremost, leading figures in the current Israeli government such as Prime Minister Benjamin Netanyahu and Minister of Defense Ehud Barak, as well as high-ranking officers in the IDF's general staff. It should be noted that some of these figures have explicitly referred to the Iranian Question as an existential threat to Israel as well as generally (though other members of the security network rejected this argument). Netanyahu, for example, has argued several times that "The year is 1938 and Iran is Germany," and that Iran's president, Mahmoud Ahmadinejad, "is a problem for Jews, like Hitler was, but he is also a problem for the entire world" (see, e.g., *Ynet* December 19, 2006; *NRG* May 21, 2012).

But Israel's policy toward the Iranian Question has also featured profound disagreements within its powerful security network. One subnetwork, led by Netanyahu and Barak, is reportedly in favor of launching an attack against Iran's nuclear facilities, and they are joined by other security officials, especially in the IDF. However, there seems to be serious opposition to such a move by a number of ministers in the Israeli government, including some with background in Israel security sector, by former security officials such as Meir Dagan and Yuval Diskin, who spoke publicly against an Israeli attack against Iran, and reportedly also by serving senior officers in the IDF. The debate between these two subnetworks on the Iranian Question is followed with great concern and attention by the Israeli public, which is divided not only about the particular policy that Israel should adopt, but also on how to perceive the Iranian threat: As an existential threat, and therefore one that necessitates a preemptive Israeli strike, particularly if the world fails to stop Iran's quest for nuclear weapons, or as a threat that does not require immediate action by Israel. In the meantime, as the Iranian Problem is discussed and debated, particularly among members of the security network, other domestic and external issues and problems that beleaguer Israel, including some that might be detrimental its future (especially its policy toward the Palestinians but also a host of other political, social, and economic issues), are put on hold.

We here present our main conclusions from our analysis of Israel's security network and its impact on the domestic and external arenas, as well as from our attempt to situate the Israeli case in a broader, comparative and theoretical perspective. These conclusions relate to Israel, to the category of continuously threatened small states to which Israel belongs, and to more general discussions of the relationship between the state's civilian and security spheres, especially in non-Western states. An important aspect in this discussion is the various roles performed by the security sector and by informal security networks (and subnetworks within them) in the security and foreign affairs of these states and, occasionally, within these states.

As far as Israel is concerned, we have shown that there has been a close connection between the history of the Jewish people, the actual domestic and external circumstances in which the state and its formal democratic regime were established, the collective memory of the Jewish community in Palestine then and in later periods, and the imagined and real domestic and external threats facing the Yishuv and, later, the state. Moreover, all these factors enhanced the close and intricate ties between serving and retired security officials and their partners in various civilian spheres in the Yishuv and later also in the independent state, resulting in the emergence of Israel's security network. As we noted a number of times in this book, this informal security network, and subnetworks within it, has acquired a considerable and, at times, overriding influence on policymaking and implementation domestically as well as externally. What our analysis reveals is that Israel's informal security network has been a basic and continuous feature of the relationship between Israel's civilian and security spheres, particularly since the 1967 War, and that this has become a major factor in accounting for the formal and not the effective civilian control over Israel's large and powerful security sector, especially the IDF.

The other side of the coin is the formal nature of Israel's democracy, in which major institutions such as the government, the bureaucracy, the Knesset, the political parties, and the court system are effectively short-circuited by the security network in major policy areas, most notably in the area of national security. The perpetual weakness of these institutions and other civilian actors in Israel, particularly its civil society, renders them incapable of preventing the security network from influencing and even determining policymaking and implementation in crucial areas, internal as well as external. Indeed, these civilian actors, who are themselves penetrated by the security network, are compelled to share power with the latter or acquiesce to its dominant role. Efforts made by some civilian actors to present themselves as security experts in order to tap onto the dominant security network, especially in recent years, only underscore their weakness. Indeed, these efforts have themselves become a major destabilizing force in Israel's domestic and external arena, as demonstrated for example in the early stages of the war between Israel and Hizbullah in 2006, as well as in the recent struggle over the best strategy that Israel should adopt to prevent Iran from acquiring a nuclear capability.

At the same time, it should be emphasized that Israel's security network is not a homogeneous actor: A number of competing and even clashing subnetworks have occasionally emerged within this security network, especially in recent years. This was manifested, for example, in the Galant Affair, which was essentially a power struggle between two rival informal subnetworks in Israel's security network. In this case, each of these subnetworks sought to appoint its preferred candidate as the IDF's new chief of staff and, ultimately, to shape Israel's national security policy. Still, members of the security network do exhibit uniformity in the preponderance of Israel's security over all other considerations and in the pivotal role accorded to the security sector (particularly the IDF) in determining the state's security needs and interests. This can be seen in the strong support the security network lends to the security sector and to its budgetary requirements. In sum, while members of Israel's security network are sometimes divided over concrete policies, and while there are disagreements and even bitter rivalries between them, they are united in their unequivocal support of what they regard as the cornerstone of the Israeli state.

Above all, these conclusions suggest that the Israeli case is marked by considerable continuity on both the domestic and external levels, particularly from 1967 onward. Again as mentioned in the various chapters of the book, this is closely connected to the long history of existential threats that in the 1950s contributed to the adoption of an offensive–defensive military strategy to defend Israel against all the real and imagined threats that have encountered it. This means particularly and significantly that basic structures, intersystems and interorganizational relations, strategies, and policies in major areas of the polity persist for years, and even decades. All these are pronounced, publicized, and intentionally carried on from one government to another despite domestic political, social, and economic changes, and notwithstanding major external (i.e., regional and international) developments and challenges.

In some cases, such as the Palestinian Territories and Lebanon, these policies have persisted for long periods of time despite their considerable costs. While this continuity can be lauded in a volatile region such as the present-day Middle East, it does have significant drawbacks. In particular, decisions regarding Israel's ultimate identity and many interconnected factors, such as its borders, main social-economic policies, and budgets, are constantly delayed, and Israel's civil society remains weak, fragmented, and thus highly ineffective.

When comparing our main findings in the Israeli case to the four additional cases that have been discussed in Chapter 6 – South Korea, Taiwan, South Africa, and Singapore – several important conclusions can be drawn.

First, despite the fact that these five states differ in their size and population, they have experienced quite similar security predicaments. Indeed, all of these states have faced actual and perceived continuous domestic or external, or both, existential threats that have had a significant impact on these states' regimes in general, on their civilian and security sectors in particular, as well as on the relationship between these sectors. The perception of continuous existential threats to these states was sustained by their security sectors and widely disseminated in order to influence their citizens, especially over the long term. The inclusion of these five states in the category of continuously threatened small states is, thus, justified.

Second, important consequences of the continuous existential threats facing these states have been the considerable power acquired by their security sector and the blurring of the boundaries between the security and civilian sectors. This often resulted in the emergence of security networks composed of acting and retired security officials and actors operating in various civilian spheres, such as the cultural, educational, social, political, and economic ones. These security networks, whose exact nature varies in degree from case to case, are nevertheless similar in their considerable, and at times dominant, influence over security matters and also over utterly civilian issues. Also, because of the existential threats facing the state and the fact that the political system is not fully democratic, these arrangements and positions are accepted by many people in these states, including in Israel.

Third, the process whereby security networks were created in these five continuously threatened small states has been markedly different. In Israel, for example, as noted earlier, the security network, which had existed in embryonic form already during the pre-state period, developed in the first decades after independence and became fully blown in the wake of the 1967 War. Moreover, during most of the period, the acting and retired security officials in Israel's security network, rather than their civilian allies, played the major role. In Singapore, by contrast, civilian–military fusion emanated from the civilian government and not from the military (Huxley 1993: 19), and the country's civilian leaders managed to retain effective control of the security sector despite the latter's growing power. This factor, in turn, may account for Singapore's prudent national security policy: It has refrained from naming its enemies, and its defense budget is a fixed percent of its Gross Domestic Product (GDP), a factor that prevents the security sector from amplifying security threats to receive additional resources and at the same time turns this sector itself into a stakeholder in the state's economic success (Yong 2001). A different trajectory from that in Singapore can be observed in South Korea and Taiwan, where long periods of military rule resulted in the expansion of informal connections and ties among security officials and between them and civilian actors into the state's civilian realms. Finally, in South Africa the security network had clear formal attributes and the security sector itself was sometimes referred to as the "security network."

Fourth, in all five cases, the dominant position of the security network, especially in the area of national security, stemmed from the securitization of civilian spheres and issues as a response to the perceived continuous existential threats facing the state. This was done mainly through the total strategies that all of these states adopted, which led to the militarization of their political system, society, economy, and public discourse, and, ultimately, resulted in even more porous boundaries between the state's security and civilian sectors.

Fifth, apart from the growing power of both the security sector and the security network in these states, the continuous existential threats facing them and the particular relationship that emerged between their civilian and security sectors have affected the nature of their regime. Three of these states – South Africa, South Korea, and Taiwan – have witnessed a transformation from an authoritarian regime to a formal democracy, but not to an effective democracy. The other two states – Israel and Singapore – have, on the other hand, exhibited a marked continuity: Israel has remained a formal democracy whereas Singapore is partially democratic. In the former group of states, democratization seems to have been related to the relative relaxation of the continuous existential threats in recent decades and the reduced critical need for actual defense by the security sector. But despite the relative declining political role of both the security sectors and the security networks, effective civilian control of the military in these states has, thus far, not been attained. In the second group of states, the decline of the continuous existential threats facing the state has not led to a transition to an effective democracy in Israel, or to a formal democracy in Singapore. This can be explained, at least in part, by examining their particular pattern of civil–security relations.

Finally, with the notable exception of Singapore throughout the period under discussion and the cases of South Korea and Taiwan in recent years, these continuously threatened small states have, for long periods of time, been characterized by the absence of robust civilian institutions capable not only of imposing effective, as opposed to formal, control over the security sector, especially the military, but also of cultivating their own political and administrative cadres. What follows is that even if the security sectors and the security networks in these states were to be weakened considerably, possibly on account of the decline of the continuous existential threats facing the state and the imposition of effective civilian control over the security sector, it is not at all clear who could fill the void.

A more general issue that can be inferred from the category of continuously threatened small states, is that the continuous existential threats, be they domestic, external, or both, facing these states since their independence, have had a considerable impact on the particular pattern of civil–security relations that emerged in each state, but these threats were also affected by this particular relationship. Indeed, in all of these states, it was the security sector, especially the military, that acquired considerable influence, and the boundaries between the security sector and the civilian sector became increasingly blurred. This was evident through the emergence of security informal networks composed of acting and retired security officials and actors operating in various civilian spheres.

The analysis in this book has clearly demonstrated that the connection between existential threats and the roles of the security sector and informal security networks and subnetworks in shaping and influencing the type and functioning of democracies is extremely complex. Hence we suggest that our analysis in this book is only an initial step for further analyses of such developments and situations in additional states that face existential threats and wish for further democratization. We hope that we supplied quite a number of initial theoretical and analytical tools for further studies of the significant questions discussed here.

These analytical tools include, first and foremost, the examination of the history of a state and its society, the development of its regime, the need to make distinctions between real and imagined existential threats facing these states, and the emergence, survival, and impacts of informal security networks. All these and additional aspects discussed in our book should be further explored and analyzed, thus contributing to the general political theory.

From the comparative perspective, we suggest that the informal security networks that emerged in these continuously threatened small states have been similar in their considerable and, at times, dominant influence not only in the area of national security but also over politics, society, the economy, and culture. Moreover, while in all of these cases the considerable power of the security sector, especially the military, initially stemmed from the need to respond to the continuous existential threats facing the state, in later stages of these states' political developments, its influential position, as well as that of the informal security networks, led to the securitization of additional civilian spheres and issues. This made the establishment of an effective democracy in these states all the more difficult.

Also from a comparative perspective, we have argued that the total strategy adopted by most of these continuously threatened small states to counter the challenges they faced has resulted, over time, in varying degrees of militarization of their culture, political system, society, economy, and public discourse. This practice, in turn, led to more porous, or even nonexistent, boundaries between the state's security and civilian sectors and between its external and domestic spheres. While some of these states have witnessed significant political change in recent years, in particular democratization, none is considered an effective democracy, and this outcome is, or so it seems, closely related to their complex civil–security relationship.

On the more general theoretical level, we have shown that traditional theories of civil–military relations, which were formulated in and about Western democracies (most particularly the United States) in the period of the Cold War, are applicable to Israel and other similar cases only in a very limited way. This is not because the underlying premise of these theories that war is a political instrument and therefore the military should be under effective civilian control has become obsolete. This principle is as important today as it was when these theories were first formulated. The problem is that in democratic, democratizing, and partially democratic non-Western states, especially those that face severe security threats, the means that are prescribed for different public policies intended to attain this goal are sometimes counterproductive. This is because in these states both the political system and civil society are generally weak in comparison to the security sector, which presents itself as the state's foremost protector against the threats to its secure existence. This enables the security sector to avert effective civilian control and to penetrate into the civilian sphere, regardless of whether civilian control of the security sector is supposed to be attained through institutional or informal, including cultural, means.

The result of this penetration is the creation of informal security networks that further obstruct effective civilian control of the security sector, especially the military. Some of the new states in Asia, the Balkans, and the former Soviet Union can be mentioned in this context. Additional research is needed to determine the nature of the security networks that have emerged in these states, as well as to explore the possible interplay between the emergence and persistence of these security networks and the partial or nondemocratic regimes in these states.

To conclude, this book has identified the informal security network that emerged in Israel, and its domestic and external impacts, and then juxtaposed it to similar phenomena in other continuously threatened small states. It is our hope that this study will encourage scholars, policymakers, and also the general public to pay more attention to these and other informal aspects of the relationship between the state's civilian and security spheres, which, despite their critical importance, have only recently begun to receive the attention they deserve.

Bibliography

Abulof, Uriel. 2009. "'Small Peoples': The Existential Uncertainty of Ethnonational Communities." *International Studies Quarterly* 53: 227–48.

Achary. N.d. "The Achary Project: A Preparation Course for a Meaningful Service in the IDF." At: http://w2.kfarolami.org.il/Site/Dormitory/EduSupervision/Sport/achary+army.htm (Accessed December 7, 2010) [Hebrew].

Adler, Emanuel. 1997. "The Emergence of Cooperation: National Epistemic Communities and the International Evolution of the Idea of Nuclear Arms Control." In *Knowledge, Power and International Policy Coordination*, ed. Peter Haas, pp. 101–45. Columbia, SC: University of South Carolina Press.

2005. *Communitarian International Relations: The Epistemic Foundations of International Relations*. New York: Routledge.

Alagappa, Muthia, ed. 2001. *Coercion and Governance: The Declining Political Role of the Military in Asia*. Stanford, CA: Stanford University Press.

Aldrich, Howard E., and Catherine Zimmer. 1986. *Entrepreneurship through Social Networks*. Urbana-Champaign: University of Illinois at Urbana-Champaign's Academy for Entrepreneurial Leadership Historical Research Reference in Entrepreneurship, at: http://papers.ssrn.com/sol3/papers.cfm?abstract_id=1497761 (Accessed May 29, 2012).

Amstrup, Niels. 1976. "The Perennial Problem of Small States: A Survey of Research Efforts." *Cooperation and Conflict* 11 (3): 163–82.

Anderson, Benedict. 1991. *Imagined Communities*. 2nd ed. New York: Verso.

Anderson, Lisa. 1987. "The State in the Middle East and North Africa." *Comparative Politics* 20 (1): 1–18.

Arian, Asher. 1999–2003. *Israeli Public Opinion on National Security, 1999–2003*. Tel Aviv: Jaffee Center for Strategic Studies, Tel Aviv University.

Attorney General Elyakim Rubinstein. 2001. "Opinion–The Sharon–Ben-Gal–Gosinsky Affair." At: http://www.news1.co.il/Archive/004-D-176-00.html (Accessed February 21, 2011) [Hebrew].

Avant, Deborah. 2000. "From Mercenary to Citizen Armies: Explaining Change in the Practice of War." *International Organization* 54 (1): 41–72.

2005. *The Market for Force*. Cambridge: Cambridge University Press.

Ayalon, Ami. 2003. "A Shattered Dream: An Analysis of the Israeli-Palestinian Peace Process. In *The Collapse of the Oslo Process and the Violent Israeli-Palestinian Conflict*, ed. Yaacov Bar-Siman-Tov, pp. 5–12. Jerusalem: Leonard Davis Institute for International Relations, The Hebrew University of Jerusalem [Hebrew].

Aydinli, Ersel. 2009. "A Paradigmatic Shift for the Turkish Generals and an End to the Coup Era in Turkey." *Middle East Journal* 63 (4): 581–96.

2011. "Ergenekon, New Pacts, and the Decline of the Turkish 'Inner State'." *Turkish Studies* 12 (2): 227–39.

Baehr, Peter. 1975. "Small States: A Tool for Analysis." *World Politics* 27 (3): 456–66.

Barak, Oren. 2009. *The Lebanese Army: A National Institution in a Divided Society*. Albany: State University of New York Press.

2010. "Ambiguity and Conflict in Israeli-Lebanese Relations." *Israel Studies* 15 (3): 163–88.

2011. "Studying Middle Eastern Militaries: Where Do We Go from Here?" *International Journal of Middle East Studies* 43 (3): 406–7.

Barak, Oren, and Chanan Cohen. 2006. *The Future of Israel's Ministry of Foreign Affairs*. Jerusalem: Leonard Davis Institute for International Relations, The Hebrew University of Jerusalem [Hebrew].

Barak, Oren, and Gabriel Sheffer. 2006. "Israel's 'Security Network' and Its Impact: An Exploration of a New Approach." *International Journal of Middle East Studies* 38 (2): 235–61.

2007. "The Study of Civil-Military Relations in Israel: Traditional Approaches, Gaps, and a New Approach." *Israel Studies* 12 (1): 1–27.

2009a. Eds. *Existential Threats and Civil-Security Relations*. Lanham, MD: Lexington Books.

2009b. "Introduction." In *Existential Threats and Civil-Security Relations*, eds. Oren Barak and Gabriel Sheffer, pp. 1–16. Lanham, MD: Lexington Books.

2010. Eds. *Militarism and Israeli Society*. Bloomington: Indiana University Press.

Barak, Oren, and Eyal Tsur. 2012. "The Military Careers and Second Careers of Israel's Military Elite." *Middle East Journal* 66 (3): 1–20.

Barakat, Cherbel R. 2011. *Madameek: A Struggle for Peace in a Zone of War*. Bloomington, IN: AuthorHouse.

Barany, Zoltan. 2009. "Building Democratic Armies." In *Is Democracy Exportable*, eds. Zoltan Barany and Robert G. Moser, pp. 178–204. Cambridge: Cambridge University Press.

Barnett, Michael N. 1996. "The Politics of Uniqueness: the Status of the Israel Case." In *Israel in Comparative Perspective: Challenging the Conventional Wisdom*, ed. Michael N. Barnett, pp. 3–25. Albany: State University of New York Press.

Bar-Or, Amir, and Karl Haltiner. 2009. "Democratic Control of the Armed Forces in Israel and Switzerland in Times of Security Threats." In *Existential Threats and Civil-Security Relations*, eds. Oren Barak and Gabriel Sheffer, pp. 153–78. Lanham, MD: Lexington Books.

Bar-Siman-Tov, Yaacov. 1980. *The Israeli-Egyptian War of Attrition*. New York: Columbia University Press.

Bar-Siman-Tov, Yaacov, ed. 2003. *The Collapse of the Oslo Process and the Violent Israeli-Palestinian Conflict*. Jerusalem: Leonard Davis Institute for International Relations, The Hebrew University of Jerusalem [Hebrew].

Bar-Tal, Daniel, Eran Halperin, and Tamir Magal. 2009. "The Paradox of Security Views in Israel: A Social-psychological Explanation." In *Existential Threats and Civil-Security Relations*, eds. Oren Barak and Gabriel Sheffer, pp. 219–48. Lanham, MD: Lexington Books.

Bar-Zohar, Michael. 1975. *Ben-Gurion*. 3 vols. Tel Aviv: Am Oved [Hebrew].

Bäumel, Yair. 2007. *A Blue and White Shadow: Israeli Establishment Policy and Actions among Its Arab Citizens, 1958–1968*. Haifa: Pardes [Hebrew].

Bechtol, Bruce. 2005. "Civil Military Relations in the Republic of Korea: Background and Implications." *Korea Observer* 36 (4): 603–30.

Ben-Ari, Eyal, Zeev Rosenhek, and Daniel Maman. 2001. "Military, State and Society in Israel: An Introductory Essay." In *The Military, State and Society in Israel*, eds. Daniel Maman, Eyal Ben-Ari, and Zeev Rosenhek, pp. 1–39. New Brunswick, NJ: Transaction.

Ben-Eliezer, Uri. 1995. "A Nation-in-Arms: State, Nation, and Militarism in Israel's First Years." *Comparative Studies in Society and History* 37: 264–85.

　　1997. "Rethinking the Civil-Military Relations Paradigm: The Inverse Relation between Militarism and Praetorianism through the Example of Israel." *Comparative Political Studies* 30 (3): 356–74.

　　1998. *The Making of Israeli Militarism*. Bloomington: Indiana University Press.

　　2000. "Do the Generals Rule Israel?" In *A Society in the Mirror*, ed. Hanna Herzog, pp. 235–67. Tel Aviv: Ramot [Hebrew].

　　2004. "Post-Modern Armies and the Question of Peace and War: The Israeli Defense Forces in the 'New Times.'" *International Journal of Middle East Studies* 36 (1): 49–70.

Ben-Meir, Yehuda. 1995. *Civil-Military Relations in Israel*. New York: Columbia University Press.

Benvenisti, Meron. 2007. *Son of the Cypresses: Memories, Reflections, and Regrets from a Political Life*. Berkeley: University of California Press.

Berent, Moshe. 2010. "The Ethnic Democracy Debate: How Unique is Israel?" *Nations and Nationalism* 16 (4): 657–74.

Bergman, Ronen, and Gil Meltzer. 2003. *The Yom Kippur War*. Tel Aviv: Yedioth Ahronoth [Hebrew].

Betts, Richard. 2009. "Are Civil-Military Relations Still a Problem?" In *American Civil-Military Relations: The Soldier and the State in a New Era*, eds. Suzanne C. Nielsen and Don M. Snider, pp. 11–41. Baltimore: The Johns Hopkins University Press.

Bialer, Uri. 1990. *Between East and West: Israel's Foreign Policy Orientation, 1948–1956*. Cambridge: Cambridge University Press.

Bichler, Shimshon, and Jonathan Nitzan. 2001. *From War Profits to Peace Dividends*. Jerusalem: Carmel [Hebrew].

Bland, Douglas. 2001. "Patterns in Liberal Democratic Civil-Military Relations." *Armed Forces & Society* 27 (4): 525–40.

Brecher, Michael. 1972. *The Foreign Policy System of Israel: Setting, Images, Process*. New Haven: Yale University Press.

Breznitz, Dan. 2005. "Collaborative Public Space in a National Innovation System: A Case Study of the Israeli Military's Impact on the Software Industry." *Industry and Innovation* 12 (1): 31–64.

　　2007. *Innovation and the State: Political Choice and Strategies for Growth in Israel, Taiwan, and Ireland*. New Haven: Yale University Press.

Bruneau, Thomas C. 2006. "Introduction." In *Who Guards the Guardians and How: Democratic Civil-Military Relations*, eds. Thomas C. Bruneau and Scott T. Tollefson, pp. 1–14. Austin: University of Texas Press.

Burk, James. 2002. "Theories of Democratic Civil-Military Relations." *Armed Forces & Society* 29 (1): 7–29.

Burt, Ronald. 1982. *Structural Holes*. New York: Academic Press.

    2001. "The Social Capital of Structural Holes." In *New Directions in Economic Sociology*, eds. Mauro Guillen, Randall Collins, Paula England, and Marshall Meyer. New York: Russell Sage Foundation.

Buzan, Barry, Ole Wæver, and Japp De Wilde. 1998. *Security*. Boulder: Lynne Rienner.

Cawthra, Gavin. 2003. "Security Transformation in Post-Apartheid South Africa." In *Governing Insecurity*, eds. Gavin Cawthra and Robin Luckham, pp. 31–56. London: Zed.

Cawthra, Gavin, and Robin Luckham, eds. 2003. *Governing Insecurity: Democratic Control of Military and Security*. London: Zed.

Cha, Victor. 2001. "Strategic Culture and the Military Modernization of South Korea." *Armed Forces & Society* 28 (1): 99–127.

Chang, Felix. 2003. "In Defense of Singapore." *Orbis* 47 (1): 107–23.

Chen-Shany, Shmuel. 2002. *From the Battlefield to the Negotiation Table*. Tel Aviv: Maarachot [Hebrew].

Choi, Seung-Whan, and Patrick James. 2008. "Civil-Military Structure, Political Communication, and the Democratic Peace." *Journal of Peace Research* 45 (1): 37–53.

Clifford, Mark. 1994. *Troubled Tiger: Businessmen, Bureaucrats and Generals in South Korea*. New York: M. E. Sharpe.

Clough, Ralph. 1998. "The Enduring Influence of the Republic of China on Taiwan Today." In *Contemporary Taiwan*, ed. David Shambaugh, pp. 10–27. Oxford: Clarendon.

Cock, Jacklyn, and Laurie Nathan. Eds. 1989. *War and Society*. Cape Town: David Phillip.

Cohen, Avner. 1998. *Israel and the Bomb*. New York: Columbia University Press.

Cohen, Eliot. 2002. *Supreme Command: Soldiers, Statesmen, and Leadership in Wartime*. New York: The Free Press.

Cohen, Hillel. 2010. *Good Arabs: The Israeli Security Agencies and the Israeli Arabs, 1948–1967*. Berkeley: University of California Press.

Cohen, Stuart. 1995. "Small States and Their Armies: Restructuring the Militia Framework of the Israel Defence Force." *Journal of Strategic Studies* 18 (4): 78–93.

    2008. *Israel and Its Army: From Cohesion to Confusion*. London: Routledge.

Cohen, Yoram, and Jeffrey White. 2009. *Hamas in Combat: The Military Performance of the Palestinian Islamic Resistance Movement*. Washington, DC: The Washington Institute for New East Policy. At: http://washingtoninstitute.org/pubPDFs/PolicyFocus97.pdf (Accessed August, 18, 2011).

Cordesman, Anthony H., and William D. Sullivan. 2007. *Lessons of the 2006 Israeli-Hezbollah War*. Washington, DC: Center for Strategic and International Studies.

Croissant, Aurel. 2004. "Riding the Tiger: Civilian Control and the Military in Democratizing Korea." *Armed Forces & Society* 30 (3): 357–82.

Croissant, Aurel, and David Kuehn. 2009. "Patterns of Civilian Control of the Military in East Asia's New Democracies." *Journal of East Asian Studies* 9: 187–217.

Croissant, Aurel, David Kuehn, Paul Chambers, and Siegfried O. Wolf. 2010. "Beyond the Fallacy of Coup-ism: Conceptualizing Civilian Control of the Military in Emerging Democracies." *Democratization* 17 (5): 950–75.

da Cunha, Derek. 1999. "Sociological Aspects of the Singapore Armed Forces." *Armed Forces & Society* 25 (3): 459–75.

2002. "Defence and Security: Evolving Threat Perceptions." In *Singapore in the New Millennium*, ed. Derek da Cunha, pp. 133–53. Singapore: Institute of Southeast Asian Studies.

Dahan-Kalev, Henriette, and Udi Lebel. 2004. "Security and Education: Generals as Israeli School Managers." *Politika* 11–12: 27–40 [Hebrew].

David, Steven R. 2009. "Existential Threats to Israel." In *Contemporary Israel: Domestic Politics, Foreign Policy and Security Challenges*, ed. Robert O. Freedman, pp. 299–316. Boulder, CO: Westview.

Davis, Eric. 1991. "Theorizing Statecraft and Social Change in Oil-Producing Countries." In *Statecraft in the Middle East: Oil, Historical Memory, and Popular Culture*, eds. Eric Davis and Nicholas Gavrielides, pp. 122–31. Miami: Florida International University Press.

Dayan, Moshe. 1976. *Story of My Life*. Tel Aviv: Dvir [Hebrew].

1981. *Shall the Sword Devour Forever?* Jerusalem: Edanim [Hebrew].

Defense Update Business Report. 2010. "Israel's Defense Exports Soar to $6.75 Billion in 2009." *Defense Update Business Report*. At: http://www.worldaffairsboard. com/international-defense-topics/54345-israels-defense-exports-soar-6–75-billion-2009-a.html (Accessed December 1, 2010).

Desch, Michael. 1996. "Threat Environments and Military Missions." In *Civil-Military Relations and Democracy*, eds. Larry Diamond and Marc F. Plattner, pp. 12–29. Baltimore: The Johns Hopkins University Press.

1999. *Civilian Control of the Military: The Changing Security Environment*. Baltimore: The Johns Hopkins University Press.

2009. "Liberalism and the New Definition of 'Existential' Threats." In *Existential Threats and Civil-Security Relations*, eds. Oren Barak and Gabriel Sheffer, pp. 37–60. Lanham, MD: Lexington Books.

Diamond, Larry. 2001. "How Democratic Is Taiwan? Five Key Challenges to Democratic Consolidation." At: http://www.stanford.edu/~ldiamond/papers/ taiwan.pdf (Accessed May 12, 2011).

Dowty, Alan. 1998. *The Jewish State*. Berkeley: University of California Press.

Dvir, D. and A. Tishler. 2000. "The Changing Role of the Defense Industry in Israel's Industrial and Technological Development." *Defense Analysis* 16: 33–52.

Eilam, Uzi. 2009. *Eilam's Arc: Advanced Technology, the Secret of Israeli Strength*. Tel Aviv: Yedioth Ahronoth [Hebrew].

Eisenhower, Dwight. 1961. "Farewell Radio and Television Address to the American People." At: http://www.presidency.ucsb.edu/ws/index.php?pid=12086 (Accessed December 14, 2010).

Eisenstadt, S. N. 1967. *Israeli Society*. London: Weidenfeld & Nicolson.

1985. *The Transformation of Israeli Society*. Boulder, CO: Westview.

Eitan, Raphael. 1985. *Story of a Soldier*. Tel Aviv: Maariv [Hebrew].

Elman, Miriam. 1995. "The Foreign Policies of Small States: Challenging Neo-Realism in Its Own Backyard." *British Journal of Political Science* 25 (2): 171–217.

Elran, Meir. 2010. *The Carmel Fire: Another Opportunity to Build a Strategy of Preparedness for the Civilian Front.* Tel Aviv: Institute for National Security Studies. At: http://www.inss.org.il/upload/(FILE)1292169211.pdf (Accessed June 29, 2011) [Hebrew].

Enloe, Cynthia. 1980. *Ethnic Soldiers.* Athens: University of Georgia Press.

Erez, Ram. 2009. *The Politics of Innovation: Networks as an Arena for Change in Israel's Security Policy: The Cases of the Lavi and the Arrow.* Ph.D.diss. Jerusalem: The Hebrew University of Jerusalem [Hebrew].

Erlich, Reuven. 1997. "The Conception of the Security Zone and Its Ability to Pass the Test of Reality." In *The Security Zone in Lebanon*, ed. Yaacov Bar-Siman-Tov, pp. 9–28. Jerusalem: Leonard Davis Institute for International Relations, The Hebrew University of Jerusalem [Hebrew].

Evans, Peter, Dietrich Rueschmeyer, and Theda Skocpol, eds. 1985. *Bringing the State Back In.* Cambridge: Cambridge University Press.

Evron, Yair. 1987. *War and Intervention in Lebanon.* London: Croom Helm.

Eyal, Gil. 2002. "Dangerous Liaisons between Military Intelligence and Middle Eastern Studies in Israel." *Theory and Society* 31: 653–93.

Feaver, Peter D. 2005. *Armed Servants. Agency, Oversight, and Civil-Military Relations.* Cambridge, MA: Harvard University Press.

Feaver, Peter D., and Erika Seeler. 2009. "Before and After Huntington: The Methodological Maturing of Civil-Military Studies." In *American Civil-Military Relations: The Soldier and the State in a New Era*, eds. Suzanne C. Nielsen and Don M. Snider, pp. 72–90. Baltimore: The Johns Hopkins University Press.

Finer, Samuel. 1962. *The Man on Horseback: The Role of the Military in Politics.* London: Pall Mall.

1975. "State- and Nation-Building in Europe: The Role of the Military." In *The Formation of National States in Western Europe*, ed. Charles Tilly, pp. 84–163. Princeton: Princeton University Press.

Folman, Yeshayahu. 2004. *The Story of the Security Fence.* Jerusalem, Carmel [Hebrew].

Foucault, Michel. 1979. *Discipline and Punish.* Trans. Alan Sheridan. New York: Vintage Books.

Frankel, Philip. 1984. *Pretoria's Praetorians.* Cambridge: Cambridge University Press.

Fravel, Taylor. 2002. "Towards Civilian Supremacy: Civil-Military Relations in Taiwan's Democratization." *Armed Forces & Society* 29 (1): 57–84.

Freedom House. 2010. "Combined Average Ratings – Independent Countries." 2010 edition, at: http://www.freedomhouse.org/template.cfm?page=546&year=2010 (Accessed November 5, 2010).

2011. "Freedom in the World 2011." At: http://www.freedomhouse.org/images/File/fiw/Tables%2C%20Graphs%2C%20etc%2C%20FIW%202011_Revised%20I_11_11.pdf (Accessed April 2, 2011).

Freilich, Charles D. 2006. "National Security Decision-Making in Israel: Processes, Pathologies, and Strengths." *Middle East Journal* 60 (4): 635–63.

Galant, Yoav. 2007. *The Strategic Challenge of Gaza.* Jerusalem: Jerusalem Center for Public Affairs. At: http://www.jcpa.org/JCPA/Templates/ShowPage.asp?DBID=1&LNGID=1&TMID=111&FID=253&PID=0&IID=1549 (Accessed April 19, 2011) [Hebrew].

Gavison, Ruth. 1999. "Jewish and Democratic? A Rejoinder to the 'Ethnic Democracy' Debate." *Israel Studies* 4 (1): 44–72.

Gazit, Orit. 2011. *Betrayal, Morality and Transnationalism: Identity Construction Processes of the 'South Lebanese Army' in Israel since May 2000*. Ph.D. diss. Jerusalem: The Hebrew University of Jerusalem [Hebrew].

Gazit, Shlomo. 2003. *Trapped Fools: Thirty Years of Israeli Policy in the Territories*. London: Frank Cass.

Gelber, Yoav. 1986. *The Emergence of a Jewish Army*. Jerusalem: Yad Ben-Zvi [Hebrew].

1992. *Growing a Fleur-de-lis*. Tel Aviv: Ministry of Defense [Hebrew].

Gellner, Ernest. 1983. *Nations and Nationalism*. Oxford: Blackwell.

Gibson, Christopher, and Don Snider. 1999. "Civil-Military Relations and the Potential to Influence: A Look at the National Security Decision-Making Process." *Armed Forces & Society* 25 (2): 193–218.

Gledenhuys, Deon. 1990. *Isolated States*. Cambridge: Cambridge University Press.

Gluska, Ami. 2004. *Eshkol, Give the Order!* Tel Aviv: Maarachot [Hebrew].

Golani, Motti. 1997. *There Will Be War Next Summer*. Tel Aviv: Maarachot [Hebrew].

2001. "Chief of Staff in Quest of a War: Moshe Dayan Leads Israel into War." *Journal of Strategic Studies* 24: 49–70.

2002. *Wars Don't Just Happen*. Ben-Shemen: Modan [Hebrew].

Goldstein, Yossi. 2003. *Eshkol – Biography*. Jerusalem: Keter [Hebrew].

Gonzalez, Michael. 2002. "Making the Nuclear Choice: Strategic and Regional Factors in State Acquisition of Nuclear Weapons." *International Affairs Review* 11 (2): 38–53.

Gorenberg, Gershom. 2006. *The Accidental Empire: Israel and the Birth of the Settlements, 1967–1977*. New York: Times Books.

Graham, Norman. 1991. "The Role of the Military in the Political and Economic Development of the Republic of Korea." In *Civil Military Interaction in Asia and Africa*, eds. Charles H. Kennedy and David J. Louscher, pp. 114–31. Leiden: Brill.

Greenberg, Joel. 1997. "Israelis Turn Military Skills into Software Export Boom." *New York Times on the Web,*. At: http://www.nytimes.com/library/cyber/week/081897ware.html (Accessed December 14, 2010).

Griffiths, Robert. 1991. "The South African Military: The Dilemmas of Increased Influence in Decision Making." In *Civil military Interaction in Asia and Africa*, eds. Charles H. Kennedy and David J. Louscher, pp. 76–95. Leiden: Brill.

2010. "Democratizing Civil-Military Relations in South Africa: A Blueprint for Post-Conflict Reform?" In *War and Peace in Africa: History, Nationalism, and the State*, eds. Toyin Falola and Raphael C. Njoku, pp. 583–97. Durham, NC: Carolina Academic Press.

Grundy, Kenneth. 1988. *The Militarization of South African Politics*. Oxford: Oxford University Press.

Gur, Mordechai. 1998. *Chief of the General Staff*. Tel Aviv: Maarachot [Hebrew].

Haas, Peter. 1990. *Saving the Mediterranean: The Politics of International Environmental Cooperation*. New York: Columbia University Press.

1997. "Introduction: Epistemic Communities and International Policy Coordination." In *Knowledge, Power and International Policy Coordination*, ed. Peter Haas, pp. 1–35. Columbia, SC: University of South Carolina Press.

Hadar, Yael. 2009. "The Israeli Public's Trust of the State's Institution in the Last Decade." *Parliament* 63, at: http://www.idi.org.il/Parliament/2009/Pages/2009_63/B/b_63.aspx (Accessed December 14, 2010) [Hebrew].

al-Haj, Majid, and Uri Ben-Eliezer, eds. 2003. *In the Name of Security*. Haifa: Haifa University Press [Hebrew].

Hamizrachi, Beate. 1988. *The Emergence of the South Lebanon Security Belt*. New York: Praeger.

Hamizrachi, Yoram. n.d. "Memoirs." At: http://www.blabla4u.com/sites/blabla4u/ShowMessage-eng.asp?LangCode=Heb&ID=2533920 (Accessed February 3, 2011) [Hebrew].

Handel, Michael. 1981. *Weak States in the International System*. London: Frank Cass.

   1994. "The Evolution of Israeli Strategy: The Psychology of Insecurity and the Quest for Absolute Security." In *The Making of Strategy: Rulers, States, and War*, eds. Williamson Murray, MacGregor Knox, and Alvin H. Bernstein, pp. 534–78. Cambridge: Cambridge University Press.

Harkavy, Robert. 1977. "The Pariah State Syndrome." *ORBIS* 21 (3): 623–49.

   1981. "Pariah States and Nuclear Proliferation." *International Organization* 35 (1): 135–63.

Heichal, Gabriella. 1998. *Civil Control over the Israel Defense Forces*. Jerusalem: Ariel [Hebrew].

Heller, Patrick. 2000. "Degrees of Democracy: Some Comparative Lessons from India." *World Politics* 52: 484–519.

Henriksen, Thomas. 2001. "The Rise and Decline of Rogue States." *Journal of International Affairs* 54 (2): 349–73.

Hickey, Dennis. 2001. *The Armies of East Asia*. London: Lynne Rienner.

Hirschfeld, Yair. 2000. *Oslo: A Formula for Peace*. Tel Aviv: Am Oved [Hebrew].

Hobsbawm, Eric. 1990. *Nations and Nationalism since 1780*. Cambridge: Cambridge University Press.

Horovitz, David. 1996. *Shalom, Friend: The Life and Legacy of Yitzhak Rabin*. New York: New Market Press.

Horowitz, Dan. 1982. "The Israel Defense Forces: A Civilianized Military in a Partially Militarized Society." In *Soldiers, Peasants, and Bureaucrats*, eds. Roman Kolkowicz and Andrzej Korbonski, pp. 77–106. London: Allen & Unwin.

   1993. *The Heavens and the Earth: A Self-Portrait of the 1948 Generation*. Jerusalem: Keter [Hebrew].

Horowitz, Dan, and Moshe Lissak. 1977. *The Origins of the Israeli Polity*. Tel Aviv: Am Oved [Hebrew].

   1989. *Trouble in Utopia: The Overburdened Polity of Israel*. Albany: State University of New York Press.

Horowitz, Donald. 1985. *Ethnic Groups in Conflict*. Berkeley: University of California Press.

Huntington, Samuel. 1957. *The Soldier and the State: The Theory and Politics of Civil-Military Relations*. Cambridge, MA: Harvard University Press.

   1968. *Political Order in Changing Societies*. New Haven, CT: Yale University Press.

   1996. "Reforming Civil-Military Relations." In *Civil-Military Relations and Democracy*, eds. Larry Diamond and Marc F. Plattner, pp. 3–11. Baltimore: The Johns Hopkins University Press.

Huxley, Tim. 1993. *The Political Role of the Singapore Armed Forces' Officer Corps*. Canberra: Strategic and Defence Studies Center, Australian National University.

2000. *Defending the Lion City*. St. Leonards, N.S.W.: Allen & Unwin.

Im, Hyug Baeg. 2004. "Faltering Democratic Consolidation in South Korea: Democracy at the End of the 'Three Kims' Era." *Democratization* 11 (5): 179–98.

Inbar, Efraim, and Gabriel Sheffer, eds. 1997. *The National Security of Small States in a Changing World*. London: Frank Cass.

Ingebritsen, Christine Iver Neumann, Sieglinde Gstohl, and Jessica Beyer, eds. 2006. *Small States International Relations*. Seattle: University of Washington Press.

International Crisis Group. 2010. *Loose Ends: Iraq's Security Forces between U.S. Drawdown and Withdrawal*. At: http://www.crisisgroup.org/en/regions/middle-east-north-africa/iraq-syria-lebanon/iraq/099-loose-ends-iraqs-security-forces-be-tween-us-drawdown-and-withdrawal.aspx (Accessed March 29, 2011).

Ish-Shalom, Piki. 2006. "Theory as a Hermeneutical Mechanism: The Democratic-Peace Thesis and the Politics of Democratization." *European Journal of International Relations* 12 (4): 565–98.

Israel Diplomatic Network. N.d. "Israel's Security & Safety Industries." At: http://sofia.mfa.gov.il/mfm/Data/70481.doc (Accessed December 14, 2010).

Janowitz, Morris. 1960. *The Professional Soldier: A Social and Political Portrait*. Glencoe, IL: The Free Press.

1977. *Military Institutions and Coercion in the Developing Nations*. Chicago: University of Chicago Press.

Jinsok, Jun. 2001. "South Korea: Consolidating Democratic Civilian Control." In *Coercion and Governance*, ed. Muthia Alagappa, pp. 121–142. Stanford, CA: Stanford University Press.

Johnson, Chalmers. 2004. *The Sorrows of Empire*. New York: Metropolitan Books.

Kanaaneh, Rodha Ann. 2009. *Surrounded: Palestinian Soldiers in the Israeli Military*. Stanford, CA: Stanford University Press.

Kaufman, Asher. 2002. "Who Owns the Shebaa Farms? Chronicle of a Territorial Dispute." *Middle East Journal* 56 (4): 576–96.

Kaya, Serdar. 2009. "The Rise and Decline of the Turkish 'Deep State': The Ergenekon Case." *Insight Turkey* 11 (4): 99–113.

Keohane, Robert. 1969. "Lilliputians Dilemmas: Small States in International Politics." *International Organization* 23 (2): 291–310.

Kerbs, Gil. 2007. "The Unit." *Forbes.Com*. At: http://www.forbes.com/2007/02/07/israel-military-unit-ventures-biz-cx_gk_0208israel.html (Accessed January 20, 2011).

Kimmerling, Baruch. 1993. "Patterns of Militarism in Israel." *European Journal of Sociology* 34:196–223.

Knesset Research and Information Center. 2011. *The "Galei Zahal" Station: Various Aspects of its Activity*. Jerusalem: Knesset Research and Information Center, at: http://www.knesset.gov.il/mmm/data/pdf/m02853.pdf (Accessed June 22, 2011) [Hebrew].

Knoke, David. 1990. *Political Networks*. Cambridge: Cambridge University Press.

Kohn, Richard. 2002. "The Erosion of Civilian Control of the Military in the United States Today." *Naval War College Review* 55 (3): 9–59.

2009. "The Danger of Militarization in an Endless 'War' on Terrorism." *Journal of Military History* 73 (1): 177–208.

Krebs, Ronald. 2006. *Fighting for Rights: Military Service and the Politics of Citizenship*. Ithaca, NY: Cornell University Press.

Kuehn, David. 2008. "Democratization and Civilian Control of the Military in Taiwan." *Democratization* 15 (5): 870–890.

Lake, David A., and Donald Rothchild. 1998. "Spreading Fear: The Genesis of Transnational Ethnic Conflict." In *The International Spread of Ethnic Conflict*, eds. David A. Lake and Donald Rothchild, pp. 3–32. Princeton: Princeton University Press.

Lasswell, Harold. 1941. "The Garrison State." *American Journal of Sociology* 46 (4): 455–68.

Ledbetter, James. 2011. *Unwarranted Influence: Dwight D. Eisenhower and the Military-Industrial Complex*. New Haven, CT: Yale University Press.

Lee, Wei-chin Lee. 2007. "The Greening of the Brass: Taiwan's Civil–Military Relations since 2000." *Asian Security* 3 (3): 204–27.

Leifer, Michael. 2000. *Singapore's Foreign Policy*. London: Routledge.

Levy, Yagil. 2007. *Israel's Materialist Militarism*. Lanham, MD: Lexington Books.

2009. "Untangling the Imbroglio." *Haaretz*. At: http://www.haaretz.com/print-edition/opinion/untangling-the-imbroglio-1.2126 (Accessed March 17, 2011) [Hebrew].

2010a. *Who Governs the Military? Between Control of the Military and Control of Militarism*. Jerusalem: The Magness Press [Hebrew].

2010b. "The Second Lebanon War: Examining 'Democratization of War' Theory." *Armed Forces & Society* 36 (5): 786–803.

Liberman, Paul. 2001. "The Rise and Fall of the South African Bomb." *International Security* 26 (2): 45–86.

Lichbach, Mark. 1997. "Social Theory and Comparative Politics." In *Comparative Politics: Rationality, Culture, and Structure*, eds. Mark Lichbach and Alan Zuckerman, pp. 239–76. Cambridge: Cambridge University Press.

Liel, Alon. 1999. *Black Justice: The South African Upheaval*. Tel Aviv: Hakibutz Hameuchad [Hebrew].

Lin, Nan. 2001. "Building a Network Theory of Social Capital." In *Social Capital: Theory and Research*, eds. Lin Nan, Karen S. Cook, and Ronald S. Burt, pp. 3–29. New York: Aldine.

Lissak, Moshe. 2001. "Uniqueness and Normalization in Military-Government Relations in Israel." In *The Military, State and Society in Israel*, eds. Daniel Maman, Eyal Ben-Ari, and Zeev Rosenhek, pp. 395–422. New Brunswick, NJ: Transaction.

Lissak, Moshe, and Uri Cohen. 2010 "'Scientific Strategists' in the Period of *Mamlachtiut*: Reciprocity between the Academic Community and Political Power Centers." *Iyunim Bitkumat Israel* 20 (2010): 1–27 [Hebrew].

Lo, Chih-Cheng. 2001. "Taiwan: The Remaining Challenges." In *Coercion and Governance*, ed. Muthia Alagappa, pp. 143–161. Stanford, CA: Stanford University Press.

Luckham, A. R. 1971. "A Comparative Typology of Civil-Military Relations." *Government and Opposition* 6 (1): 5–35.

Luckham, Robin. 2003. "Democratic Strategies for Security in Transition and Conflict." In *Governing Insecurity*, eds. Gavin Cawthra and Robin Luckham, pp. 3–28. London: Zed.

Lumsky-Feder, Edna, and Eyal Ben-Ari, eds. 1999. *The Military and Militarism in Israeli Society*. Albany: State University of New York Press.

Luttwak, Edward, and Dan Horowitz. 1975. *The Israeli Army*. London: Allen Lane.

Malet, David. 2010. "Why Foreign Fighters? Historical Perspectives and Solutions." *Orbis* 54 (1): 97–114.

Maman, Daniel, and Moshe Lissak. 1996. "Military-Civilian Elite Networks in Israel: A Case Study in Boundary Daniel Structure." In *A Restless Mind*, ed. Benjamin Frankel, pp. 49–79. London: Frank Cass.

Mandel, Robert. 2002. *Armies without States: The Privatization of Security*. Boulder: Lynne Rienner.

Mann, Michael. 1986. "The Autonomous Power of the State: Its Origins, Mechanisms and Results." In *States in History*, ed. John Hall, pp. 109–36. Oxford: Blackwell.

Maoz, Zeev. 2006. *Defending the Holy Land*. Ann Arbor: Michigan University Press.

2009. "Threat Perception and Threat Manipulation: The Uses and Misuses of Threats in Israel's National Security, 1949–2008." In *Existential Threats and Civil-Security Relations*, eds. Oren Barak and Gabriel Sheffer, pp. 179–218. Lanham, MD: Lexington Books.

Margalit, Dan, and Ronen Bergman. 2011. *The Pit*. Or Yehuda: Kinneret, Zmora-Bitan, Dvir [Hebrew].

Marin, Bernd, and Renate Mayntz. 1991. "Studying Policy Networks." In *Policy Networks*, eds. Bernd Marin and Renate Mayntz, pp. 11–23. Frankfurt: Campus.

Marsh, David, and Rod Rhodes, eds. 1992. *Policy Networks in British Government*. Oxford: Oxford University Press.

Marsh, David, and Martin Smith. 2000. "Understanding Policy Networks: Towards a Dialectical Approach." *Political Studies* 48 (1): 4–21.

Marsh, David, and Gerry Stoker. 1995. "Conclusions." In *Theory and Methods in Political Science*, eds. David Marsh and Gerry Stoker, pp. 292–4. London: Macmillan.

Mauzy, Diane, and R. S. Milne. 2002. *Singapore Politics under the People's Action Party*. London: Routledge.

Mayzel, Matitiahu. 2001. *The Golan Heights Campaign*. Tel Aviv: Maarachot [Hebrew].

McVadon, Eric. 2003. "Bolstering Trust between Taiwan's Government and Military – A Two Way Process." *Issues and Studies* 39 (4): 163–8.

Michael, Kobi. 2007. "The Dilemma behind the Classical Dilemma of Civil–Military Relations: The 'Discourse Space' Model and the Israeli Case during the Oslo Process." *Armed Forces & Society* 33 (4): 518–46.

Migdal, Joel S. 1997. "Studying the State." In *Comparative Politics: Rationality, Culture, and Structure*, eds. Mark Lichbach and Alan Zuckerman, pp. 208–38. Cambridge: Cambridge University Press.

2001. *Through the Lens of Israel: Explorations in State and Society*. Albany: State University of New York Press.

Mills, C. Wright. 1956. *The Power Elite*. New York: Oxford University Press.

Mills, Greg. 1993. "Armed Forces in Post-Apartheid South Africa." *Survival* 35 (3): 78–96.

Ministry of Foreign Affairs. 2001. "Shimon Peres: Curriculum Vitae." At: http://www.mfa.gov.il/mfaheb/mfaarchive/2001/shimon_peres.htm (Accessed April 17, 2011) [Hebrew].

Mintz, Alex. 1985. "The Military-Industrial Complex: American Concepts and Israeli Realities." *Journal of Conflict Resolution* 29: 623–39.

Miro, Michael. 2004. "The Impact of the IDF on the Israeli Media." Paper presented at the Van Leer Institute in Jerusalem, Jerusalem, Israel, November 18 [Hebrew].

Mitchell, Timothy. 1991. "The Limits of the State: Beyond Statist Approaches and Their Critics." *American Political Science Review* 85: 77–96.

Moon, Chung-in and Sang-young Rhyu. 2011. "Democratic Transition, Persistent Civilian Control over the Military, and the South Korean Anomaly." *Asian Journal of Political Science* 19 (3): 250–69.

Moskos, Charles. 2000. "Towards a Postmodern Military: The United States as a Paradigm." In *The Postmodern Military*, eds. Charles Moskos, John Allen Williams, and David Segal, pp. 14–31. New York: Oxford University Press.

Mosse, George. 1990. *Fallen Soldiers*. Oxford: Oxford University Press.

Mutalib, Hussin. 2002. "The Socio-Economic Dimension in Singapore's Quest for Security and Stability." *Pacific Affairs* 75 (1): 39–56.

Narayanan, Arjunan. 1997. "Singapore's Strategy for National Survival." *Asian Defence Journal* 1: 6–16.

Nielsen, Suzanne C., and Don M. Snider, eds. 2009. *American Civil-Military Relations: The Soldier and the State in a New Era*. Baltimore: The Johns Hopkins University Press.

Oren, Amiram. 2002. "'The Order of Battle – An Assessment, 1953–1960' as a Milestone and Turning Point in Israel's Changing Defense Policy and the IDF's Enlargement in the 1950s." *Iyunim Bitkumat Israel* 12: 123–41 [Hebrew].

   2009. *'Drafted Territories': The Creation of Israeli Army Hegemony over the State's Land and Its Expanses during Its Early Years (1948–1956)*. Tel Aviv: Madaf [Hebrew].

Oren, Amiram, and Rafi Regev. 2008. *'Land in Uniform': Territory and Defense in Israel*. Jerusalem: Carmel [Hebrew].

Oren, Amiram, Oren Barak and Assaf Shapira. 2013. "'How the Mouse Got His Roar': The Shift to an 'Offensive-Defensive' Military Strategy in Israel in 1953 and its Implications." *International History Review* 35 (2): 1–21.

Ostfeld, Zehava. 1994. *An Army Is Born*. Tel Aviv: Ministry of Defense [Hebrew].

Owen, Roger. 2000. *State, Power, and Politics in the Making of the Modern Middle East*. 2nd ed. London: Routledge.

Pa'il, Meir. 1979. *From the Hagana to the Defense Forces*. Tel Aviv: Zmora Bitan Modan [Hebrew].

Pedatzur, Reuven. 1996. *The Triumph of Embarrassment: Israel and the Territories after the Six-Day War*. Tel Aviv: Yad Tabenkin–Galili Research Institute and Bitan Publishers [Hebrew].

Peled, Alon. 1998. *A Question of Loyalty: Military Manpower Politics in Multiethnic States*. Ithaca, NY: Cornell University Press.

Peres Center for Peace. N.d. "Shimon Peres." At: http://www.peres-center.org/ AboutUsheb.asp?cc=020202 (Accessed April 17, 2011) [Hebrew].

Peres, Shimon. 1978. *Tomorrow Is Now*. Jerusalem: Mabat [Hebrew].

Peri, Yoram. 1983. *Between Battles and Ballots*. Cambridge: Cambridge University Press.

   1996. "The Radical Social Scientists and Israeli Militarism." *Israel Studies* 1: 230–66.

   2002. *The Israeli Military and Israel's Palestinian Policy*. Washington, DC: United States Institute of Peace.

2003. "The Democratic Putsch of 1999." In *In the Name of Security*, eds. Majid Al-Haj and Uri Ben-Eliezer, pp. 125–44. Haifa: Haifa University Press [Hebrew].

2006. *Generals in the Cabinet Room: How the Military Shapes Israeli Policy.* Washington, DC: United States Institute of Peace Press.

2007. "Intractable Conflict and the Media." *Israel Studies* 13 (1): 79–102.

Peri, Yoram, and Amnon Neubach. 1985. *The Military-Industrial Complex in Israel: A Pilot Study.* Tel Aviv: International Center for Peace in the Middle East.

Perlmutter, Amos. 1969. *Military and Politics in Israel.* New York: Praeger.

1974. *Egypt: The Praetorian State.* New Brunswick, NJ: Transaction.

Perman, Stacy. 2005. *Spies, Inc.: Business Innovation from Israel's Masters of Espionage.* Upper Saddle River, NJ: Pearson/Prentice Hall.

Peterson, John. 2003. *Policy Networks.* Vienna: Institute for Advanced Studies.

Philips, Steven. 2006. "Identity and Security in Taiwan." *Journal of Democracy* 17 (3): 58–71.

Pion-Berlin, David. 2010. "Informal Civil-Military Relations in Latin America: Why Politicians and Soldiers Choose Unofficial Venues." *Armed Forces & Society* 36 (3): 526–44.

Polakow-Suransky, Sasha. 2010. *The Unspoken Alliance: Israel's Secret Relationship with Apartheid South Africa.* New York: Pantheon Books.

Prime Minister's Office. N.d. "Prime Minister–Curriculum Vitae." At: http://www.pmo. gov.il/PMOEng/PM/Resume (Accessed November 17, 2010).

Purkitt, Helen, and Stephan Burgess. 2005. *South Africa's Weapons of Mass Destruction.* Bloomington: Indiana University Press.

Quinlivan, James. 1999. "Coup-Proofing: Its Practice and Consequences in the Middle East." *International Security* 24 (2): 131–65.

Rabin, Yitzhak. 1996. *The Rabin Memoirs: Expanded Edition with Recent Speeches, New Photographs, and an Afterword.* Berkeley: University of California Press.

Rahim, Lily Zubaidah. 2012. "Governing Muslims in Singapore's Secular Authoritarian State." *Australian Journal of International Affairs* 66 (2): 169–85.

Randal, Jonathan C. 1983. *Going All the Way: Christian Warlords, Israeli Adventurers, and the War in Lebanon.* New York: Viking Press.

Roman, Peter J., and David W. Tarr. 1998. "The Joint Chiefs of Staff: From Service Parochialism to Jointness." *Political Science Quarterly* 113 (1): 91–111.

Ron, James. 2003. *Frontiers and Ghettos: State Violence in Serbia and Israel.* Berkeley: University of California Press.

Rosenblum, Doron. 1996. *Israeli Blues.* Tel Aviv: Am Oved [Hebrew].

Rosenhek, Zeev, Daniel Maman, and Eyal Ben-Ari. 2003. "The Study of War and the Military in Israel: An Empirical Investigation and a Reflective Critique." *International Journal of Middle East Studies* 35 (3): 461–84.

Rotberg, Robert. 1988. "The Process of Decision Making in Contemporary South Africa." In *South Africa: In Transition to What?* ed. Helen Kitchen, pp. 12–34. New York: Praeger.

Ruach Tzevet. 2009. "Guarding the Pension: The Last Mile." *Ruach Tzevet* 91 (December): 2–3 [Hebrew].

2010a. "The Change in the Linkage of the Pension: The Last Mile." *Ruach Tzevet* 92 (March): 2 [Hebrew].

2010b. "The Struggle for the Pension." *Ruach Tzevet* 93 (June): 4, 6–7 [Hebrew].

2011. "There Was No Agenda to Increase the Salaries of the Active Members at the Expense of the Pensioners" *Ruach Tzevet* 100 (March): 12–15 [Hebrew].

Salem, 'Ali. 1996. *A Journey to Israel*. Cairo: Madbuli [Arabic].

Salih, Khaled. 1996. *State-Making, Nation-Building and the Military: Iraq, 1941–1958*. Goteborg: Department of Political Science, Goteborg University.

Saxer, Carl. 2004. "Generals and Presidents: Establishing Civilian and Democratic Control in South Korea." *Armed Forces & Society* 30 (3): 383–408.

Schiff, Rebecca. 1992. "Civil-Military Relations Reconsidered: Israel as an 'Uncivil' State." *Security Studies* 1: 636–58.

1995. "Civil-Military Relations Reconsidered: A Theory of Concordance." *Armed Forces & Society* 22 (1): 7–24.

2009. *The Military and Domestic Politics: A Concordance Theory of Civil-Military Relations*. New York: Routledge.

Schiff, Zeev, and Ehud Yaari. 1984. *Israel's Lebanon War*. New York: Simon & Schuster.

Sechser, Todd S. 2004. "Are Soldiers Less War-Prone than Statesmen?" *Journal of Conflict Resolution* 48 (5): 746–74.

Seegers, Annette. 1991. "South Africa's National Security Management System, 1972–1990." *Journal of Modern African Studies* 29 (2): 253–73.

1996. *The Military in the Making of Modern South Africa*. London: Tauris.

Segal, David. 1994. "Civil-Military Relations in Democratic Societies." In *Armed Forces at the Dawn of the Third Millennium*, eds. Jurgen Kuhlmann and David Segal, pp. 37–48. Munich: Sozialwissenschaftliches Institut der Bundeswehr.

Segev, Tom. 2000. *One Palestine, Complete: Jews and Arabs under the Mandate*. New York: Henry Holt & Co.

2007. *1967: Israel, the War, and the Year that Transformed the Middle East*. New York: Metropolitan Books.

Sela, Avraham. 2007. "Civil Society, the Military, and National Security: The Case of Israel's Security Zone in South Lebanon." *Israel Studies* 13 (1): 53–78.

2009. "Difficult Dialogue: The Oslo Process in Israeli Perspective." *Macalester International* 23 (11), at: http://digitalcommons.macalester.edu/macintl/vol23/iss1/11 (Accessed April 8, 2011).

Senor, Dan, and Shaul Singer. 2009. *Start-Up Nation: The Story of Israel's Economic Miracle*. New York: Twelve.

Sharett, Moshe. 1978. *Personal Diary*. 8 vols. Tel Aviv: Maariv [Hebrew].

Sharkansky, Ira. 1999. *Ambiguity, Coping, and Governance: Israeli Experiences in Politics, Religion, and Policymaking*. Westport, CT: Praeger.

Sheffer, Gabriel. 1996a. *Moshe Sharett: Biography of a Political Moderate*. Oxford: Oxford University Press.

1996b. "Has Israel Really Been a Garrison Democracy?" *Israel Affairs* 3 (1): 13–38.

Sheffer, Gabriel, Oren Barak, and Amiram Oren. 2008. Eds. *New Approaches to Israel's Civil-Security Relationship*. Jerusalem: Carmel [Hebrew].

Shelah, Ofer. 2003. *The Israeli Army: A Radical Proposal*. Or Yehuda: Kinneret [Hebrew].

Shiffer, Zalman F. 2007. "The Debate over the Defense Budget in Israel." *Israel Studies* 12 (1): 193–214.

Shlaim, Avi. 1988. "Israeli Interference in Internal Arab Politics: The Case of Lebanon." In *The Politics of Arab Integration*, eds. Giacomo Luciani and Ghassan Salamé, pp. 232–255. New York: Croom Helm.

Shuman, Ellis. 2001. "El Al's Legendary Security Measures Set Industry Standards." *Israelinsider*. At: http://www.israelinsider.com/channels/security/articles/sec_0108. htm (Accessed December 14, 2010).

SIPRI (Stockholm International Peace Research Institute). 2012. "The SIPRI Military Expenditure Database." At: http://milexdata.sipri.org (Accessed May 17, 2012).

Smith, Anthony. 1986. *The Ethnic Origins of Nations*. Oxford: Blackwell.

Smooha, Sammy. 2002. "The Model of Ethnic Democracy: Israel as a Jewish and Democratic State." *Nations and Nationalism* 8 (4): 475–503.

Sobelman, Daniel. 2004. *New Rules of the Game: Israel and Hizbollah after the Withdrawal from Lebanon*. Tel Aviv: Jaffee Center for Strategic Studies, Tel Aviv University.

State Comptroller. 2009. *Annual Report No. 59A for the Year 2009*. At: http://www.mevaker.gov.il/serve/contentTree.asp?bookid=532&id=191&contentid=&parentcid=undefined&sw=1024&hw=698 (Accessed April 17, 2011) [Hebrew].

2010a. *The Appointment Processes of the IDF's Senior Officers*. Jerusalem: Office of the State Comptroller [Hebrew].

2010b. *The Preparedness of the Israel Fire and Rescue Services for Emergencies*. Jerusalem: Office of the State Comptroller [Hebrew].

2012. *Annual Report for the Year 2012*. Jerusalem: Office of the State Comptroller [Hebrew].

Steinmetz, George, ed. 1999. *State/Culture: State-Formation after the Cultural Turn*. Ithaca, NY: Cornell University Press.

Stepan, Alfred. 1988. *Rethinking Military Politics: Brazil and the Southern Cone*. Princeton: Princeton University Press.

Sternhell, Zeev. 1995. *Nation-Building or a New Society? The Zionist Labor Movement (1904–1940) and the Origins of Israel*. Tel Aviv: Am Oved [Hebrew].

Stritzel, Holger. 2007. "Towards a Theory of Securitization: Copenhagen and Beyond." *European Journal of International Relations* 13 (3): 357–83.

Tamir, Moshe. 2005. *Undeclared War*. Tel Aviv: Ministry of Defense [Hebrew].

Tan, Andrew. 1999. "Singapore's Defence: Capabilities, Trends, and Implications." *Contemporary Southeast Asia* 21 (3): 451–74.

2012. "Punching Above Its Weight: Singapore's Armed Forces and Its Contribution to Foreign Policy." *Defence Studies* 11 (4): 672–97.

Tilly, Charles. 1975. "Reflections on the History of European State-Making." In *The Formation of National States in Western Europe*, ed. Charles Tilly, pp. 3–84. Princeton: Princeton University Press.

1990. *Coercion, Capital, and European States: AD 990–1992*. Oxford: Blackwell.

Tzeng, Yi-suo. 2009. *Civil-Military Relations in Democratizing Taiwan, 1986–2007*. Ph.D. diss. Washington, DC: George Washington University.

Ünver, H. Akin. 2009. *Turkey's "Deep-State" and the Ergenekon Conundrum*. Policy Brief No. 23. Washington, DC: The Middle East Institute, at: http://mei.edu/Portals/0/Publications/turkey-deep-state-ergenekonconundrum.pdf (Accessed January 11, 2011).

Van Creveld, Martin. 1998. *The Sword and the Olive: A Critical History of the Israeli Defense Force*. New York: Public Affairs.

Wæver, Ole. 2009. "What Exactly Makes a Continuous Existential Threat Existential – and How Is It Discontinued." In *Existential Threats and Civil-Security Relations*, eds. Oren Barak and Gabriel Sheffer, pp. 19–45. Lanham, MD: Lexington Books.

Wald, Emanuel. 1992. *The Wald Report*. Boulder, CO: Westview.

Walsh, Sean. 2007. "The Roar of the Lion City: Ethnicity, Gender, and Culture in the Singapore Armed Forces." *Armed Forces & Society* 33 (2): 265–85.

Wasserman, Stanley, and Katherine Faust. 1994. *Social Network Analysis*. Cambridge: Cambridge University Press.

Wedel, Janine R. 2009. *Shadow Elite: How the World's New Power Brokers Undermine Democracy, Government, and the Free Market*. New York: Basic Books.

Weizman, Ezer. 1982. *The Battle for Peace*. Jerusalem: Edanim [Hebrew].

Wellman, Barry, ed. 1999. *Networks in the Global Village*. Boulder, CO: Westview.

Wiberg, Håkan. 1987. "The Security of Small Nations: Challenges and Defenses." *Journal of Peace Research* 24 (4): 339–63.

Wilkinson, Claire. 2007. "The Copenhagen School on Tour in Kyrgyzstan: Is Securitization Theory Useable Outside Europe?" *Security Dialogue* 38 (5): 5–25.

Williams, Michael. 2003. "Words, Images, Enemies: Securitization and International Politics." *International Studies Quarterly* 47 (4): 511–31.

Winograd Commission [The Commission of Inquiry into the Events of Military Engagement in Lebanon 2006]. 2007. *Interim Report*. At: http://go.ynet.co.il/vinograd/300407.pdf (Accessed August 18, 2011) [Hebrew].

Wolfsfeld, Gadi. 2004. *Media and the Path to Peace*. New York: Cambridge University Press.

Woo, Jongseok. 2011. *Security Challenges and Military Politics in East Asia: From State Building to Post-Democratization*. New York: Continuum.

Wood, Geoffrey. 1996. "The South African Military in Transition." *Australian Journal of Political Science* 31 (3): 387–99.

Yaniv, Avner. 1987. *Dilemmas of Security: Politics, Strategy, and the Israeli Experience in Lebanon*. New York: Oxford University Press.

Yew, Lee Kwan. 2007. "The United States, Iraq, and the War on Terror: A Singaporean Perspective." *Foreign Affairs* 86 (1): 2–7.

Yiftachel, Oren. 2006. *Ethnocracy: Land and Identity Politics in Israel/Palestine*. Philadelphia: University of Pennsylvania Press.

Yong, Tan Tai. 2001. "Singapore: Civil-Military Fusion." In *Coercion and Governance*, ed. Muthia Alagappa, pp. 276–93. Stanford, CA: Stanford University Press.

Zertal, Idith. 2005. *Israel's Holocaust and the Politics of Nationhood*. Cambridge: Cambridge University Press.

Zertal, Idith, and Akiva Eldar. 2004. *Masters of the Land: The Settlers and the State of Israel*. Tel Aviv: Dvir [Hebrew].

Zisser, Eyal. 2009. "The Israeli-Syrian-Lebanese Triangle: The Renewed Struggle over Lebanon." *Israel Affairs* 15 (4): 397–412.

Index